learning with
intuto™

D1305188

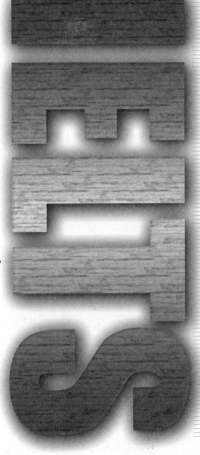

LISTENING

雅思听力

新东方雅思考试指定辅导教程——基础培训

新东方教育科技集团雅思研究院 ◎ 著

西安交通大学出版社
XI'AN JIAOTONG UNIVERSITY PRESS

图书在版编目(CIP)数据

雅思听力 / 新东方教育科技集团雅思研究院著. —西安：西安交通大学出版社，2009（2013.11 重印）
ISBN 978-7-5605-3117-5

Ⅰ. 雅… Ⅱ. 新… Ⅲ. 英语—听说教学—高等教育—自学参考资料 Ⅳ. H319.9

中国版本图书馆 CIP 数据核字(2009) 第 061197 号

Acknowledgements

This publication was designed by Madelize Bekker and Dorothy Cleary.
We would also like to thank the following authors for their contributions:

The Curriculum Factory Team

Sheryl Read

All rights reserved.

No part of this publication may be reproduced or transmitted in any form or by any means, electronic or mechanical, including photocopying, recording, taping, or any information and retrieval system, without the written permission of the publisher.

Copyright © 2009 by New Oriental

书　　名	雅思听力	
著　　者	新东方教育科技集团雅思研究院	
责任编辑	刘会婷	
封面设计	赵文康	
出版发行	西安交通大学出版社	
地　　址	西安市兴庆南路 10 号(邮编：710049)	
电　　话	(010)62605588　62605019(发行部)　(029)82668315(总编室)	
读者信箱	bj62605588@163.com	
印　　刷	北京朝阳新艺印刷有限公司	
字　　数	266 千	
开　　本	889mm×1194mm　1/16	
印　　张	12	
版　　次	2013 年 11 月第 1 版第 15 次印刷	
书　　号	ISBN 978-7-5605-3117-5/H·914	
定　　价	48.00 元	

Overview

This book covers the following points:

Strategies and Practice for Answering the IELTS Listening Question Types

- using the question sheet to predict the kind of information you will need to listen for
- listening for factual information, including times, dates, places and names
- listening for detail / description
- listening for main ideas
- listening for opinions

Four Sections of the IELTS Listening Test

Each section of the IELTS listening test has a different kind of listening.
You will practice listening to:

- dialogues between two people — Section 1
- monologues (where one person is speaking by themselves) — Section 2
- conversations between three or more people — Section 3
- lectures from a course of study — Section 4

Common Listening Topics

You will hear topics which are often used in the IELTS listening test. For example:

- social needs such as asking for directions, prices or information (Sections 1 and 2)
- education topics such as courses of study, or common academic topics (Sections 3 and 4)

Vocabulary

Each unit contains exercises to help you to recognise and learn useful vocabulary for the listening texts.
There are lists of useful phrases which are common in the IELTS listening test.
You will practice:

- recognising sounds
- recognising words
- homonyms — e.g. their and there
- synonyms — e.g. clever, smart, intelligent, bright
- paraphrases — phrases with the same or similar meanings

All four sections of the IELTS listening test are covered and practised in this book.

We hope you will enjoy using this book, and that you will learn useful language and skills to help you to pass the IELTS listening test.

Work hard, take every opportunity to practice, enjoy your study and succeed in the IELTS listening test!

Dear Student,

Welcome to this New Oriental IELTS preparation course and the Listening Book in particular.

IELTS, the International English Language Testing System, is one of the world's most popular English language tests for entry into university or higher education where English is the language of communication. In other words, it is your academic passport!

You may find that listening is one of the more difficult modules in IELTS because you have to listen, process the language, read the questions and write the answers all at the same time. You will get a lot of practice in this book.

This book is designed to help you prepare for the test in a systematic way. You will learn a lot of useful vocabulary and you will learn how to predict and listen for different kinds of information.

The exercises have been created to give you practice in the various skills and strategies you will need to answer the different kinds of questions in the test.

You will further develop your listening skills by listening to dialogues and monologues spoken with a variety of accents on topics that typically occur in the IELTS listening test.

Congratulations on choosing to study IELTS with New Oriental!

Ready? Let's go!

Rod Ellis
第二语言教学之父
"Task Base" 教学法创始人

Preface

Dear Student,

Thank you for choosing to study for the IELTS with New Oriental.

This book is the long anticipated result of a close cooperation between New Oriental and international IELTS experts to develop our own IELTS training materials. We believe it offers a different approach, with the following features:

First of all, the language used is likely what you will encounter in a real classroom or work setting while living abroad. The setting of each dialogue is also consistent with how you might encounter English as used by native speakers in their own country.

Also, under the guidance of renowned professor Rod Ellis, our partner international research team has delivered a proven methodology for ensuring the intended acquisition of needed skills for IELTS test takers in speaking, listening, reading and writing.

And most importantly, this book incorporates ten years of IELTS training experience by the very best teachers at New Oriental, and therefore has been customized to suit the needs of Chinese students.

I sincerely hope that together with these materials New Oriental teachers can make your IELTS classroom fruitful and rewarding. Enjoy your learning time with New Oriental!

周成刚
新东方教育科技集团

Contents

Unit 1	Music	2
Unit 2	Eating Healthily	8
Unit 3	Sport	14
Unit 4	Media	20
Unit 5	Giving Directions	26
Unit 6	Advertising	34
Unit 7	Education	40
Unit 8	Recycling	46
Unit 9	Food	54
Unit 10	Technology	60
Unit 11	Censorship	68
Unit 12	Leisure Activities	74
Unit 13	Social Issues	80
Unit 14	Money	86
Unit 15	Youth Issues	92
Unit 16	Commodities	100
Unit 17	Dieting	106
Unit 18	International Events	112
Unit 19	Online Safety	118
Unit 20	Environment	124
	Answer Key	133

IELTS

Listening

"Chance favors the prepared mind."
(Louis Pasteur)

po sition 取位

This Unit and IELTS

In Section 1 of the IELTS Listening test, you listen to a conversation. You are often required to listen for factual information and then complete a form, notes, table, flow-chart or summary. There is no chance to listen a second time. In this unit, you will listen for information about music exams and complete **forms**.

Introducing the topic

Many students take exams for different subjects. Many exams are national or local, but there are also important international exams for some subjects, including music and languages.

Piano violin

1 *Discuss these questions with a partner.*

    a.   What was the last exam you took?
    b.   What was it for?
    c.   Where did you take it?
    d.   Have you ever sat an international exam?
    e.   Have you ever sat an exam for language or music?

Vocabulary

2 *Pay attention to how the words sound.*

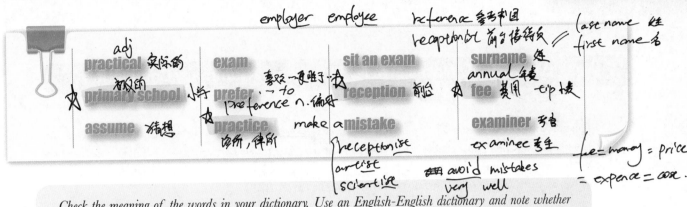

employer employ~~ee~~ reference 参考书目
receptionist 前台接待员 // last name 姓
                                        first name 名

adj
practical 实际的   **exam**   **sit an exam**   **surname** 姓
机灵的   勤奋一夏难子~~~   **annual** 年度
primary school 小学 **prefer** ~~to~~   **reception** 前台   **fee** 费用 tip 小费
                        preference n. 偏爱
assume 猜想   **practice** make a mistake   **examiner** 考官
                        诊所,律所
                        receptionist   examinee 考生
                        artist   ~~err~~ avoid mistakes   fee = money = price
                        scientist   very well   = expense = cost.

Check the meaning of the words in your dictionary. Use an English-English dictionary and note whether the dictionary provides a pronunciation guide.

Music-related vocabulary

kate
kite 回纹 key

grade	violin	viola	diary 日记
pianos	instruments 乐器	piece (of music)	money diary 账本
√ scales 双模 片 键片	accuracy n. 精确 accurate 有精确的	fluency 流利	

large

3 *Write the words to complete each sentence.* 造新句, 地道

a. In most countries, children go to __primary school__ at the age of five or six.

b. I don't like coffee very much. I __prefer__ tea. 吧! You may have to

c. When you enrol at a language school, you may have to 2t may be __sit__ a placement test. 分班考试 a good idea

d. At my son's music club, the __fee__ for a year is $400. 音乐俱乐部

e. The double bass and cello are stringed __instruments__

f. My given name is Irene. My __surname__ is Wilson.

g. I try to __practice__ on the viola for at least 30 minutes each day.

TIP
Understanding numbers is very important in IELTS Listening. You need to practise listening to numbers and identifying them then writing them accurately. Also, remember to write numbers very clearly; if the marker cannot decide, for example, whether you have written 1 or 7, you will not get a mark.

4 *Write the numbers as words and numbers.*

a.	12	f.	187
b.	16	g.	1345
c.	30	h.	7894
d.	67	i.	520000 = 5h est
e.	90	j.	1000000 = 1 M

TIP

For summary completion in the IELTS Listening test, usually more words than required are given in a box. For table completion, you are not usually given the words in writing. You may see an instruction 'Write NO MORE THAN THREE WORDS AND /OR A NUMBER'. The number of words may vary from ONE to THREE, so check carefully.

Predicting the type of answer

Look carefully at the question sheet. You can often predict what type of answers is required.

5 _Predict_ the type of answers required. Circle the type of answer.

a.	$ _____	number / word / 2+ words
b.	_____ Road	number / word / 2+ words
c.	_____ kg	number / word / 2+ words
d.	_____ Williams	number / word / 2+ words
e.	Specific learning goals: _____	number / word / 2+ words

Practising writing numbers, proper nouns, time and dates

6 *Write the names, numbers and dates that you hear.*
Write NO MORE THAN THREE WORDS AND /OR A
NUMBER.

a. Grade _____
b. _____ Rd
c. July _____
d. _____ School
e. Meeting to be held: _____

TIP

In the IELTS Listening exam, units of measurement and amounts are usually written for you, and you are normally required to write a number or words, rather than symbols. For example, you may see $ ____ or ____ kg. Proper names are usually spelled out. For example, you may hear 'I live in Seddon St. That's S-E-D-D-O-N...'.

Language focus – Homonyms (words that sound the same)

TIP

There are many words in English that have exactly the same sound but quite different meanings. For example, 'there' and 'their' are pronounced identically. These words are easier to understand if you hear them in a particular context.

7 Match the words in the box to the homonyms below. Saying the words will help you.

over weight 超过,在上面 overdo 过分
over due 过度

seat [seats]
[rooms]

aisle	forth	~~mourning~~	cite 引用	there	heel 高跟鞋
greyed	read	pear	symbol 象征 weight 重量	banned 禁止,停止=not
heal	base	allowed	your	hire	site websites capsites 营地

basement 地下室   database 数据库
131

a. aloud _____   i. reed _____
b. band _____   j. sight _____
c. bass _____   _____
d. fourth _____   k. their _____
e. grade _____   l. he'll _____
f. higher _____   _____
g. I'll _____   m. wait _____
h. pair _____   n. you're _____

anonymous 匿名的

Getting ready to listen – Prediction

8 You will hear the introduction to Listening 1. First, try to answer the following questions. Write ONE word or A NUMBER in the gap.

a. The audio will be a conversation between _____ people.

b. The conversation is about a Grade 7 viola _____.

c. The people are speaking on the _____.

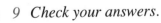

9 Check your answers.

Complete the form. Write NO MORE THAN THREE WORDS OR A NUMBER for each answer.

WOODLANDS SCHOOL OF MUSIC
EXAMINATION ENTRY FORM 2008

Candidate's name	Example *John Kepler*
Grade exam this weekend	1 Grade ___7___
Grade attained in 2007	2 Grade ___6___
Instrument	3 ___viola___
Date and time of examination	4 Date: Saturday, July ___17th___ 可以更加多的字 你自己罐 5 Time: ___2:00 (pm)___ ✗
Examination fee	6 $ ___205___
Examination Room	7 Room ___26___ 8 in ___D___ Block 单名 / A.B. C.D
Candidate's choice of three pieces	9 List A No. 1 List B No. ___B___ List C No. 6
Number of scales candidates must play 双提	10 ___5___

11th
21st

Check your answers.

Complete the form. Write NO MORE THAN THREE WORDS OR A NUMBER for each answer.

John Kepler's Memo

11 Exam at _____Hillcrest_____ Primary School

12 Arrive at the school by __1:30 pm__

13 Tuning: four strings C, G, ___D___, A

14 Take: a spare bow / a cleaning cloth / a ___pencil___

15 Also, take own music ___stand___

16 Order of three-part exam

    First part: sight-reading

    Second part: ___three___ prepared pieces of music

    Third part: ___scales___

17 Marking of first and third part is out of ___20___ %

18 Examiner looking for ___accuracy___ and fluency

19 Results made available on the Woodlands ___website___ and through the mail

20 Aim for 2009: Grade ___8___

(handwritten margin notes: crest 山顶；wave crest n. 波峰；1:30 pm / half past one / one thirty)

Final activity

A *Do a survey of your friends or family.*

  a. Find out if anyone has sat a music exam.
  b. Find out if anyone has sat a language exam.
  c. If so, ask them about it.
  d. If not, ask them about the last test or exam they sat at work or at school.
  e. Ask them: 'What do you need to do to be successful in any exam?'
  f. Do they have any tips or advice for exam candidates for the day of their exam?

B *With a partner, discuss how you go about sitting the IELTS exam in your area.*

  a. Can you sit the exam in your city?
  b. Do you have to travel to another city?
  c. Who do you have to phone or talk to initially to book a place to sit the exam?

C *Share the information with your classmates in your next English class.*

This Unit and IELTS

In Section 2 of the IELTS Listening test, you listen to a monologue, which consists of one person speaking.

You will often hear factual information and need to answer multiple choice type questions. There is no chance to listen a second time. In this unit, you will listen for information about eating healthily and answer **multiple choice** questions.

Introducing the topic

1 Discuss these questions with a partner.

    a.   Which of the pictures shows a doughnut, a filled roll, a sausage roll?

    b.   Would you eat these foods for lunch?

    c.   Do you think they are healthy or unhealthy?

    d.   What would you prefer to eat for lunch?

Vocabulary

2 Write the word or words to complete each sentence.

    a.   In order to stay healthy, we should eat ___wholesome___ foods, such as fruit, vegetables and whole grains.

wholesome book 有益的书

TIP
A useful method for learning the meaning of new vocabulary items is to write a sentence for each word. This way, you can remember how to use the word in context.

b. A person who is _____obese_____ is extremely overweight, and in danger of becoming ill because of it.

c. Schools are _____responsible_____ teaching pupils subjects such as maths, science and geography.

d. We go to school and university in order to gain a good _____education_____. 眼睛症 regular lifestyle

e. People who have an unhealthy ~~lifestay~~ lifestyle are generally unfit and get sick more often. irregular lifestyle 不规律

f. At school we have _____physical education_____ classes outside, where we run and learn to play different kinds of sports. physics 物理 physical education 体育 = 身体教育 physiology 生理学 不规律

g. A _____nutritionist_____ is someone who specialises in the areas of food and diet.

h. People who are _____active_____ 活跃的 spend a lot more time moving around and doing things than people who are not. activity, activate, an action,

i. Doing something in ~~moderations~~ moderation means not doing it too much. 适当的 适度的

j. _____Traditional_____ methods are methods that have been used for a long time and passed from one generation to another. 代代相传

k. The school ~~expert specialist~~ is the place where you can go to buy snacks and light meals.

l. An _____expert = specialist_____ is someone who knows a lot about a particular subject area. 3水

m. The term _____youth_____ refers to young people—usually children and teenagers. 术语 adults 语太规则 youth think 词太闲 use sink

If you are unsure of the meaning of any of the words you wrote above, check your dictionary. If possible, check them in an English - English dictionary as well as a translation dictionary.

3 *Pay attention to how these words sound.*

organic farm 有机农场 chubby 婴儿肥 big 大块头
fat-free 不要脂肪 Instant milk tea 速溶
bakery 烘焙 half - boiled eggs
baker 面包师 半熟热煮蛋
steamed eggs 蒸鸡蛋

Food-related vocabulary

low-fat high-fat	wholegrain 全麦	serving 一份	celery
high-sugar	bread	portion	rice cooker
low-fat	junk food = fast food 垃圾食物 banana	banana	to steam
meat pie	chips 快餐	cereal 谷物	to boil
egg roll 蛋卷 sausage roll 卷	fried chicken	sugary	to bake
鸡肉卷		饮料	
cream doughnut	filled roll	apple	to stir-fry 大火翻炒
	milk tea 奶茶		
fruit	yoghurt 酸奶	pear	oil 油 olive oil 橄榄油
salad	vegetables	kiwi fruit 猕猴桃	raw material 原材料
sandwich	grain 谷物	carrot	dressing 沙拉酱 difficult = no easy
		uncooked 没煮	safe = not dangerous

Check the meaning of the words above in your dictionary. If possible, check them in a picture dictionary as well as a translation dictionary.

4 *Classify the words you hear. Write them in the order that you hear them.*

TIP
Another useful method for learning new vocabulary items is to group them according to categories.

Types of fruit	
Types of vegetables	
Grains	
Prepared food (healthy)	
Prepared food (unhealthy)	
Food preparation (verbs)	
Adjectives to describe food	

Task type: Multiple choice questions

Here are the first two multiple choice questions for Listening 1.

5 *In pairs, quickly discuss the following questions.*

   a.   How many possible answers are given for each question?
   b.   Which letters are written beside the answer options?

---

1. What are they doing in school tuck shops?
   A. selling more healthy food
   B. selling more junk food
   C. offering more meat pies and sausage rolls

2. What do most adults think about this?
   A. It's a bad idea.
   B. It's a good idea.
   C. Tuck shops should sell more cream doughnuts.

TIP
In the IELTS Listening test, you will usually have to answer multiple choice questions. A multiple choice question is a question with three or more possible answers. You need to listen to the audio and decide the correct answer. You need to circle the letter of the correct answer on your question sheet.

TIP
Before the audio is played, you will have some time to read the questions and possible answers. Say the key words in the questions and answer options silently to yourself. This way, you will 'fix' them in your head and better be able to recognise them when you hear them.

 6 *Can you hear the answer to question 1?*

Language focus – Synonyms

7 *Write the words you hear next to their synonyms.*

a. good   _____

b. principal   _____

c. greater amounts   _____

d. tired   _____

e. advertisements   _____

f. overweight   _____

g. to choose   _____

h. tuck shop   _____

i. fast food   _____

j. sport   _____

k. healthy   _____

l. help   _____

m. to suggest   _____

n. uncooked   _____

o. specialist   _____

p. serving   _____

Now read the pairs of words out loud to yourself to help 'fix' the sounds in your head.

Getting ready to listen – Prediction

8 *You will hear the introduction to Listening 1. First, try to answer the following questions.*

a. What type of text do you think this will be?

   A. a conversation between two people
   B. a conversation between more than two people
   C. a monologue (just one person talking)

b. What is the main topic?

   A. supermarkets
   B. school food shops
   C. food markets

c. What changes do you think they might be talking about?

   A. new types of food
   B. increasing prices
   C. increasing numbers of shoppers

9 *Check your answers.*

Instead of X
but √ (前面不重 但后面重)
replace 不 with √ (要 with 后面的)
rather than X A and C 要选 B.

Listening 1

*Choose the correct letter, **A**, **B** or **C**.*

1. What are they doing in school tuck shops?

   A. selling more wholesome food

   B. selling more junk food

   C. offering more meat pies and sausage rolls

2. What do most adults think about this?

   A. It's a bad idea.

   B. It's a good idea.

   C. Tuck shops should sell more cream doughnuts.

3. Which opinion is NOT expressed?

   A. Children should be free to decide what they eat.

   B. There should be more sport at school.

   C. The school is responsible for teaching healthy eating to children.

4. What will some of the children do?

   A. bring healthy food from home

   B. buy junk food on the way to school

   C. bring junk food from home

5. How much does it cost for chicken and chips?

   A. $4.00

   B. $4.50

   C. $2.50

6. How could parents be educated about healthy eating?

   A. magazine advertisements

   B. public meetings

   C. advertisements on television

7. How can schools help children eat healthily?

   A. check children's lunchboxes

   B. sell mainly healthy food

   C. ban junk food in school

Listening 1 – check

Check your answers.

Listening 2

*Choose the correct letter, **A**, **B** or **C**.*

8. Mr White is a

   A. nutritionist.

B. school principal.

C. health expert.

9. The children will be happier and healthier by

A. eating less fruit and vegetables.

B. eating greater amounts of fast food.

C. eating great amounts of fruit and vegetables.

10. How many servings of vegetables per day do health specialists recommend?

A. five

B. two

C. three

11. What happens to people when they don't eat breakfast?

A. They feel tired.

B. They usually eat a banana late in the morning.

C. They don't feel hungry at lunch time.

12. Which food item is NOT suggested for lunch?

A. a wholesome sandwich

B. steamed vegetables

C. fried chicken

13. What recommendations does the speaker make for summer?

A. select green, white and purple vegetables

B. make a salad with uncooked vegetables

C. use a high-fat cooking method

14. How much exercise per day does she recommend for young people?

A. 30 minutes

B. 13 minutes

C. 20 minutes

15. What should children do if they can't walk or bike to school?

A. take a taxi

B. play sports with friends

C. join a chess club

Final activity

A Do a survey of the people in your class.

- First, work with a partner in class to write questions about what food people eat for breakfast, lunch and dinner.
- Do they eat snacks between meals?
- Do they prefer junk food or healthy food?

B Next, carry out your survey. Talk to your classmates, and write down their answers as you listen.

C Finally, discuss with the whole class whether most people eat healthily or unhealthily.

This Unit and IELTS

In Section 1 of the IELTS Listening test, you listen to a conversation. You are often required to match a list of items from the audio to a set of items in a box. In this unit, you will listen for information about sports competitions and complete **matching** exercises.

Introducing the topic

Athletics is an important part of sports events such as the Olympic Games, and this includes running events, from 100 metre sprints to the marathon. In a relay race, teams of runners take turns to complete part of the race.

1 Discuss the following questions with your partner.

a. Do you prefer to watch sprinting (fast, short distance) or long distance races? Why?
b. Have you ever watched relay running events live or on television?
c. In a relay running event, are all the runners equally important?
d. If you were in a relay race with four people, which runner would you like to be—the first, second, third or fourth?
e. What is cross-country running?

Vocabulary

TIP

A useful method for learning vocabulary for listening is to say the words out loud as you read them. Check your pronunciation with your teacher or a native speaker, or use a dictionary that gives pronunciation guidance. Also, check the meanings of the words.

2 *Pay attention to how these words sound.*

ready	favourite	ankle	schedule
successful	organise	challenging	turn up
registration	First Aid	question	accident

Sport-related vocabulary

runners	100 metres sprint	400 metres relay	team speed
baton	long jump	hurdles	high jump
cross country	course	timekeeper	start line
starting gun	water jump		

Check the meaning of the words in your dictionary. Use an English-English dictionary if possible and note whether the dictionary provides a guide to pronunciation.

3 *Write the word or words to complete each sentence.*

a. In a sprint race, _____ is important.

b. In the _____metre relay, four people in a team run _____ metres each.

c. In an athletics event, _____ may also try out other sports, such as the _____ jump.

d. All the runners must be ready at the _____ before the race begins.

e. Some cross country races are very _____.

f. The _____ event is a sprint race with jumps.

g. A race starts when the _____ is fired.

h. Runners and teams must go to the _____ table to enter a race or to find out their time.

4 *Choose the words from the box that match the meanings you hear. Write the correct letters **A-F** next to questions **a-f**.*

A course	B to organise …	C high jump
D to turn up	E timekeeper	F baton

a. _____

b. _____

c. _____

d. _____

e. _____

f. _____

5 *Write the letters, **A-F**, in the order that you hear the words in the box.*

A First Aid	B schedule	C favourite
D successful	E accident	F ankle

a. _____

b. _____

c. _____

d. _____

e. _____

f. _____

Language focus – Listening to names, places and times

TIP

In the IELTS Listening test, you will often hear the names of people or places. Proper names are often spelled out. You may also hear references to clock time, such as an appointment or the time of an event on a schedule.

6 *Write the names you hear next to questions **a-h**.*

a. _____

b. _____

c. _____

d. _____

e. _____

f. _____

g. _____

h. _____

7   *Write the correct letters, **A-G**, next to questions **a-g**.*

A	9 am
B	10 am
C	11 am
D	12 noon
E	1 pm
F	1:30 pm
G	2 pm

a. What time is the 800 metre race? _____

b. What time is the 400 metre relay? _____

c. What time is the high jump event? _____

d. What time is the long jump event? _____

e. What time was the 100 metre sprint? _____

f. What time was the hurdles event? _____

g. What time is the cross-country race? _____

Task type: Matching

TIP

In the first part of the IELTS Listening test, you are often required to listen to an audio and match a numbered list of items from the listening to a set of items in a box. To answer each question, you write a letter from the box beside a number in the list below.

Getting ready to listen – Prediction

8   *You will hear the introduction to Listening 1. First, try to answer the following questions.*

*Write the correct letters **A-D** next to questions **a-d**.*

A	teams, colours and events
B	two athletes
C	track and field meet
D	their relay race

a.   You will hear _____

b.   at a _____

c.   talking about _____

d.   and about _____

9   *Check your answers.*

Questions 1 – 7

What do the athletes say about their relay race, and about teams, colours and events?

Choose your answers from the box. Write the correct letters **A-D** next to questions **1-4**.

A	Andy
B	Pete
C	Robbie
D	Dave

1. first runner _____
2. second runner _____
3. third runner _____
4. fourth runner _____

Choose your answers from the box. Write the correct letters **A-C** next to questions **5-7**.

A	Lancaster College
B	Ashgrove College
C	Highland Park

5. green _____
6. red _____
7. white _____

Questions 8 – 12

Choose your answers from the box. Write the correct letters **A-E** next to questions **8-12**.

A	hurdles
B	high jump
C	100 metres sprint
D	long jump
E	400 metres relay

8. 1 pm _____
9. 1:30 pm _____
10. 3 pm _____
11. 4:30 pm _____
12. 5 pm _____

Listening 1 – check

Check your answers.

Listening 2

Questions 13 – 18

What do the athletes say before the race about people's positions?

Choose your answers from the box. Write the correct letters **A-G** next to questions **13-18**.

A	Catherine
B	Elizabeth
C	Thomas
D	Jeremy
E	Tony
F	Felicity
G	Matt

13. on the start line _____

14. beside the first jump _____

15. at the registration table _____

16. in the timekeeper's tent _____

17. beside the water jump _____

18. at the First Aid tent _____

Questions 19 – 24

What is said after the race?

*Choose your answers from the box. Write the correct letters **A-K** next to questions **19-24**.*

A	everyone
B	next week
C	next year
D	to the winners
E	in the kitchen
F	in the club rooms
G	in the shower block
H	to all the helpers
I	to see
J	to eat
K	in the carpark

19. Congratulations _____

20. Well done _____

21. There's tea and coffee _____

22. There's plenty _____

23. Thank you _____

24. See you _____

Final activity

A *Talk with your partner about any race that you can remember participating in. Perhaps it was quite recent or maybe it was many years ago. Describe*

- where it was;
- your performance;
- your place;
- the other competitors in the race.

B *Puzzle question: ask your partner this question:*

- You are in a running race. You pass the runner who is second. What position are you now in?

C *Discuss your answers.*

This Unit and IELTS

In Section 2 of the IELTS Listening test, you listen to a monologue.

You may be asked to listen to factual information and complete the labels on a diagram, using the options in a list. In this unit, you will listen for information about equipment and **label diagrams**.

Introducing the topic

Media is a general term for the ways of presenting information to many people. Common forms of media are television, the internet, newspapers and magazines. Cameras are important media tools.

1 Discuss these questions with a partner.

    a.   What is your favourite form of media?

    b.   When you read a magazine or newspaper, do you usually look at the pictures or the words first?

    c.   Do you agree with the saying 'a picture is worth a thousand words'?

    d.   Do you own a camera or video camera?

    e.   Do you know how it works?

Vocabulary

2 Pay attention to how these words sound.

recommend	comfortable	operate	inspect
extremely	easily	carefully	neatly
thoroughly	on the side of	beside	in front of
behind	above	carry	design
pack away	inspect		

Check the meaning of the words in your dictionary. Use an English-English dictionary and note whether the dictionary provides a guide to pronunciation.

Camera vocabulary

lens	focus	battery	microphone
cord	hand grip	operate	

3 Write the word or words to complete each sentence.

comfortable	inspect	recommend	focus	operate

a. I _____ that you buy a video camera with an international guarantee.

b. A rubber hand grip makes the camera very _____ to hold.

c. You _____ the camera by looking through the lens and pushing the 'Record' button.

d. Quality control workers in the factory will _____ your camera carefully before it is boxed ready for sale.

e. The camera will _____ on the subject automatically.

4 Check your answers.

5 *Write the base form of the verbs you hear as past participles to complete the sentences.*

    a.   The camera is very well _____.

    b.   It can be _____ neatly into the leather carry bag.

    c.   The laptop is light, so it can easily be _____ onto a plane.

    d.   The hand grip can be _____ away.

    e.   The lens focus can be _____ on automatic or manual.

    f.   The camera can be _____ by almost anyone.

    g.   The battery should be _____ from time to time.

6 *Write the word beside each number according to the order in which you hear them.*

A. extremely	B. easily	C. carefully	D. neatly	E. especially	F. thoroughly

    a.   _____

    b.   _____

    c.   _____

    d.   _____

    e.   _____

    f.   _____

Task type: Labelling a diagram, plan or map

For this task type, candidates have to listen and to complete the labels on a diagram, plan or map. A set of possible answers is given on the question paper and candidates are required to write the letter of the option they have selected. A diagram may represent a piece of equipment, a plan may show the layout of a building or buildings and a map may show part of a city. Another possible visual is a series of pictures. The numbers of the labels follow the order of the audio that you hear.

7 *What is a label? Listen to three definitions A, B and C, and write the correct letter below.*

    A label is _____.

8 *Which type of visual do the following items probably belong to? Write the correct letter below.*

A a plan	B a diagram	C a map

    a.   The parts of a telescope   _____

    b.   The outline of an island   _____

    c.   The lay-out of a theatre   _____

9 *Label the diagram of a television.*

A. screen	F. speaker
B. mute button	G. dial
C. handle	H. volume
D. channel select	I. remote
E. colour adjustment	J. aerial

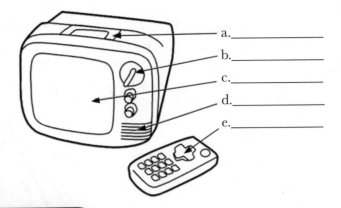

a._____

b._____

c._____

d._____

e._____

Language focus – The position of adverbs of manner, prepositions and the passive

Adverbs of manner usually follow the direct object in a sentence, or follow the verb if there is no object. For example, 'You can adjust the shutter speed quickly.' 'She listened intently.' An adverb usually comes before the adjective it qualifies. For example, 'The concert was highly successful.'

Adverbs of manner – Position

10 *Choose the correct adverbs to complete the sentences. Write the letters, **A-E**, in the correct position—in either sentence (**i**) or (**ii**).*

A extremely	B easily	C carefully	D neatly	E thoroughly

1. (i) The computer bag is roomy, so the computer fits into _____ it.
    (ii) The computer bag is roomy, so the computer fits into it _____.

2. (i) This camera is very good, but it's _____ expensive.
    (ii) This camera is very good, but it's expensive _____.

3. (i) You should take off _____ the lens.
    (ii) You should take the lens off _____ .

4. (i) The manufacturers inspect _____ each new lens.
    (ii) The manufacturers inspect each new lens _____.

5. (i) The camera bag has special pockets, so everything can _____ be packed away.
    (ii) The camera bag has special pockets, so everything can be packed away _____.

Prepositions and adverbial phrases of place

A. on top of	B. on the front of	C. underneath	D. on the left-hand side of
E. around	F. here	G. against	H. on the right-hand side of

11 Write the letters **A-H** to show the order in which you hear these words or phrases.

a. _____   c. _____   e. _____   g. _____
b. _____   d. _____   f. _____   h. _____

12 Write the correct letter for the position in relation to the tent.

A	on the side of
B	beside
C	in front of
D	behind
E	above

d._____

b._____

e._____

a._____

c._____

Passive voice

13 Write the passive verbs correctly.

1. These cameras _____ for easy handling.
2. Nearly all cameras today _____ with automatic focusing.
3. The bag _____ to allow all the parts to fit in neatly.
4. The camera is light and can _____ easily.
5. The cord and battery can _____ away neatly.

14 Tick the sentence you hear.

A. _____ In the IELTS Listening test, you often need to label parts of a plan correctly.
B. _____ In the IELTS Listening test, you often need to label parts of a map correctly.
C. _____ In the IELTS Listening test, you often need to label parts of a diagram correctly.

Getting ready to listen – Prediction

15 You will hear the introduction to Listening 1. First, try to answer the following questions.

a. What type of text do you think this will be?
   A. a conversation between two people
   B. a conversation between more than two people
   C. a monologue(just one person talking)

b. What is the main type of image?
   A. a plan
   B. a diagram
   C. a map

16 Check your answers.

Listening 1

Label the diagram below. Choose 4 answers from the box and write the correct letter next to questions 1-4.

A	filter
B	lens
C	focusing ring
D	hand grip
E	on / off button
F	microphone
G	rubber cup
H	tripod socket

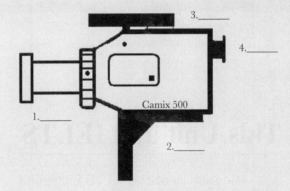

Listening 1 – check

Check your answers.

Listening 2

Label the diagram below. Choose 4 answers from the box and write the correct letter next to questions 5-8.

A	bulbs
B	cord
C	microphone
D	battery charger
E	lens
F	battery
G	camera

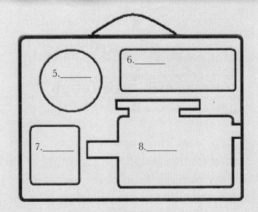

Final activity

A *Choose a diagram of something you use in your everyday life—such as a bicycle, a motorbike or a sewing machine.*

   a.   Draw it yourself first so you have a model.
   b.   Give your partner instructions on how to draw it, without allowing them to see your one.
   c.   Compare the diagrams.

B *Then repeat the activity, with your partner giving you instructions for their diagram.*

This Unit and IELTS

In Section 1 of the IELTS Listening test, you listen to a conversation.

You may be asked to listen to someone giving directions, and complete a map-labelling question. In this unit, you will listen to directions and **label maps**.

Introducing the topic

An important listening skill is being able to understand directions. For many young people, meeting friends at different places, or at each others' houses, is a popular weekend pastime. In order to meet up in unknown places, it is necessary to be able to follow someone else's explanation of how to get there.

1 Discuss these questions with a partner.

    a.   What do you usually do on the weekend?
    b.   Do you ever meet up with your friends?
    c.   Do your friends ever come to your house?
    d.   Where would you usually go to have a party?

Vocabulary

2 Pay attention to how these words sound.

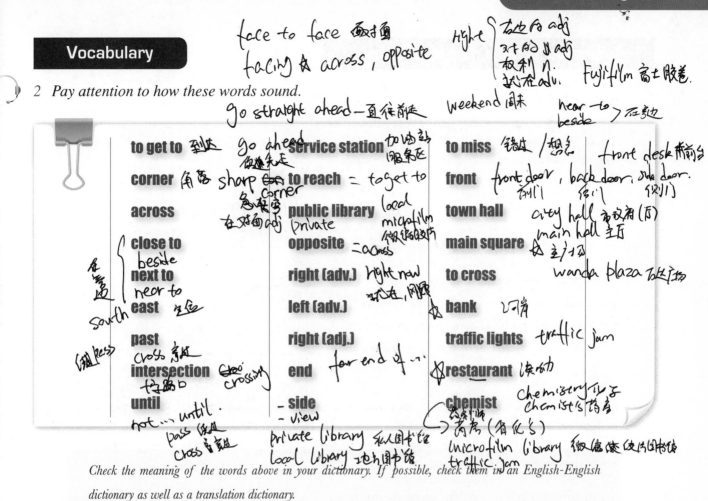

to get to	service station	to miss	
corner	to reach	front	
across	public library	town hall	
close to	opposite	main square	
beside	right (adv.)	to cross	
next to	left (adv.)	bank	
near to			
east			
past	right (adj.)	traffic lights	
intersection	end	restaurant	
until	– side	chemist	
	– view		

Check the meaning of the words above in your dictionary. If possible, check them in an English-English

dictionary as well as a translation dictionary.

TIP

A useful method for learning new vocabulary items is to write them down in groups of related meaning and/or use. We can refer to these groups of related words as categories.

3 Complete the table by writing the words you hear in the correct columns. Write them in the order that you hear them.

Verbs for asking / giving directions	Nouns related to roads and streets	Names of shops and buildings in town	Nouns referring to parts of a street or building	Direction words

Now, say the words from the key vocabulary list out loud, to help you hear them.

TIP

In the IELTS Listening test, you will sometimes have to answer questions requiring you to label things on a map. You have to listen very carefully, so that you can follow the information about where things are located in relation to other things.

The map-labelling instructions and questions for Listening 1 are in the map below.

4   *In pairs, quickly discuss the following questions.*

    a.   How many answers do you have to write? _____

    b.   What do you need to write for your answers? _____

    c.   What should you NOT write for your answers? _____

    d.   Do you have to label all of the places on the map? _____

TIP

Before the audio is played, you will have some time to look at the map. Say the names and words written on the map and in the questions silently to yourself. This way, you will 'fix' them in your head and better be able to recognize them when you hear them. Think of any vocabulary words that might relate to the map.

5   *Can you hear the answer to the example question? Listen to the first part of Listening 1 and look at the map.*

Label the map below.
Write the correct letters, **B-G**, next to questions 1 and 2.
'A' has already been given as an example.

Example	Answer
Brenda's house	A

Anne Street, Corner Store, Queen Street, Tramway Road, Bettina Road, Public Library, Service Station, Bob's House

A · B · C · D · E · F · G

1. Katie's house ....

2. Helen's house ....

Language focus – Prepositional phrases

6 *Write the prepositional phrases next to the correct pictures below.*

on the corner of   词组

a. X is ___on the corner of___

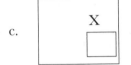

b. ___across the road from___ or ___on the opposite to___
对面

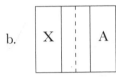

c. X is ___close to___

d. X is ___far from___

e. X is ___next to___

f. X is ___on the right of___

g. X is ___on the left of___

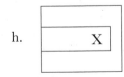

h. X is ___at the end of___
末尾处   in the end
                  结局

Now read the words out loud to yourself to help 'fix' the sounds in your head. You may see or hear some of them in Listening 1 and 2.

TIP

When we are giving directions in English, we use adverbs of movement with the verbs 'go' and 'turn' (as well as other verbs) in order to tell people where to go.

7 *Write the phrases next to the correct pictures below.*

door [room]
gate (yard)

Go along

a. 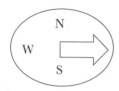   go ~~to~~ ease

~~to th~~

b. 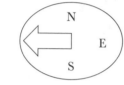   Jo west

c. 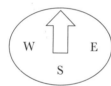   go north

d. 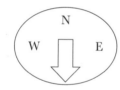   go south

e.    go along

f. 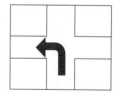   ~~turn~~ turn left

media room
[d]f [j]/ [i'] --- [dʒ]

g. 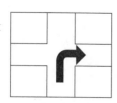   turn right

{ would you
  could you
  I need you

{ ticket office
  box office

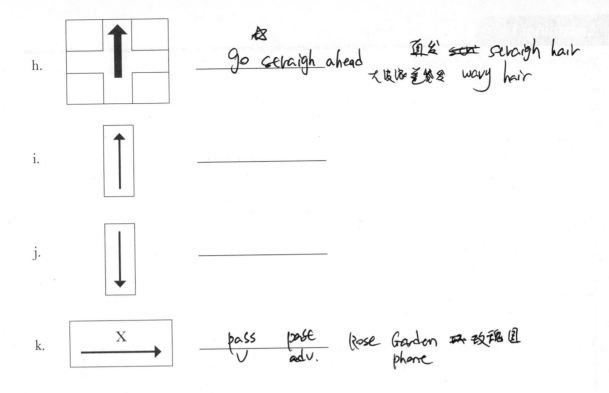

h. _go seraigh ahead_   直么 ~~seat~~ seraigh hair

大波浪至鬈发 wavy hair

i. _____

j. _____

k. _pass   pase_

pass(v)   adv.

Rose Garden 玫瑰园

phone

Now read the words out loud to yourself to help 'fix' the sounds in your head. You may see or hear some of them in Listening 1 and 2.

Getting ready to listen – Prediction

8 *You will hear the introduction to Listening 1. First, try to answer the following questions.*

a. What type of text do you think this will be?
  A. a conversation between two people
  B. a conversation between more than two people
  C. a monologue (just one person talking)

b. What is the main topic?
  A. how to find a road
  B. where to find a map
  C. how to go to a place

c. Where do you think the person wants to go?
  A. the dentist
  B. a friend's party
  C. a shopping mall

 9 *Check your answers.*

Listening 1

Label the map below. Write the correct letter next to questions 1 and 2. 'A' has already been given as an example.

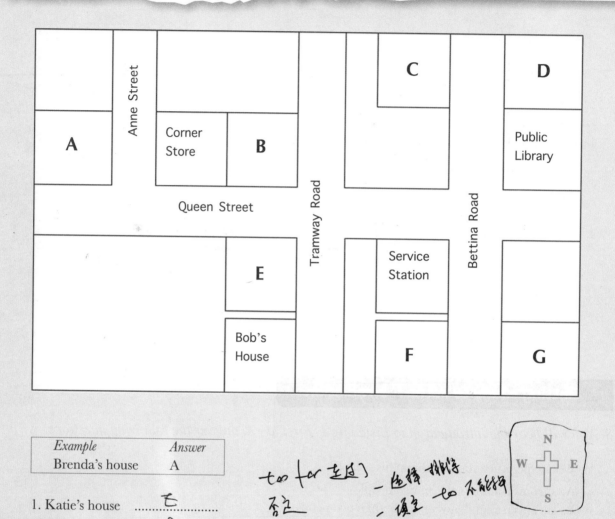

Example	Answer
Brenda's house	A

1. Katie's house ....E..........
2. Helen's house ....G..........

to far 走过了
否定

一些择 挑 挑得
一设定 too 不能接

Listening 1 – check

Check your answers.

Listening 2

Label the map below. Write the correct letter next to questions 3-7. 'A' has already been given as an example.

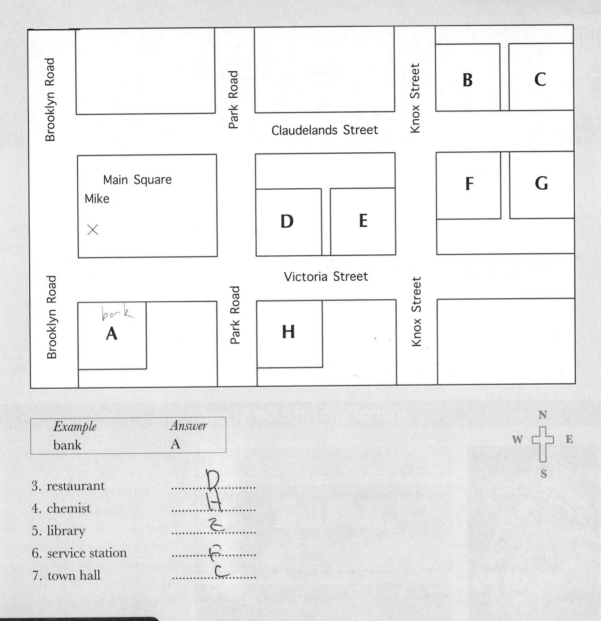

Example	Answer
bank	A

3. restaurant ....D..........
4. chemist ....H..........
5. library ....E..........
6. service station ....F..........
7. town hall ....C..........

Final activity

A In pairs, practise asking for and giving directions.

B Work with someone you don't know very well.

  a. Ask him or her how to get to their home from the school.
  b. Then your partner can ask you for directions to your house.
  c. If you already know where each other's houses are, then ask directions to your partner's sports club, or grandmother's house, or favourite restaurant, and so on.

C If you are good at drawing, you could draw a map showing how to get there while you are listening to your partner speak.

This Unit and IELTS

In Section 2 of the IELTS Listening test, you listen to a monologue.

You may need to listen to factual information and complete a table. In this unit, you will hear people advertising mobile phones and mobile phone plans and complete **tables**.

Introducing the topic

Advertising is a large part of many modern societies. Advertisers use television, radio, the internet, newspapers, journals, signs, billboards and many other ways to get their message across. Advertisers are trying to sell a product or service. They need to make their product or service as attractive as possible so that people will want to buy it. Mobile phones are a prominent part of modern life for many people, especially young people. You often see and hear advertisements for mobile phones.

1 Discuss these questions with a partner.

    a.   What kinds of advertising do you experience most often? Television? Radio? Newspapers? Billboards?

    b.   Do you think advertising ever influences what you buy?

    c.   If you have a mobile phone, did advertising influence your choice of phone?

    d.   What special features does your mobile phone have?

    e.   Do you think it is more important for a mobile phone to be fashionable or good quality?

Vocabulary

ticket office ┐售票处
box office ┘

advertising

brand 牌子

cell phone

company

convenient 方便的

coverage 覆盖的

customer 顾客

discount 折扣

fashionable

feature 特色

purchase 购买

product 产品

quality 质量

sales

service

value 价值

2 *Write the word or words you hear to complete each sentence.*

a. Many companies spend a lot of money on television ___advertising___.
b. They want you to become one of their ___customers___.
c. Advertisers want you to buy a certain ___product___.
d. They often claim that they offer the best ___value___ for money.
e. In many countries nearly everyone owns a ___cell phone___.
f. Companies may offer a ___discount___ to get you to buy something.
g. If you want it to last a long time, you should buy a ___quality___ phone.
h. If you are not sure which phone to buy, you can ask a ~~seales~~ sales to help you. person
i. Choose a phone with nationwide ___coverage___ if you travel a lot.

Syllables

3 *Write how many syllables each word has. The first one has been done.*

a.	company	3
b.	technology	
c.	comfortably	
d.	convenient	
e.	coverage	

f.	fashionable	
g.	feature	
h.	purchase	
i.	service	
j.	value	

Collocations – Words that often go together

4 *Write the word or words that often go with the word(s) given below.*

a. sales and _____
b. _____ for money
c. _____ coverage

5 *Check your answers.*

6 *Choose a synonym for these words from the vocabulary list.*

    a.   (to) buy   Purchase

    b.   easy, handy   Convenient

7 *Match the key vocabulary words to other words with similar meanings.*

fashionable	brand	customer	value

    a.   price, worth   value

    b.   popular, stylish   fashionable

    c.   company, name   brand

    d.   purchaser, buyer   customer

Task type: Form/Notes/Table/Flow-chart/Summary completion

In the IELTS Listening test you are often required to listen to a conversation or discussion containing factual information and then complete a form, notes, table, flow-chart or summary. When completing a summary, the words are usually given in a box, but when completing a table, the words are not usually given in writing. You will often see the instruction, *'Write NO MORE THAN THREE WORDS AND /OR A NUMBER'.*

Predict a word or a numeral

8 *Write 'word' or 'number' beside each symbol or*
  abbreviation below.

    a.   % _____

    b.   Dr _____

    c.   _____ year-olds

    d.   _____ months

    e.   Brand name _____

    f.   Place of previous study _____

    g.   _____ km

    h.   Confident and _____

    i.   _____ cc

    j.   Fax. no. _____

TIP

You can often predict what type of answer is coming next. For example, if you see a $ or a £, you can predict that a numeral will follow, to show an amount of money in dollars or pounds. If you see a label such as Mrs, Lake or Mount, you can predict the answer will be a word. In a table in the IELTS Listening exam you usually write a numeral rather than a word for a number; for example, '8' not 'eight'.

Number of words in answer

9 Cross out the answers that would not be acceptable in the IELTS Listening test because they contain too many words.

a. of the advertising ✓

b. quality products and happy customers ✗

c. expensive, top-quality shoes ✓→氣1个单词

d. sales and service ✓

e. ~~the~~ day before yesterday ✗

f. green, blue ~~and~~ pink ✗

g. 5 megapixel camera ✓

TIP

Read the following instruction in the IELTS Listening exam carefully.

在三个词中一做

'Write NO MORE THAN THREE WORDS AND /OR A NUMBER'. max

Hyphenated words count as one word. 3 words + 1 number

Example: 'excellent after-hours service' (3 words) would be acceptable.

Language focus: Reference words – 'this', 'that' and 'it'

TIP

'This' and 'that' refer to something that has already been referred to. The meaning of these reference words is gained by remembering what has just been said. 'This' refers to something nearby, while 'that' refers to something further away. 'It' refers to a thing already mentioned.

For example, in the sentence, ' My last assignment was easy but this one is difficult.'
'this one' refers to the present assignment.

10 Tick one box to answer the question.

What does 'this' refer to?

a.	Geoff Beck	
b.	Luna Mobiles	
c.	The radio programme, 'Technology and You'…	
d.	Another radio programme	

11 Read the following text and underline the 'this', 'that' or 'it' reference words that you see.

Let me tell you about four new products. First, the Luna 500. It's one of my favourites! This little beauty has some great games, a camera, the internet and a voice recorder. It's fashionable, too! It comes in red, green, blue and pink. The price of this beauty is $849. Now, that's not cheap but you'll love it. It's very good value for money. Secondly, the Aquila 50. My daughter loves this one. Not as many features as the Luna, but it's slimmer and lighter. It has excellent games and a 5 megapixel camera, so you get really sharp shots.

12 *Write the correct letter, **A** or **B**, to show what 'this' and 'it' refer to.*

A	Luna 500
B	Aquila 50

a.   It's fashionable …   _____

b.   … this one   _____

c.   This little beauty …   _____

d.   … you'll love it.   _____

13 *Write 'this', 'that' or 'it' in the following sentences.*

a.   We have a discount on the Luna 500. Don't miss _____ opportunity.

b.   The Luna 500 is slim and fashionable. You'll love _____.

c.   This one is expensive, but _____ one over there is being sold at a discount today.

d.   The battery is reliable. _____ will keep going for up to 48 hours of use.

e.   The first Aquila was made in 2003. _____ model sold well, but today's Aquila is even more popular.

Getting ready to listen – Prediction

In the Listening text monologue, you will hear advertising and information about cell phones.

14   *Discuss these questions with a partner.*

a.   How many voices do you expect to hear? _____

b.   How many features are there for the phones in the table for Listening 1? _____

c.   Do you think all the phones will have all the features? If not, why not? _____

_____

Listening 1

Complete the table. Write Y in the table to show the features for each phone.

	Games	Camera	Internet connectivity	Voice recorder
LUNA	Y	Y	Y	Y
AQUILA 50	Y	Y		
HERMES	Y	Y		
RIVA	Y			

Listening 1 – check

Check your answers.

Listening 2

Complete the table.

Phone company	BASIC	PEAK HOUR	OFF PEAK	COVERAGE
COMMIX	$24	26c	4. 20c	Nationwide
PHONTIC	$27	3. 26 C	20c	6. _____ Main cities
PLUTO	1. $27	26c	20c	Nationwide
WORLD	$28	28c	27c	Nationwide
DIALOG	2. $29.5	32c	5. 27C	7. National islands

Final activity

A *Discuss with your partner the cell phone plan you have. How do you pay for cell phone use?*

B *Has advertising influenced your choice of plan? How?*

C *If you were asked to write an advertisement for radio for your own cell phone and plan, what features would you advertise?*

This Unit and IELTS

In section 1 of the IELTS Listening test, you listen to a conversation and answer questions, such as matching labels to descriptions. In this unit, you will listen to a conversation about school teachers and complete **matching** exercises.

Introducing the topic

Your teachers, subjects and classmates at school make your education experience good or bad. Most students have favourite subjects at school. These may or may not be the same as the subjects that they are good at. Many students also have favourite teachers.

1 Discuss these questions with a partner.

a. What are your favourite subjects?
b. Why do you like them?
c. Are there any subjects that you are good at, but that you don't like?
d. Why don't you like them?
e. After all your years of school, do you have a favourite teacher?
f. What makes them your favourite?

Vocabulary

2 Pay attention to how these words sound.

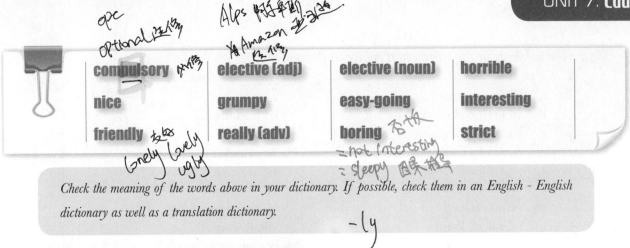

compulsory | elective (adj) | elective (noun) | horrible
nice | grumpy | easy-going | interesting
friendly | really (adv) | boring | strict

Check the meaning of the words above in your dictionary. If possible, check them in an English - English dictionary as well as a translation dictionary.

Positive and negative descriptions

3 Write the adjectives that describe people in the correct column of the table (positive or negative).

| nice | friendly | grumpy | easy-going | boring | horrible | interesting | strict |

positive	negative

Antonyms

4 Circle the underlined word you hear in each sentence.

a. Ms Taylor can be really <u>nice / horrible</u> sometimes.
b. Mr Harris is a really <u>easy-going / strict</u> teacher.
c. Miss Williams teaches really <u>interesting / boring</u> classes.
d. Mr Smith seems to be quite <u>friendly / grumpy</u>, doesn't he?
e. Maths and science are <u>compulsory / elective</u> subjects at our school.

School subjects

5 Pay attention to how these words sound.

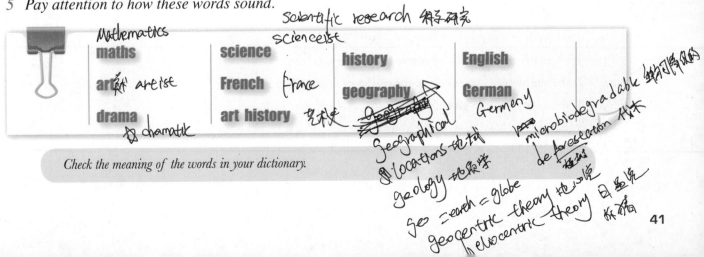

maths | science | history | English
art | French | geography | German
drama | art history | |

Check the meaning of the words in your dictionary.

41

6   *Match the subjects to the words that relate to them.*

a. language, travel	i. art
b. laboratory, experiments	ii. art history
c. language, Germany	iii. drama
d. numbers, equations	iv. English
e. past, events	v. French
f. drawing, painting	vi. German
g. acting, actor	vii. geography
h. language, France	viii. history
i. paintings, styles	ix. maths
j. countries, map	x. science

7   *Check your answers. Say the words quietly to yourself, to help you recognise them when you hear them.*

8   *Circle the subject that the person is talking about.*

a. French	geography	maths
b. German	drama	history
c. geography	science	art
d. science	English	geography
e. drama	art history	art
f. history	maths	French
g. English	art	science
h. art history	German	drama

Task type: Matching questions

In the IELTS Listening test, you are often required to listen to a recording comparing or discussing different items (things or people) and match each item to the correct description. When completing a matching question, either the descriptions or the items are given in a box as answer options. You will often see more answer options than you need to use.

9   *Look at the instructions and matching questions for Listening 1. In pairs, quickly discuss the following questions.*

a.   How many names are there in the box?

b.   How many descriptions are there below the box?

c.   Is the number of names the same as the number of descriptions?

d.   Is there an example given?

e.   What do you have to write for your answers?

f.   What should you not write for your answers?

Listen and match the names from the box to the descriptions. Write the correct letter next to questions 1-4. 'F' has already been done as an example.

| A. Mr Smith |
| B. Miss Williams |
| C. Mr Jones |
| D. Mrs Brown |
| E. Mr Harris |
| F. Ms Taylor |

Example: teaches art history   F

1. is new to the school   ....

2. teaches geography   ....

3. only teaches the upper classes   ....

4. is often sick   ....

Say the names and words quietly. Will you be able to recognise them when you hear them?

10 *Can you hear the answer to the example question?*

Language focus – Common surnames

TIP

In the IELTS test, you sometimes have to identify names of people or places. Below are some common surnames that you might hear.

11 *Pay attention to how these common English surnames sound.*

		Brown	Black
Anderson	Andrews	Brown	Black
Campbell	Collins	Davis	Dawson
Edwards	Evans	Fisher	Ford
Granger	Green	Harris	Hill
Johnson	Jones	King	Lewis
Marshall	Oliver	Palmer	Patterson
Reed	Robinson	Stevens	Smith
Taylor	Turner	Watson	Williams

12 *Tick the surnames you hear. You will not hear all the names in the box.*

13 *Circle the surname you hear. You will only hear one name in each set of three.*

a.	Anderson	Evans	Harris
b.	Brown	Marshall	Patterson
c.	Collins	Turner	King
d.	Palmer	Stevens	Oliver
e.	Reed	Black	Dawson
f.	Smith	Campbell	Fisher
g.	Taylor	Williams	Hill
h.	Watson	Robinson	Edwards
i.	Green	Lewis	Andrews

14 Pay attention to how the titles sound.

    a. Miss Brown
    b. Ms Brown
    c. Mrs Brown
    d. Mr Brown
    e. Dr Brown

TIP

Surnames usually have a title in front of them. The most common title for men is 'Mr'. The most common titles for women are 'Miss', 'Ms' and 'Mrs'. 'Dr' (doctor) can be either a man or a woman.

15 Circle the title you hear.

a. Miss	Ms	Mrs	<u>Mr</u>	Dr
b. Miss	Ms	Mrs	Mr	Dr
c. Miss	Ms	Mrs	Mr	Dr
d. Miss	Ms	Mrs	Mr	Dr
e. Miss	Ms	Mrs	Mr	Dr

TIP

You will usually have to identify surnames 'in context'. That means you have to understand them while someone is speaking about some other topic.

16 Circle the surname you hear.

a. Green	Jones	Turner
b. Ford	Campbell	Oliver
c. Patterson	Hill	Robinson
d. Fisher	Granger	Collins
e. Marshall	Black	Williams

Getting ready to listen – Prediction

17 You will hear the introduction to Listening 1. First, try to answer the following questions.

a. What type of text do you think this will be?

    A. a conversation between two people
    B. a conversation between more than two people
    C. a monologue (just one person talking)

b. What is the main topic?

    A. Bill's math's class
    B. Sarah's electives
    C. the art history classes

c. What do you think will happen next?

    A. Ms Taylor will tell them to go to class.
    B. Bill will give Sarah advice.
    C. Sarah will give Bill advice.

18 Check your answers.

Listening 1

What do the students say about each teacher?

Choose your answers from the box and write the correct letters A-F next to questions 1-4.

'F' has already been done as an example.

A.	Mr Smith
B.	Miss Williams
C.	Mr Jones
D.	Mrs Brown
E.	Mr Harris
F.	Ms Taylor

Example: teaches art history   F

1. is new to the school   D
2. teaches geography   B
3. only teaches the upper classes   A
4. is often sick   C

Listening 1 – check

Check your answers.

Listening 2

What do the students say about each teacher?

Choose your answers from the box and write the correct letters A-F next to questions 5-8.

'F' has already been done as an example.

A.	Ms Palmer
B.	Mr Turner
C.	Dr Reed
D.	Mrs Fisher
E.	Miss Edwards
F.	Mr Green

Example: teaches German   F

5. teaches art history   A
6. no longer works at the school   D
7. is very strict   E
8. teaches drama   B

Final activity

A In pairs, ask each other about the subjects that you study.

- Which subjects are compulsory?
- Which subjects are electives (i.e. you can choose to do them)?
- Which teachers do you have for each subject?

B When you have finished, do a survey with the whole class.

- How many people study each subject?
- How many people have the same teachers?

UNIT 8 Recycling

This Unit and IELTS

In Section 2 of the IELTS Listening test, you listen to a monologue. You may need to listen to factual information and complete a flow-chart. In this unit, you will listen to monologues about recycling and complete **flow-charts**.

Introducing the topic

The environment is an important issue around the world. One problem is what to do with all the waste we produce. We can help to minimise this problem by reusing and recycling. This means making sure that we use things more than once, instead of throwing them away, and processing used products to make new ones.

1 Discuss these questions with a partner.

    a.   What do you know about recycling?

    b.   Why is it important?

    c.   What kinds of products can be recycled?

    d.   Do you usually recycle any products? If so, which kinds?

Technical vocabulary

2 Pay attention to how these words sound.

aluminium	fibreglass	sand
ash	gas	glass
chemical	limestone	metal

Check the meaning of the words above in your dictionary. If possible, check them in an English - English dictionary as well as a translation dictionary.

General vocabulary

3 Write the word or words you hear to match each meaning.

    a. _____ a place where rubbish is dumped and covered with earth

    b. _____ the process of reprocessing a used product so that it can be used again

    c. _____ with bubbles of washing soap in it

    d. _____ the ordinary people of a town, city or country

    e. _____ a factory, where things are processed to make new products

    f. _____ to change from solid form to liquid in hot temperatures

    g. _____ an enclosed box used for heating things to high temperatures

    h. _____ a specially-shaped container into which metal or glass is poured to give it form

    i. _____ to make something flat by moving a tube-shaped object backwards and forwards over it

4 *Write the vocabulary list word which best fits in the spaces in the sentences below.*

    a.   _____ products uses less energy than making them new.

    b.   If you recycle, you are helping to reduce the waste at your local _____.

    c.   Bottles and cans are collected and taken to a recycling _____, where they are made into new products.

    d.   Glass or metal can be heated in a _____ until it melts.

    e.   A machine can _____ out the metal to make it thin.

    f.   Hot glass can be poured into a _____ to make it into a shape.

5 *Check your answers.*

Synonyms

6 *Write the words next to their synonyms below.*

    a.   bin   _____

    b.   to separate   _____

    c.   to break   _____

    d.   to place   _____

    e.   to sterilize   _____

    f.   to pick up   _____

    g.   drink   _____

    h.   to take   _____

Task type: Flow-chart completion

Flow-charts are used to show the steps of a process. Steps are explained in note form, not full sentences, and the direction of each step is shown by arrows. In this task type, you may need to write *one or two* words to complete each part of the flowchart. You must write these words exactly as you hear them.

In the box on the next page are the instructions and the first questions for Listening 1.

7 *In pairs, quickly discuss the following questions.*

    a.   What do you have to write—words, letters or numbers?

    b.   How many items should you write for your answer?

TIP

When you are completing a flow-chart in the IELTS Listening test, you need to write the exact words that you hear. You should not change the form of the words.

Listen and complete the flow-chart. Write NO MORE THAN TWO WORDS for each answer.

Glass bottles and jars cleaned in 1. _____ water

⬇

collected in public 2. _____ or picked up by

3. _____ companies

8 *Write the words and phrases that you hear.*

a. _____

b. _____ and _____

c. _____ the _____

d. _____

e. _____ or _____

f. _____

g. _____

h. _____

i. _____

j. _____

k. _____

l. _____

TIP

You will have to choose the correct words from a whole sentence or sentences that you hear to write in a shorter phrase.

9 *Complete the phrases. Write NO MORE THAN TWO WORDS for each answer.*

a. _____ and _____ are collected

b. taken by the general public to _____

c. sorted into _____ by glass collection companies

d. millions and millions of _____

e. first step in the _____

f. melted in a very _____

g. taken to another _____ for further processing

TIP   Synonyms and paraphrasing

Often the words around the gaps on your page will be different or in a different order to those that you hear. You need to listen carefully for synonyms and paraphrasing (words with the same or similar meanings).

10 Complete the phrases. Write NO MORE THAN TWO WORDS for each answer.

a. no _____ or _____ on the glass
b. people take glass to _____
c. recycling happens at a _____
d. waste reduced in _____
e. cans cut into _____
f. aluminium _____ and _____ thin by machine

Language focus – Sequencing words and phrases

11 Look at these sequencing words and phrases, and make sure that you understand their meanings. If necessary, check in your dictionary.

First	The first step	Secondly	Thirdly
Next	Then	After that	In the final stages
Finally	Lastly		

12 Order these steps in a process. Write the letters **a-f**. One of them, **e**, has already been done for you as an example.

__**e**__   glass mixed with sand and melted in furnace
_____   bottles and jars taken to recycling plant
_____   melted glass poured to make new bottles and jars
_____   bottles and jars washed
_____   glass broken into small pieces
_____   bottles and jars collected from people's homes

Language focus – Revision: The passive

13 Complete the sentences. Write TWO WORDS for each answer.

a. The bottles and jars _____ in recycling bins.
b. The glass _____ into small pieces.
c. The aluminium _____ in a hot furnace.
d. The bottles _____ at the recycling plant.
e. The aluminium _____ to make it thin.
f. The drinks _____ to shops and supermarkets for sale.

14 *Complete the flow-chart notes. Notice how, in note form, the passive form can be shortened.*

bottles and jars **a.** _____ in recycling bins

⬇

sterilized and **b.** _____ at the plant

⬇

c. _____ and **d.** _____ to make new bottles

Getting ready to listen – Prediction

15 *You will hear the first part of Listening 1. First, try to answer the questions. Circle the correct letter, **A**, **B** or **C**.*

a. What type of text do you think this will be?

    A. a conversation between two people
    B. a conversation between more than two people
    C. a monologue(just one person talking)

b. What is the main topic?

    A. cleaning glass
    B. making glass
    C. recycling glass

c. What objects do you think they might be talking about?

    A. bottles and jars
    B. windows
    C. mirrors

16 *Check your answers.*

Complete the flow-chart. Write NO MORE THAN TWO WORDS for each answer.

glass bottles and jars cleaned in **1.** _____ water

⬇

collected in public **2.** _____ or picked up by

3. _____ companies

⬇

taken to a **4.** _____

⬇

EITHER bottles **5.** _____ and refilled

⬇

OR glass **6.** _____ into small piece

⬇

glass mixed with **7.** _____ and limestone

⬇

melted in a **8.** _____

⬇

EITHER made into new **9.** _____ and _____

⬇

OR used to make tiles or **10.** _____

Check your answers.

Listening 2

Complete the flow-chart. Write NO MORE THAN TWO WORDS for each answer.

Cans collected in **11.** _____ or picked up from houses by trucks

⬇

Checked for **12.** _____ or other materials

⬇

Taken to a **13.** _____

⬇

Cut into **14.** _____ by a machine

⬇

15. _____ in a hot furnace

⬇

Poured into **16.** _____ to cool

⬇

Heated and **17.** _____ thin

⬇

Made into **18.** _____ by another machine

⬇

Painted, dried and **19.** _____

⬇

Filled with **20.** _____ and _____

Final activity

A *First, talk with a partner.*

    a. Ask them if they recycle any products.
    b. If so, which ones. / If not, ask why not.

B *Next, work with your partner to write some questions to ask people about their recycling habits.*

    a. Share your questions with the whole class, and design a class survey.
    b. Finally, in pairs, take your survey questions to another English class.
    c. Interview the students.
    d. Note down their information as you listen.

C *Report back to your class afterwards.*

This Unit and IELTS

In Section 1 of the IELTS Listening test, you listen to a conversation.

You may need to complete a variety of question types. In this unit, you will listen to restaurant conversations and answer **multiple choice** and **form-completion** questions.

Introducing the topic

dessere seated (着席)
desert

This unit is about eating out. In many Western countries, people usually eat breakfast and dinner at home and lunch at their school or place of work. However, sometimes, they meet up with friends to have lunch at a cafe or restaurant, and sometimes they go out with family or friends to have dinner in a restaurant. In some countries, it is also quite common to eat breakfast out at a cafe. Cafes usually serve lighter meals than restaurants, and are only open during the day, for breakfast, lunch and coffee. Restaurants usually serve larger meals, and generally only open at night, although some also open for lunch. Often, the food that people eat in cafes and restaurants is different to the food they usually eat at home. It can be richer, and generally contains different ingredients to those that people buy to cook for themselves.

1 *Discuss the following questions with a partner.*

   a. How often do you eat out?
   b. Do you eat out for breakfast, lunch and dinner?
   c. What type of food do you eat when you eat out? Is it different to the food you cook for yourself?
   d. Have you ever eaten at a Western-style restaurant? What type of food did they serve? Did you like it?

Vocabulary

2 *Pay attention to how these words sound.*

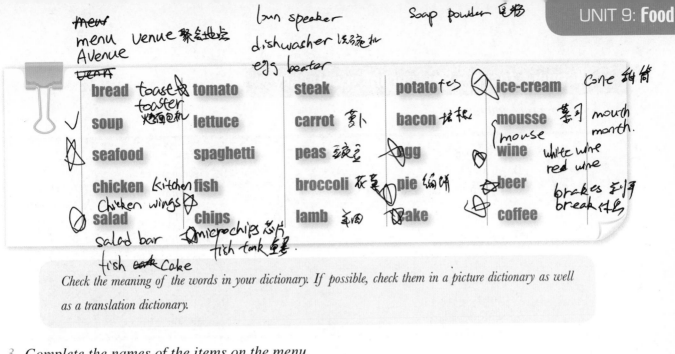

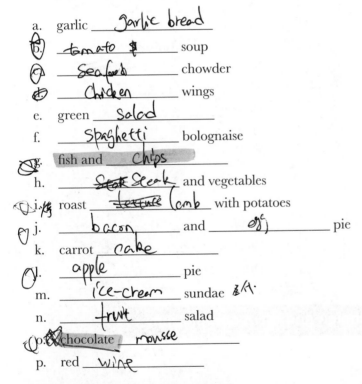

menu *venue* 聚会地点
Avenue

bun speaker
dishwasher 洗碗机
egg beater

Soap powder 皂粉

bread *toast* *toaster*	tomato	steak	potatoes	ice-cream	*Cone 舒筒*
soup *烤面包机*	lettuce	carrot 胡萝卜	bacon 培根	mousse 慕斯 *mouse* *mouth* *month*	
seafood	spaghetti	peas 豌豆	egg	wine *white wine* *red wine*	
chicken *Kitchen* fish *Chicken wings*		broccoli 花菜 pie 馅饼	beer	*brakes 刹车* *break 休息*	
salad	chips	lamb 羊肉 cake	coffee		

salad bar *microchips 芯片*
fish tank 鱼缸
fish cake

Check the meaning of the words in your dictionary. If possible, check them in a picture dictionary as well as a translation dictionary.

3 *Complete the names of the items on the menu.*

a.   garlic ___garlic bread___

b.   ___tomato___ soup

c.   ___Seafood___ chowder

d.   ___Chicken___ wings

e.   green ___salad___

f.   ___Spaghetti___ bolognaise

g.   fish and ___chips___

h.   ___Steak___ and vegetables

i.   roast ___lamb___ with potatoes

j.   ___bacon___ and ___egg___ pie

k.   carrot ___cake___

l.   ___apple___ pie

m.   ___ice-cream___ sundae 圣代

n.   ___fruit___ salad

o.   chocolate ___mousse___

p.   red ___wine___

Restaurant vocabulary

4 *Complete the questions.*

a.   What would you like to _____?

b.   Will you be having a _____?

c.   Would you like a green _____?

d.   What will you have for your _____ course?

e.   Would you like to order a _____?

f.   Would you like any _____ with your meal?

5 *Choose the one you hear.*

a.	A. apple pie B. steak pie C. bacon and egg pie	b.	A. carrot cake B. chocolate cake C. chocolate mousse
c.	A. fish and chips B. fish and vegetables C. fish and potatoes	d.	A. roast lamb with carrots B. roast lamb with broccoli C. roast lamb with peas
e.	A. fruit salad B. green salad C. seafood salad	f.	A. chicken pie B. chicken soup C. chicken wings

6 *Complete the menus.*

a.

Menu

Starter: _____

Main: _____

Dessert:_____

Drink: _____

b.

Menu

Starter: _____

Main: _____

Dessert:_____

Drink: _____

c.

Menu

Starter: _____

Main: _____

Dessert:_____

Drink: _____

d.

Menu

Starter: _____

Main: _____

Dessert:_____

Drink: _____

Task type: Revision – Multiple choice and form completion

Multiple choice

7 *Answer the multiple choice questions.*

a. What does Michelle want for her main course?

   A. garlic bread

   B. steak and vegetables

   C. spaghetti bolognaise

b. What vegetables come with the steak?

   A. carrots and peas

   B. broccoli and potatoes

   C. They don't know.

c. What does Paul want for his main?

    A. green vegetables and steak

    B. roast lamb with potatoes

    C. He hasn't decided.

d. What does Michelle order for dessert?

    A. nothing

    B. ice-cream

    C. mousse

Form completion

8 *Complete the form. Write NO MORE THAN TWO WORDS for each answer.*

<table>
<tr><td colspan="2" align="center">**Menu**</td></tr>
<tr><td>Starters:</td><td>green salad</td></tr>
<tr><td></td><td>**a.** _____</td></tr>
<tr><td>Mains:</td><td>fish and chips</td></tr>
<tr><td></td><td>**b.** _____</td></tr>
<tr><td>Desserts:</td><td>carrot cake</td></tr>
<tr><td></td><td>**c.** _____</td></tr>
<tr><td>Drinks:</td><td>**d.** _____</td></tr>
<tr><td></td><td>beer</td></tr>
</table>

Getting ready to listen – Prediction

9 *You will hear the introduction to Listening 1. First, try to answer the following questions.*

a. What type of text do you think this will be?

    A. a conversation between two people

    B. a conversation between more than two people

    C. a monologue(just one person talking)

b. What is the main topic?

    A. cooking a meal

    B. ordering a meal

    C. shopping at the supermarket

c. Where are they?

    A. in the kitchen

    B. in the supermarket

    C. in a restaurant

10 *Check your answers.*

Listening 1

Part A
*Choose the correct letter, **A**, **B** or **C**.*

1. Where are they sitting?
   - A. next to the window
   - B. next to the door
   - C. in the centre of the room

2. What is Dan having as a starter?
   - A. tomato soup
   - B. green salad
   - C. He isn't having a starter.

3. When did Lucy last eat?
   - A. in the morning
   - B. at lunchtime
   - C. in the afternoon

Part B
Complete the form below. Write NO MORE THAN THREE WORDS for each answer.

	Menu
Starters:	tomato soup
	seafood chowder
	4. _____
Mains:	roast lamb
	bacon and egg pie
	5. _____
	spaghetti bolognaise
Desserts:	apple pie
	6. _____

Listening 1 – check

Check your answers.

Listening 2

Part A
*Choose the correct letter, **A**, **B** or **C**.*

7. What is the name of the couple?

   A. Mr and Mrs Watson

   B. Mr and Mrs Williams

   C. Mr and Mrs Wilson

8. Where do they decide to sit?

   A. next to the window

   B. next to the door

   C. in the centre of the room

9. What number is their table?

   A. 14

   B. 24

   C. 34

Part B

Complete the form below. Write NO MORE THAN THREE WORDS for each answer.

Menu	
Starters:	green salad
	10. _____
Mains:	11. _____ with potatoes
	12. _____
Desserts:	13. _____
Drinks:	coffee
	14. _____

Final activity

A *Work in groups.*

   a. Decide on a menu for a restaurant.

   b. Use the food and restaurant vocabulary you have learned in this unit.

B *Now, work in pairs to do a role play activity.*

   a. One person is the waiter, and the other person is the diner.

   b. Use a copy of the menu that you have written in your groups.

   c. The ' waiter' should note down what the other person wants to eat.

   d. The 'waiter' should then check with them at the end that this is correct.

C *When you have finished, swap roles and do the activity again.*

UNIT 10 Technology

This Unit and IELTS

In Section 2 of the IELTS Listening test, you listen to a monologue. You may be asked to listen to factual information and complete a set of notes. In this unit, you will listen to descriptions of digital cameras and notebook computers and complete **notes**. You will also revise **table-completion** and **matching** questions.

Introducing the topic

This unit is about technology. In the 21st century, technology affects almost every aspect of our lives. Whether for home, work, study, entertainment, health or travel, we rely on all sorts of mechanical, electrical and electronic devices to help us. From cars and television sets, to desktop computers and microwave ovens, the list is endless.

1 *Discuss the following questions with a partner.*

a. What are the most important pieces of technology in your life? (For example, your computer, your play station, your television set or something else?)

b. Why are these things important to you? Is one of them more important than the others?

c. How often do you use them?

d. Imagine that you had to live without them. How different do you think your life would be?

Technical vocabulary

2 *Pay attention to how these words sound.*

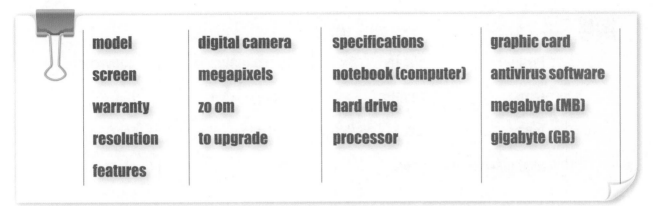

model	digital camera	specifications	graphic card
screen	megapixels	notebook (computer)	antivirus software
warranty	zo om	hard drive	megabyte (MB)
resolution	to upgrade	processor	gigabyte (GB)
features			

Check the meaning of the words in your dictionary. If possible, check them in an English - English dictionary as well as a translation dictionary.

3 *Write the word or words to complete each sentence.*

a.   I'm looking to buy a _____.

b.   Do you know which _____ you'd prefer?

c.   This one here has a large _____.

d.   The _____ is excellent.

e.   It's 8.4 _____.

f.   It also has a 5x optical _____.

g.   This one certainly has a lot of _____ for the money.

h.   If you'd like to see the exact _____, just let me know.

i.   We offer a very comprehensive 2-year _____.

j.   You can also _____ this to 5 years by paying an extra $150.

k.   This _____ is very light and easy to carry.

l.   The _____ has a lot of space for storing files.

m.   This one here has quite a fast _____.

n.   They all come with free _____.

o.   The _____ enables you to deal with a lot of images.

p.   It has a 2 _____ hard drive.

q.   The upgrade will give you an extra 500 _____.

4 *Check the meaning of the words below in your dictionary. If possible, check them in an English-English dictionary as well as a translation dictionary.*

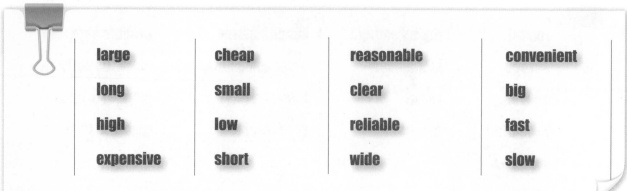

large	cheap	reasonable	convenient
long	small	clear	big
high	low	reliable	fast
expensive	short	wide	slow

5 *Write the word or words to complete each sentence.*

a. The price for this one is very _____.

b. The screen size makes it very _____ for viewing photos and movies.

c. This model is quite _____.

d. This television has a very _____ picture.

e. The screen on this one is a bit too _____.

f. These all come with a _____ warranty.

g. This camera has a nice _____ zoom.

h. This model here is very _____.

i. If you want a _____ model, you can't expect as many features.

j. The processor on this computer is quite _____.

k. This one has quite a _____ capacity.

l. This one here only comes with a _____ warranty.

m. This digital camera has a _____ megapixel count.

n. This one offers a lot of features for a _____ price.

o. The hard drive on this computer isn't _____ enough.

p. I need one with a _____ processor.

Language focus – Comparative and superlative adjectives

6 *Write the words and phrases you hear.*

a. _____

b. _____

c. _____

d. _____

e. _____

f. _____

g. _____

h. _____

i. _____

j. _____

k. _____

l. _____

m. _____

n. _____

o. _____

p. _____

7 *Complete the sentences. Write NO MORE THAN THREE WORDS for each answer.*

a. This model is _____ than that one.

b. This computer is _____ than the other one.

c. This camera has _____ zoom.

d. This one has _____ screen.

e. This television is _____ of the three.

f. This one here has _____ processor than that one.

g. This notebook comes at _____ price than the other one.

h. You'll find that this screen size is _____ for viewing photos.

i. This model has _____ hard drive.

j. This one comes with _____ warranty.

k. This model definitely has _____ processor.

l. This screen gives you a _____ picture.

m. This one comes at _____ price because of all the features.

n. This notebook has _____ warranty.

o. The price of this television here is _____.

p. The one here definitely has _____ screen.

Task type: Note completion

Here are the instructions and questions for a practice note-completion task.

8 *In pairs, consider the table below. Discuss the following questions.*

    a.   What do you have to write—words, letters or numbers?

    b.   How many items should you write for your answer?

    c.   Which words and numbers do you need to write?

    d.   Try to guess some of the answers before you hear the listening text. Which answers seem most logical?

Listen and answer the note-completion questions. Use the words and numbers from the box. Write NO MORE THAN THREE WORDS AND/OR A NUMBER for each answer.

longest	most
cheaper	best
2-year	shorter
lowest	30-inch
smaller	highest

Comparison of three televisions:

- Movie Max 2 has **1.** _____ screen.
- Movie Max 2 has **2.** _____ resolution.
- Movie Max 2 is **3.** _____ expensive.
- Teleview XT is **4.** _____ Movie Max 2.
- Teleview XT has **5.** _____ screen.
- Teleview XT has **6.** _____ warranty than Movie Max 2.
- Teleview XT offers **7.** _____ value for money.
- Vistotron has **8.** _____ screen than Teleview XT.
- Vistotron has **9** _____ resolution.
- Vistotron has **10.** _____ warranty.

9 *Complete the notes above. When you have finished, check your answers with your partner.*

    a.   Did you guess any of the answers correctly before you listened?

    b.   Did you both get all the same answers?

Getting ready to listen – Prediction

10 *You will hear the introduction to Listening 1. First, try to answer the following questions.*

a. What type of text do you think this will be?

    A. a conversation between two people

    B. a conversation between more than two people

    C. a monologue (just one person talking)

b. What is the main topic?

    A. televisions

    B. computers

    C. cameras

c. Where is it taking place?

    A. in someone's house

    B. in a shop

    C. in a classroom

11 *Check your answers.*

Comparison of three digital cameras

Part A

Complete the notes. Write NO MORE THAN THREE WORDS for each answer.

- CF Superzoom:
    — has **1.** _____ zoom
    — has **2.** _____ screen size
    — is **3.** _____ model

- Photo-Pal A23:
    — has **4.** _____ megapixel count
    — screen is **5.** _____ size for viewing photos
    — warranty is **6.** _____ that for CF Superzoom

- QT Easishot:
    — is **7.** _____ model
    — has **8.** _____ megapixel count
    — screen is **9.** _____ size

Part B

Complete the table. Write NO MORE THAN TWO WORDS AND/OR A NUMBER for each answer.

Specifications	CF Superzoom	Photo-Pal A23	QT Easishot
Megapixels	12	**10.** _____	7
Zoom range	**11.** _____	4x	3x
Screen size	3.5 inches	3 inches	**12.** _____
Standard warranty	**13.** _____ warranty	1-year warranty	**14.** _____ warranty

Check your answers.

Comparison of three notebook computers

Part A

Answer the note-completion questions. Write NO MORE THAN THREE WORDS for each answer.

- Speedy Z:
  - has **15.** _____ processor
  - has **16.** _____ graphic card
  - comes with free **17.** _____

- Maestro Supalite:
  - has **18.** _____ hard drive than Speedy Z
  - has **19.** _____ screen
  - comes at **20.** _____ price

- Genius XT:
  - has **21.** _____ graphic card
  - comes with **22.** _____ warranty
  - is one of **23.** _____ models

Part B

*Complete the matching questions. Write ONE letter from **A-H** beside each number.*

A. has 266 MB graphic card
B. has 15-inch screen
C. costs $1,950
D. has 2.5 GB hard drive
E. costs $1,295
F. 3-year warranty
G. costs $899

24. the Speedy Z ....
25. the Maestro Supalite ....
26. the Genius XT ....

Final activity

A *In pairs, choose one item of technology that you want to research—perhaps a digital camera, a television set or a notebook computer.*

B *Then, do some research to find out the main specifications and features of each model, as well as the price. To do this, you could either look on the internet or go to an electronics store.*

C *When you have the information, make a table like the one from Listening 1, Part B to display the data for each product side by side.*

D *Finally, make a presentation to the rest of the class, where you show them the data, and explain which model is cheaper, more expensive, faster, more reliable, and so on.*

This Unit and IELTS

In Section 3 of the IELTS Listening test, you listen to a longer conversation and answer a variety of questions. In this unit, you will listen to a conversation on censorship and answer **sentence completion** questions.

Introducing the topic

Internet censorship is an issue around the world, as parents and experts must decide what is safe for people, especially children, to see, and what should be controlled or restricted in some way. The censorship issue applies to television shows, movies, computer games, the internet, and more. Many people disagree about how much censorship there should be, and what form it should take. Some possible options include: age restrictions, making parents responsible, banning unsuitable material, or providing ratings so people can decide for themselves.

1 Discuss these questions with a partner.

a. Do you think that there should be censorship to prevent children from seeing unsuitable material?
b. What do you think is the best form of censorship?
c. Who do you think should be responsible for deciding what is suitable or unsuitable?

Vocabulary

2 Pay attention to how these words sound.

in real life	appropriate	behaviour
fair	scene	right
protect	responsibility	commit
violent	suitable	fighting
disturbing	frighten	be allowed to
battle	nightmare	rating

Check the meaning of the words above in your dictionary. If possible, check them in an English - English dictionary as well as a translation dictionary.

TIP

A useful method for learning new vocabulary items is to write a sentence for each word. This way, you can remember how to use the word in context.

3 Write the word or phrase from the box to complete each sentence. *Note: you will not need all of the items in the box.*

rating	battle	violent	nightmare	protect
responsibility	appropriate	scene	commit	in real life

a. Some people worry that television crime shows or violent computer games may show how to _____ a crime.

b. If you have a bad dream, it's called a _____.

c. Sometimes it is necessary to distinguish between what can happen on television or in a game and what happens _____.

d. Who should take _____ for what children see on television?

e. The _____ of a movie is the score it receives, either to say how good it is, or to show who it is suitable for, and whether it contains anything offensive.

f. Parents want to be sure that their children are watching television that is _____ for their age.

4 Match the vocabulary list words to their synonyms.

right	battle	fair	allow
disturbing	suitable	behaviour	restrictions

a. _____ actions, conduct   e. _____ limits, rules

b. _____ permit, let   f. _____ correct, true

c. _____ appropriate, fitting   g. _____ upsetting, distressing

d. _____ fight, war   h. _____ equal, reasonable

5 *Write the synonym you hear to complete the sentences.*

a. Do violent computer games affect children's _____?

b. Some parents may _____ their children watch violent movies.

c. Ratings tell parents if a movie is _____ for their children.

d. A computer game may have graphic _____ scenes.

e. Age restrictions can prevent children from seeing _____ material.

f. There may be more than one _____ way to restrict movies and games.

g. Some television shows may be _____ to small children.

h. Any rules about censorship need to be _____.

6 *Write the noun form of these adjectives and verbs.*

a. violent _____   d. restrict _____

b. criminal _____   e. protect _____

c. act _____   f. behave _____

7 *Identify the word you hear.*

a. violent   violence   violently

b. crime   criminal   crimes

c. acting   action   act

d. restrict   restriction   restricting

e. protection   protected   protective

f. behaves   behaviour   behave

8 *Consider which type of word is missing from each space—circle your choice (noun, verb, adverb or adjective).*

a. Some parents worry their children will behave _____ after playing computer games. [noun, verb, adverb *or* adjective]

b. Some movies and television shows show how to commit _____. [noun, verb, adverb *or* adjective]

c. Do you ever try _____ like a character from a movie? [noun, verb, adverb *or* adjective]

d. Some countries have laws to _____ the content of computer games. [noun, verb, adverb *or* adjective]

e. Children need to be _____ from some of the sites on the internet. [noun, verb, adverb *or* adjective]

f. Some people say that watching violent movies doesn't affect their _____. [noun, verb, adverb *or* adjective]

9 *Write the words you hear in the gaps above.*

Identifying opinion

Stating an opinion

- **In my opinion ...**
- **I think / I guess / I suppose / It makes sense that ...**

Saying you have the same opinion

- **I agree** (with you/that) **/ I think so / suppose so.**
- **That's right.** or **You're right.**

Saying you have a different opinion

- **I disagree** (with you/that) **/ I don't think so.**

TIP

In Sections 3 and 4 of the IELTS Listening test, you may be asked questions about the speakers' opinions. Here are some ways of giving an opinion that you may hear.

10 *Write the opinion words you hear.*

a. _____. I'd never thought of it like that before.

b. _____ that there are the same rules for everyone.

c. _____ with the idea that computer games are dangerous.

d. _____ . Those games are not suitable for children.

e. _____ we'll have to make a decision tomorrow.

f. _____ . It isn't fair to have different rules for games and movies.

11 *Work in pairs and take turns to do the following: one person reads a sentence below, the other person listens and replies to the sentence by choosing an expression from Exercise 10.*

a. What do you think about children viewing violent television shows? (*state opinion*)

b. Some computer games are designed for adults, so they should have an age restriction. (*agree*)

c. Only parents should be responsible for what computer games their children play. (*disagree*)

d. Violent television shows should not be shown on television at all. (*agree*)

e. Adults should be able to choose what they can watch on television. (*disagree*)

Alternatively, *use the audio, and write appropriate responses. Pause the audio after each sentence to allow enough time to write.*

a. state opinion: _____

b. agree: _____

c. disagree: _____

d. agree: _____

e. disagree: _____

Task type: Sentence completion

In this task type, you must write *one or two words* to complete each sentence, exactly as you hear them. To become good at this, try dictation exercises: listen to words and write them down exactly as you hear them. The sentence you must complete may not contain exactly the same words as you hear. The words you see on the paper will have the same meaning, but they may be synonyms of the words you hear.

Language focus – Dictation

TIP

A useful method to practise answering sentence completion questions is dictation. Listen to words and write them down exactly as you hear them.

12 *Write the words that are missing from these sentences.*

a. _____ show if a game is suitable for parents to buy.
b. Children might try and _____ a game when playing with their friends.
c. That game is not suitable for _____.
d. People younger than sixteen are not _____ buy this game.
e. _____ on television should be banned.
f. These kinds of shows might _____ children.
g. Even worse, young people might _____ after playing violent computer games.

13 *These sentences are not exactly the same as those that you will hear. First, read the sentences and look at the key words. Think of synonyms for those key words.*

a. Age restrictions on games help us _____ young people.
b. Young people could be _____ by seeing violence on television.
c. Children may have _____ from watching battle scenes.
d. Adults who watch violent television shows might become _____.
e. Computer programs can contain graphic fighting _____.
f. Some television shows might show how to _____.
g. In my opinion, it is the children's parents' _____ to choose what is suitable for them to watch.

14 *Complete the sentence with the words you hear. Were you right?*

Getting ready to listen – Prediction

15 *You will hear the introduction to a listening text. First, try to answer the following questions.*

a. What type of text do you think this will be?
   A. a conversation between two people
   B. a conversation between more than two people
   C. a monologue (just one person talking)

b. The people speaking are:
   A. a man and a woman.
   B. two boys and a girl.
   C. four girls.

c. What is the main topic?
   A. a computer game
   B. buying a computer
   C. a television show

TIP

Before you listen, look at the sentence completion task and think about what the missing word or words might be. For example, do you think there will be: a description, an action, a thing? Will the missing words be adjectives, nouns, verbs or adverbs?

16 *Check your answers.*

Listening 1

Complete the sentences below. Write NO MORE THAN TWO WORDS for each answer.

1. Paul can't buy the game because he is not _____.
2. The game contains _____ scenes that young people shouldn't see.
3. Children may get injured if they mimic the game's violence in _____.
4. Games that are not designed for young people should have an _____.
5. Paul thinks that _____ should decide which games to buy their family.
6. Paul's friends agree that restrictions on games should be just like restrictions on _____.

Listening 1 – check

Check your answers.

Listening 2

Complete the sentences below. Write NO MORE THAN TWO WORDS for each answer.

7. The television show that Carla is watching is about _____.
8. Jack and Sally agree that it is not appropriate for _____ to see that type of show.
9. Carla believes that violent crime shows should not be shown to _____.
10. There's a possibility people may attempt to repeat a _____ that they saw on television.
11. Jack believes that _____ should not have restrictions on their television viewing.
12. The three friends decide to _____ about this topic.

Final activity

A *In groups of three or four, talk about your opinions of age restrictions on games, movies and television shows.*

- Use the language you have learned to state your opinion.
- Listen carefully, and take turns to agree or disagree with the opinions of other members of your group.

B *Interview someone in your family to find out their opinions on violence in computer games, movies and television shows.*

C *Report back to your class—state whether you agree or disagree with that person's opinions.*

This Unit and IELTS

In Section 4 of the IELTS Listening test, you listen to a monologue. There will not be any pauses for you to write your answers and there is no chance to listen a second time. In this unit, you will learn how to listen for main ideas. You will complete a **summary**. You will also practise **paraphrasing**, which is an essential skill for completing a summary.

Introducing the topic

These days, adventure sports are very popular with young people. Some examples of adventure sports are kite-surfing, rock climbing, kayaking, scuba diving, surfing, skiing, mountain biking and paragliding. These are all exciting outdoor sports with a risk of injury. Many of these are water sports, while others are land-based sports.

1 Discuss these questions with a partner.

    a.   Have you seen any of these sports on TV or for real?

    b.   Which ones are you interested in watching?

    c.   Would you like to try any of them yourself?

    d.   Which ones do you think are the most dangerous?

    e.   Do you think anyone should ever do any of these sports alone?

Vocabulary

2 *Try to classify the words below according to the number of syllables [1-4] in each word.*

> **TIP**
> A key to successful listening is being able to understand the language you are hearing. Understanding pronunciation is therefore a very important part of listening. Learning how to listen for syllables is an essential step in understanding the words you hear.

Words	No. of syllables	Words	No. of syllables
e.g. popular	**3**		
a. dangerous		g. techniques	
b. fatal		h. protective	
c. experienced		i. vital	
d. certified		j. hazard	
e. launch		k. forecast	
f. emergency		l. proportion	

3 *Check your answers.*

4 *Choose the letter of the word you hear which best matches the meaning of the word in the table.*
   You will hear two words after each number.

Target vocabulary		Answer
e.g ***focus***		***ii)***
a. fatal	i)	ii)
b. experienced	i)	ii)
c. vital	i)	ii)
d. proportion	i)	ii)
e. dangerous	i)	ii)
f. have a go	i)	ii)
g. techniques	i)	ii)
h. emergency	i)	ii)
i. certified	i)	ii)
j. hazards	i)	ii)

5 *Write the word or words to complete each sentence.*

1. Even _____ kite-surfers sometimes have serious accidents.

2. Bad weather causes a significant _____ of rock climbing accidents.

3. _____ techniques are things you need to do to protect yourself in a crisis.

4. Going kite-surfing in stormy weather is very _____.

5. If you have training with a _____ instructor, you are less likely to hurt yourself.

6. Natural _____ are things like rocks that are not man-made but occur naturally.

7. If you _____ at kite-surfing, it means you try to do it.

8. It is _____ to check the weather before going rock climbing.

9. There are a number of _____ accidents every year in sports such as kite-surfing and rock climbing.

6　*Consider these words for some clothing and equipment used in two sports.*

Vocabulary – Clothing and equipment			
first aid kit	gloves	harness	helmet
life jacket	ropes	waterproof	wetsuit

Check the meaning of the words in your dictionary.

7　*Complete the sentences using the vocabulary for clothing and equipment.*

a.　A _____ is used to keep people warm in the water.

b.　A _____ is used to keep you afloat if you fall in the water.

c.　A _____ is used to protect your head.

d.　_____ are important for keeping your hands warm.

e.　It is wise to have a _____ if there is any chance of injury in your sport.

f.　A _____ is an important piece of equipment for a climber who uses ropes.

g.　Take _____ clothing if it looks like rain.

8　*Complete these sentences.*

a.　It looks like it's going to rain. Take your _____ jacket.

b.　Kayakers wear a _____ in case they fall out of the kayak and into the water.

c.　Wear _____ in cold weather so your hands don't get too cold.

d.　If you're going out surfing today, it's cold, so wear your _____!

e.　Your guide will have a _____ to use if you get injured.

f.　Wear a _____ when climbing to protect your head from falling rocks.

g.　Make sure all your _____ are correctly fastened before starting to climb.

9　*Check your answers.*

Language focus – Giving advice

10 *Choose the options that you hear.*

a. (Looking out / Look out) for natural hazards such as loose rocks.

b. (You need to / You shouldn't) try kayaking if you don't know how to swim.

c. (Getting / Get) specialized climbing shoes. You'll really notice the difference!

d. Never (go / going) climbing in the mountains if storms are forecast.

e. You shouldn't try (sailing / sail) if you don't know how to swim.

f. (You should / Make sure) you take extra food and clothes in case you get caught in a storm.

g. You need to (checking / check) wind speed and direction before you launch your kite.

h. Always (choosing / choose) a location that suits your level of skill.

i. (Make sure / You need to) there is a safety release system for your kite.

Task type: Summary completion

In Section 4 of IELTS listening, you may have to write down words to complete a summary. The words you hear may not be the same as the ones on the paper, but they will have a similar meaning. Before you listen, think carefully about the words around each space, and other ways of stating the same information. Try and predict what language will be used. You also need to read the instructions carefully. Usually you will write no more than ONE, TWO or THREE words and / or a number. In this unit, you will practise writing only ONE word and / or a number.

Paraphrase

11 *Match the sentences you hear [a -d] to the sentences below [i - iv].*

a - d	Paraphrases
	i. Don't go skateboarding if it is rainy and windy in case you get hurt.
	ii. When you start skateboarding, you should buy the proper safety devices and make sure you know how to use them.
	iii. This lecture will focus on some of the safety issues for skateboarders.
	iv. If you get some lessons from a teacher, you can learn how to skateboard properly.

12 *Read the summary below and circle the correct options.*
If you choose 'noun', think about singular or plural. If
you choose 'verb', think about the correct ending.

TIP
Try to guess what kind of word you
will be listening for BEFORE you
hear the audio. This will help you
hear the right answer.

A growing number of people are **(a)** *(verb / adjective)* all over the world, resulting in a number of serious and even **(b)** *(noun / adjective)* accidents every year.

You should get proper training in basic skills, the use of safety devices and **(c)** *(verb / adjective)* techniques. Make sure you have **(d)** *(noun / adjective)* clothing, such as a helmet and life jacket. Don't try kite-surfing unless you can swim.

Once you have done your training, there are two **(e)** *(verb / adjective)* things that you should remember. First, choose a good place to practise, without a lot of other people around and with few natural **(f)** *(noun / adjective)*. Second, always check the **(g)** *(noun / verb)*. Avoid strong winds, which might result in **(h)** *(noun / verb)*. That usually causes serious injuries.

13 *You will hear the introduction to Listening 1. First, try to answer the following questions.*

a. What type of text do you think this will be?

    A. a conversation between two people
    B. a conversation between more than two people
    C. a monologue (just one person talking)

b. What is the topic of this lecture likely to be?

    A. some information on kite-surfing accidents
    B. some instructions on how to control your kite
    C. some safety advice for people learning kite-surfing

 14 *Check your answers.*

Listening 1

Complete the summary. Write NO MORE THAN ONE WORD AND/OR A NUMBER for each answer.

A growing number of people are **(1)** _____ all over the world, resulting in a number of serious and even **(2)** _____ accidents every year.

You should get proper training in basic skills, the use of safety devices and **(3)** _____ techniques. Make sure you have **(4)** _____ clothing, such as a helmet and life jacket. Don't try kite-surfing unless you can swim.

Once you have done your training, there are two **(5)** _____ things that you should remember. First, choose a good place to practise, without a lot of other people around and with few natural **(6)** _____. Second, always check the **(7)** _____. Avoid strong winds, which might result in **(8)** _____. That usually causes serious injuries.

Listening 1 – check

Check your answers.

Listening 2

Complete the summary. Write NO MORE THAN ONE WORD AND/OR A NUMBER for each answer.

A growing number of people are **(9)** _____ climbing all over the world, resulting in a number of **(10)** _____ falls every year.

You should get proper training in basic skills, the use of safety devices and emergency **(11)** _____. Make sure you have protective equipment, such as a helmet and **(12)** _____. Don't try rock climbing unless you have first practised on a training wall.

Once you have done your **(13)** _____, there are two vital things that you should remember. First, choose a good place to practise, without a lot of other people around and with few **(14)** _____ hazards. Second, always check the **(15)** _____. Avoid storms with rain, snow and strong gusts that might cause a climber to **(16)** _____.

Final activity

A *Make notes on the safety issues and equipment related to a sport that you enjoy.*

B *Work with a partner.*

    a.   Give a 1 – 2 minute talk on the sport you have chosen.

    b.   Answer your partner's questions.

    c.   Listen to your partner give a talk on their sport.

    d.   Ask 3 – 4 questions.

Social Issues

This Unit and IELTS

In Section 3 of the IELTS Listening test, you listen to a longer conversation and answer a variety of questions. In this unit, you will listen to conversations on city life and **label plans**.

Introducing the topic

In large cities with limited public transport, most people travel by car. In cities with a good rail network, many people travel by train or subway. They often use bicycles to get to the train station, or to travel short distances.

1 Discuss these questions with a partner.

a. How do you prefer to travel—by bus, train, subway, bike, car, or on foot(walking)?
b. How do you usually travel to work or school?
c. When you travel by bicycle, where do you leave it?
d. How do you make sure your bicycle is safe?

Vocabulary

2 Pay attention to how these words sound.

leave	entrance 入口	upgrade 升级	racks ✗
cover	roof	surveillance ✗	security 安全体
conscious 意识到的	store 自在	locker 储物柜	baggage 行李
ticket	machine 信手机 机器	mall 购物中心 shopping mall	exit 紧急出口

degrade 恶化

Check the meaning of the words in your dictionary. If possible, check them in an English-English dictionary as well as a translation dictionary.

3 *Write the word or words from the box to complete each sentence. Note: use each item once only.*

| roof | stored | lockers | racks | security | leave |
| conscious | cover | tickets | baggage | machine | |

a. If you worry about safety, you are _security conscious_

b. Bikes are often __stored__ on bike __racks__, which are metal bars that hold bikes upright.

c. You can buy train __ticket__ from a ticket office or (ticket) __machine__.

d. __Lockers__ are locked cupboards used to store ~~baggage~~ or maybe bikes.

e. It's a good idea to __leave__ your bike under __cover__, which means leaving it in a place with a ~~roof~~ _It is may be a good idea to do →_

4 *Choose the option that you hear.*

a. He is waiting by the (entrance, exit) to the International Centre.

b. These lockers are for storing (bikes, baggage).

c. She wants to know if there is a safe (locking, parking) area for her bike.

d. The station has video (surveillance, security).

e. I'm going to park my bike outside that (mall, store).

Review: Prepositions of place

5 *Number these expressions in the order that you hear them.*

1. ____ just inside the door

2. ____ outside the door

3. ____ in the far corner

4. ____ to your right

5. ____ between two people

6. ____ opposite the door

Remember to listen for these expressions when labelling a plan.

6 *Pay attention to how these words sound.*

clothes store   food court   menswear store

department store   art supplies shop   ice cream parlour

electronics store   jewellery store   supermarket

Check the meaning of the words in your dictionary.

7 *Write the store names into the plan.*

You are here: **X**

a. _____ _____			electronics store
b. _____ _____	c. _____ _____	d. _____ _____	e. _____ _____

Negotiating meaning

TIP

In the IELTS Listening test, speakers may negotiate meaning. This means that speakers may repeat information, ask questions to check information or say something wrong and then correct themselves, or they may be corrected by someone else. Here are some ways of checking, confirming and changing information.

Checking information

• using questions: Did you just say ...? / What about ...? / Can I make sure?
• restating in a question (saying the same information, but as a question)

Confirming information

• Yes / That's right / Sure

Changing information

• In a statement: Sorry ... / Wait ... / No ...
• In a question: Don't you mean ... / If ... / Isn't it ...
• Restating information correctly: I mean ... / What I meant to say was ... / Instead ...

8 *Decide whether these are questions or statements.*

a. question / statement
b. question / statement
c. question / statement
d. question / statement
e. question / statement

TIP
Remember:
in question intonation, the voice is higher at the end;
in statement intonation, the voice stays the same or goes down.

9 *Choose check, confirm or change.*

Kelly: Where can I buy a ticket at the station?
Ben: Well, there's no ticket office, so use the ticket machines just outside the door.
Kelly: The ticket machines are just outside the door?   check / confirm / change
Ben: Oh no, sorry, they are just inside the door.   check / confirm / change
Kelly: Just inside the station door?   check / confirm / change
Ben: That's right.   check / confirm / change

Task type: Label a plan

In this task type, you must listen to a conversation and decide where options are on a plan. Before you listen, look closely at the plan, and the list of options. Keep the option words in your mind, and listen out for these words.

Listen carefully to the whole conversation, because not all of the options will be on the plan. However, the speakers may mention an option that doesn't appear on the plan in their conversation, or they could give wrong information, and then correct themselves.

Language focus – Listening for signpost words

TIP
A useful method to practise labelling a plan questions is to listen for signpost words. Listen to the signpost words in conversations and decide what the speaker is trying to say. Are they checking, confirming or correcting information?

10 *Decide if the speaker is checking, confirming or changing information. Remember to listen for question or statement intonation.*

a. checking / confirming / changing
b. checking / confirming / changing
c. checking / confirming / changing
d. checking / confirming / changing
e. checking / confirming / changing

11 You will hear the introduction to Listening 1. First, try to answer the following questions.

a. What type of text do you think this will be?

    A. a conversation between two people
    B. a conversation between more than two people
    C. a monologue (just one person talking)

b. The people speaking are:

    A. a man and a woman.
    B. two males and a female.
    C. two females and a male.

c. What is the main topic?

    A. riding bikes
    B. leaving a bike at the train station
    C. catching a train

12 Check your answers.

Look at the options **A-I** for **Listening 1**.

- Read each option and say the words in your head.
- Think about how the words sound, so you will notice them during the listening.

Look at the plan for **Listening 1**.

- Look at the information written on the plan (Platform 1, Station Entrance).
- Say these words in your head.
- Think about where the numbers are in relation to the information on the plan.
- Try and predict what language will be used to describe the location of these numbers.

> **TIP**
> A useful skill for this type of question is reading before you listen, and thinking about what you will hear.

Listening 1

*Label the plan below. Choose SIX answers from the box and write the correct letters **A-I** next to questions **1-6**.*

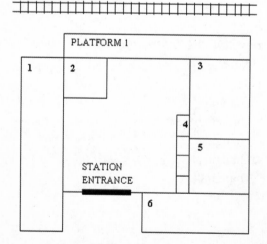

A. cafe
B. information desk
C. baggage lockers
D. open-air bike parking
E. bike lockers
F. covered bike parking
G. ticket office
H. ticket machines
I. tourist information

1. _____   4. _____
2. _____   5. _____
3. _____   6. _____

Listening 1 – check

Check your answers.

Listening 2

*Label the plan below. Choose SIX answers from the box and write the correct letters **A-I** next to questions **7-12**.*

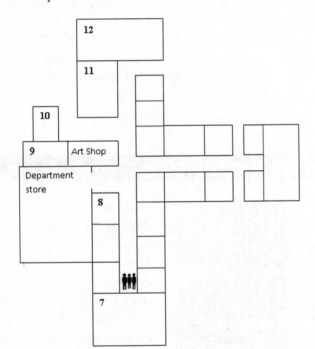

A   jewellery store
B   supermarket
C   menswear store
D   Music-Music store
E   baby clothes store
F   electronics store
G   food court
H   video store
I   bookstore

7. _____   10. _____
8. _____   11. _____
9. _____   12. _____

Final activity

A   *Draw a plan of a station, mall or other building you know well.*

   a.   Write numbers in some parts of the building, and give a list of possible labels.
   b.   Give your plan to your partner.
   c.   Tell them about the building; they must listen and label the plan.
   d.   Check their answers.

B   *Then, look at your partner's plan.*

   a.   Listen to your partner telling you about their building.
   b.   Label their plan.
   c.   Check your answers.

This Unit and IELTS

In Section 4 of the IELTS Listening test, you listen to a monologue. There will not be any pauses for you to write your answers. In this unit, you will learn how to listen for main ideas, with a focus on distinguishing imperatives from suggestions. You will complete a set of **short-answer questions**, which is a typical IELTS listening task.

Introducing the topic

A person who takes things that belong to other people is a thief; the plural of 'thief' is 'thieves'. Taking other people's things is called 'theft'. Theft is often a problem for tourists and for students in schools and universities.

1 Discuss these questions with a partner.

   a. Is there a problem of theft in your school or university?

   b. If you use a bicycle, do you have to lock it?

   c. Do you think tourists in your country have to worry about theft of money or things such as their cameras?

Vocabulary

2 Choose the word that matches the meaning.

TIP

It is important to try and work out what words used in the question paper mean, as this will help you predict what you are going to listen to.

Words	Meanings
Example:	
i ... ii ...	*things you wear on your feet*

Words		Meanings
i	ii	a. two or more things used or put together
i	ii	b. a good price for something—the buyer is happy
i	ii	c. to inform someone
i	ii	d. the common opinion of a person or place
i	ii	e. able to be seen
i	ii	f. people who take things
i	ii	g. things that are worth a lot of money
i	ii	h. to take someone's attention away from their main focus
i	ii	i. to think someone might be dishonest
i	ii	j. the main site of a school or university

3 *Classify these words according to the stress patterns in the table below. First, listen to the examples from the stress pattern table.*

combination	reputation	documents	traditional
visible	valuables	suspicious	distract
bargain	campus	notify	transaction

Pronunciation		
Stress patterns		**Words**
a.	oO *e.g. advise*	
b.	Oo *e.g. focus*	
c.	Ooo *e.g. realise*	
d.	oOo *e.g. proportion*	
e.	oOoo *e.g. experienced*	
f.	ooOo *e.g. celebration*	

4 *Check your answers.*

5 *Dictation: write the words to complete each sentence.*

a. It is important to _____ and possessions safe, wherever you are.

b. Don't carry a _____ or give out your bank account details to strangers on the telephone.

c. Your passport, sunglasses, laptop and wallet are all valuable, so don't _____ _____ in your car.

d. Tissues, pens, eye drops or make-up are not as valuable and can be carried _____ _____ or a waist bag.

e. If things go missing from your hotel room, _____ the tour leader and the police.

6 *Complete the sentences, using the words below.*

combination	reputation	documents	thieves
visible	valuables	suspicious	distract
bargain	campus	notify	transaction

1. To be _____ means you think there is something wrong or dishonest.

2. Your bank statement will list all your _____. Always check that there are no errors.

3. Some markets have a _____ for theft. You have to be very careful.

4. Essential travel _____ include your passport and air tickets.

5. Accommodation for first year students is usually available on a university _____.

6. The tour guide says that a group of people may try to _____ you so they can take something such as your camera.

7. Thieves in crowded places often use a _____ of crowds and distractions to take cameras and other valuables.

8. Make sure your money isn't _____ and easy to take without you noticing.

9. It is important that you know where your _____ are at all times.

7 *Check your answers.*

Task type: Short-answer questions

In Section 4 of IELTS listening, there may be short-answer questions. You must read the instructions carefully. Usually you will write no more than TWO or THREE words and / or a NUMBER. If you write more, your answer will be wrong even if it includes the correct words.

Remember to use the reading time to read the questions. This will introduce some of the vocabulary in the listening text. It will also help you think about the kind of answers to write.

8 *Answer the short answer questions. Write no more than ONE word for each answer.*

What is the tour guide talking about?

       tomorrow's **1.** _____

What are they going to do?

- go to the **2.** _____ in the old part of the city
- visit the palace

What should they all wear?

       comfortable **3.** _____

Language focus – Distinguishing imperatives from suggestions / Use of modals for suggestions

9 *Write the letter for each statement you hear in the correct column to complete the table.*

Imperatives – instructions	Suggestions
e.g. a	

TIP

In IELTS listening, you may need to understand how instructions are different from suggestions. In English, we use imperative verbs to give a direct instruction. Suggestions usually have a modal verb such as 'should' or 'may' to make them less definite and also more polite.

10 *Listen again to the same statements and write the word / words to complete each sentence.*

a. _____ a waist bag for valuables; it's not safe.

b. _____ of local people who promise to help you find a bargain.

c. _____ of your money in a money belt that is hidden under your clothes.

d. _____ money out of your money belt in a crowded place unless some of your tour group members are there with you.

e. Your passport, tickets and other essential documents _____ in the hotel.

f. _____ a lot of cash or keep cash in your hotel room.

g. If you lose your card, you _____ the bank and the police at once.

h. You _____ your bank statements to ensure that all the transactions are correct.

i. If you own a car, _____.

j. You _____ buying a steering lock or car alarm.

k. _____ valuables such as CDs or mp3 players in view on the seats.

l. People here use debit cards. It _____ a good idea for you to get one too.

11 *You will hear the introduction to Listening 1. First, try to answer the following questions.*

a. What type of text do you think this will be?

   A. a conversation between two people

   B. a conversation between more than two people

   C. a monologue (just one person talking)

b. Who is likely to be giving this talk?

   A. the hotel manager

   B. one of the tourists

   C. the tour guide

c. Who is likely to be listening to this talk?

   A. some people in the hotel dining room

   B. some people who are going to take a tour

   C. some people who work at the hotel

12 *Check your answers.*

Listening 1

Complete the short-answer questions. Write NO MORE THAN TWO WORDS AND / OR A NUMBER for each answer.

What combination of things in a marketplace makes thieves happy?

- **1.** _____
- tourists

Which two examples of essential documents are named by the speaker?

- **2.** _____
- **3.** _____

Which three minor items are said to be alright in a waist bag?

- **4.** _____
- **5.** _____
- cheap reading glasses

What information about prices did the tour guide give for when people bargain in the bazaar?

- The initial price will be **6.** _____.
- A fair price is about **7.** _____ of the initial price.

))
Listening 1 – check

Check your answers.

))
Listening 2

Complete the short-answer questions. Write NO MORE THAN TWO WORDS AND / OR A NUMBER for each answer.

When you get a debit card, what advice does the speaker give in relation to the PIN? Don't:

- use an **8.** _____.
- tell anyone what your number is.

Who must you notify if you lose your card?

- **9.** _____
- **10.** _____

Which scams does the speaker tell you to beware of?

- **11.** _____ scams
- **12.** _____ scams

What three kinds of possessions are said to be attractive to thieves in College Hall?

- **13.** _____
- mp3 players
- **14.** _____

Which car safety devices does the speaker suggest car owners should buy?

- **15.** a _____
  or
- **16.** a _____

Final activity

A *Think about issues related to the theft of money and possessions*

a. in the place where you live.
b. in the place where you study.

B *Work with a partner.*

a. Give a 1 – 2 minute talk on how students should protect themselves from theft.
b. Answer your partner's questions.
c. Listen to your partner's talk.
d. Ask 3 – 4 questions.

This Unit and IELTS

In Section 3 of the IELTS Listening test, you will listen to a dialogue between two, three or four people. The conversation is divided into two parts.

The general topic area is education and training and the discussion will be in an academic context. In this unit, the main skill focus is on listening for specific information. The main task types you will practise in this unit are **table completion** and **sentence completion**.

Introducing the topic

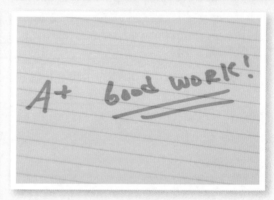

One of the biggest issues that young people face is assessment. Exams are generally an unavoidable fact of life for both high school students and university students. However, other methods of assessment are increasingly being used throughout primary, secondary and tertiary education.

1 Discuss the following questions with a partner.

    a. How do you feel about tests and exams?

    b. Are they necessary?

    c. Can you think of other ways that your teachers could test your knowledge of a subject?

    d. Do you prefer to study for one big exam worth 100% or would you prefer to have several smaller assessments adding up to 100%?

Technical vocabulary

2 *Pay attention to how these words sound.*

assessment	quiz	research	percentage
schedule	continuous	in-depth	time management
overview	specific	visual aid	discussion
spreadsheet	baseline	project	article
framework	knowledge	participation	references
exam	field trip	seminar	bibliography
assignment	presentation	proportion	lecture

Check the meaning of the words in your dictionary. If possible, check them in an English-English dictionary.

3 *Number the nouns below in the order you hear them in the sentences.*

Nouns	
presentation	assessment
assignment	schedule
references	seminar
research	participation

4 *Choose nouns from the box above to complete each sentence.*

a. I have to give an oral _____ next week. I'll have to stand up in front of everybody and talk on this topic for three to five minutes.

b. _____ in the _____ is important. Our lecturer says we must take part in the discussion.

c. Over the next few weeks I need to gather a lot of information from various sources for my _____ project.

d. Look at this timetable with all the dates of the essays and tests. It's a very busy _____ _____.

e. I've just received a terrible grade for my last _____. I forgot to make a list of all the books, articles and websites I used to get information for the essay. The lecturer said a list of _____ is essential!

5 *Check your answers.*

6 *Choose the word (i or ii) that best matches the meaning.*

Words	Meanings
i or ii	a. expedition to study something in a real or natural environment
i or ii	b. general understanding of something as a whole
i or ii	c. ongoing
i or ii	d. particular, precise, exact
i or ii	e. programme, timetable
i or ii	f. small class for study and discussion
i or ii	g. a part of the whole
i or ii	h. a list of books/articles on a particular subject or by a particular author
i or ii	i. taking part
i or ii	j. plan, structure

 7 *Look back to Exercise 2, and decide which of the words or phrases from the vocabulary list best fits each description. The first one has been done for you.*

Example: a. They have to complete one set task every two weeks.

a. They have to complete an ____**assignment**____ *every two weeks.*

b. We had a _____.

c. I have good _____.

d. The class is going on a _____.

e. We need to establish a _____.

f. Professor Brown gave a _____.

g. They are doing some _____.

h. They discussed _____.

i. Professor Knox published an _____.

j. Accountancy students often use a _____ to display numbers.

 8 *Check your answers.*

Task type: Table and sentence completion

A variety of task types is possible in any section of IELTS listening, so remember to read the instructions carefully and check the maximum number of words allowed. Use the time at the beginning and in the middle of the section to look at the questions ahead. Even while you are listening, it is a good idea to look at least one question ahead. In this way, if you miss the answer to a particular question, you can pick up the next one without getting lost. Table completion and sentence completion questions require you to listen for specific information.

Language focus – Expressing opinion/certainty/uncertainty

TIP

In IELTS Listening tasks you will hear speakers use a variety of language to give opinions and indicate certainty or uncertainty. For example:

VERBS such as, 'think', 'believe', 'suppose', 'seem';

ADVERBS such as, 'possibly', 'probably', 'perhaps', 'absolutely', 'definitely';

MODAL AUXILIARY VERBS such as, 'may', 'might', 'could'.

9 *Try to predict which kind of word you need for the answer—verb, adverb or modal auxiliary verb.*

   a. (verb / adverb / modal) there is a particular theory you'd like to challenge.

   b. This research project (verb / adverb / modal) involve costly equipment.

   c. There (verb / adverb / modal) be government funding you can apply for.

   d. I (verb / adverb / modal) we (verb / adverb / modal) look at this book.

   e. That should (verb / adverb / modal) be the second choice.

   f. I (verb / adverb / modal) a good system is important.

   g. We (verb / adverb / modal) display the posters in the hall.

   h. August is (verb / adverb / modal) the best month for handing in the research project.

10 *Complete each sentence with the words you hear.*

   a. _____ there is a particular theory you'd like to challenge.

   b. This research project _____ involve costly equipment.

   c. There _____ be government funding that you can apply for.

   d. I _____ we _____ look at this book.

   e. That should _____ be the second choice.

   f. I _____ a good system is important.

   g. We _____ display the posters in the hall.

   h. August is _____ the best month for handing in the research project.

11 *You will hear part of a discussion between a student and her academic advisor. Listen and complete the sentences below. Write NO MORE THAN TWO WORDS for each answer.*

   a. Emma has come to see her academic advisor about her _____.

   b. She's uncertain about what _____ to choose.

   c. She will have to write a _____.

   d. Emma may decide to challenge a particular _____.

   e. Some research projects might involve expensive _____ or_____.

   f. She could apply for _____ funding or a local business might give her money if her research is _____.

12 Check your answers.

13 You will hear three students discussing the reading list for their assignment. Listen and complete the table below. Write NO MORE THAN THREE WORDS OR A NUMBER for each answer.

AUTHOR	TITLE	PUBLISHER	PLACE	YEAR
Argyle and a._____	'Gaze and Mutual Gaze'	Cambridge University Press	—	1976
Berne	b. '_____, _____	Grove Press	c._____	—
Lambert	d. '_____, _____	—	—	1996
Wolfe	'A Psychology of Gesture'	Methuen	London	e._____

14 Check your answers.

Getting ready to listen – Prediction

15 You will hear the introduction Listening 1. First, try to answer the following questions.

a. What type of text do you think this will be?
  A. a conversation between two people
  B. a conversation between more than two people
  C. a monologue (just one person talking)

b. What are the teachers likely to be discussing?
  A. a subject timetable
  B. tests and assignments
  C. holiday plans

16 Check your answers.

Listening 1

1. Ms Potts prefers to work with:
   A. a computer.
   B. pencil and paper.
   C. spreadsheets.

2. She believes it is essential to have:
   A. a good system.
   B. good old days.
   C. one major assessment.

3. John thinks continuous assessment:
   A. makes him sick.
   B. affects his performance.
   C. is fair.

Questions 4 – 10

Complete the table below. Write NO MORE THAN TWO WORDS AND/OR A NUMBER for each answer.

ASSESSMENT SCHEDULE	
January	*No assessment — summer holiday*
February	**4.** _____; (set essay topics)
March	Field trip; **5.** _____ with photographs
April	**6.** _____ with visual aids. *Break.*
May	A series of **7.** _____ (short-answer questions)
June	Mid-year exams
July	*Break.* **8.** _____
August	**9.** _____
September	**10.** _____. *Break.*
October	Test
November	Final exam
December	*No assessment — summer holiday*

Check your answers.

Listening 2

Questions 1 – 4

Complete the sentences below. Write NO MORE THAN THREE WORDS OR NUMBERS for each answer.

1. Jim thinks he won't have a social life because of _____.
2. Last year Jim enjoyed the _____.
3. The _____ is scheduled for September.
4. There are _____ books and _____ articles on the reading list.

Questions 5 –10

Complete the table below. Write NO MORE THAN ONE WORD OR A NUMBER for each answer.

	ASSESSMENT SCHEDULE	Value
January	*No assessment—summer holiday*	
February	Quiz; (set essay topics)	5. _____%
March	Field trip; poster with photographs	6. _____%
April	Oral presentation with visual aids. *Break.*	7. _____%
May	A series of quizzes (short-answer questions)	10%
June	Mid-year exams	8. _____%
July	*Break.* 5,000 word essay	10%
August	Research projects	9. _____%
September	Seminar. *Break.*	5%
October	Test	10. _____%
November	Final exam	20%
December	*No assessment—summer holiday*	

Final activity

In small groups discuss your worst exam experiences.

- Are there any similarities?

Now talk about your most positive exam experiences.

- What do they have in common?

As a result of your discussion, what can you say were the main contributing factors to the negative situations?

- What can you learn from these to ensure better outcomes in the future?

Commodities

This Unit and IELTS

In Section 4 of the IELTS Listening test, you listen to a longer monologue and answer a variety of questions. There will not be any pauses for you to write your answers. In this unit, you will practise listening to a monologue on manufacturing processes and answer **flow-chart completion** questions.

Introducing the topic

Generally, commodities are goods, or things that have some value. They are bought and sold, or are traded for other goods. In economics, commodities are raw products that have standard prices. Staple foods, gold, fuel and many other things can be considered as commodities.

1 *Discuss these questions with a partner.*

    a. What kinds of things do you usually buy?
    b. Are they commodities?
    c. What do you think are the most common commodities? Compare your list with another pair.
    d. How do prices for commodities affect prices for things we buy in everyday life?

Vocabulary

2 *Pay attention to how these words sound.*

factory	soft drink	flavour	ingredients
tank	bubbles	unique	recipe
secret	syrup	pressure	sample
chewing gum	contain	packet	

Check the meaning of the words in your dictionary. If possible, check them in an English - English dictionary as well as a translation dictionary.

3 *Tick the words as you hear them.*

bubbles	packet	secret
factory	pressure	syrup
flavour	recipe	tank
ingredients	sample	unique

4 *Which word was not used?* _____

TIP

A useful method for writing difficult vocabulary items in a listening test is to write the letters of the sounds you hear, and continue listening. When the listening is finished, you can go back and correct your spelling. Otherwise, if you spend too much time thinking about how to spell a word, you could miss the next answer in the listening!

5 *Write the word or words to complete each sentence.*

a. In this _____, they make soft drinks and _____ gum.

b. The _____ used to make the gum are mixed in a big _____.

c. Both products _____ flavour and sugar _____.

d. The _____ for making soft drinks may be a secret because each flavour is

_____.

e. When you go on a factory tour, you can _____ the different flavours, and maybe take

some _____ home.

Process verbs

6 *Consider the verbs below. Check the meaning of any new words in your dictionary.*

add	collect	cut	distribute	dry
filter	grind	label	make	mix
purify	roll out	seal	sterilise	stir
test	transfer	wrap		

*7 Match the process verbs, **a-d**, with the nouns from the same family **i)-iv)**.*

a. purify
b. produce
c. add
d. mix

i) production, product
ii) mixture
iii) impurity
iv) additive

8 Write the process verbs to complete each sentence.

a. We must _____ the mixture before we _____ the other ingredients.

b. The machines _____ and then _____ the mixture.

c. The workers _____ and _____ out the ingredients.

d. We must _____ the mixture to another machine before we _____ the other ingredients in.

e. It is important to _____ and _____ the products.

Passive forms

9 Write the verbs (given in brackets) in passive form.

a. Before other ingredients are _____ (add), the mixture must be _____ (purify).

b. It is _____ (filter) and then _____ (sterilise) to remove impurities. Then it is _____ (test).

c. The ingredients need to be _____ (collect) and _____ (dry) out before they can be _____ (process).

d. The mixture is _____ (transfer) to another machine before the other ingredients are _____ (stir) in.

e. Before the products are _____ (distribute), they must be _____ (seal). Bottles and packets need to be _____ (label).

TIP
When describing a process (for example, in a flow-chart) we often do not say who does the actions. Instead, the passive form of the verb is used. Make sure you can recognise passive forms when you hear them.

10 Check your answers and your spelling.

Task type: Flow-chart completion

In this task type, you may need to write *one or two words* to complete each part of the flow-chart. You must write these words exactly as you hear them.

Flow-charts are used to show a process. A process is a series of actions that happen in a specific order. To improve your flow-chart completion skills, it is useful to know different ways of describing a process.

The information in the flow-chart that you must complete may not contain exactly the same words as you hear. The words you see on the paper will have the same meaning, but they may be written in note form, with a lot fewer words than what you hear.

Language focus – Listening for process information

11 Write the missing words into these notes as you listen to a description.

a. the water is _____ in a tank

b. the gum is _____ in a round machine

c. the packets of gum are _____ around the country

d. the syrup is _____ into the water

e. the gum is _____ into pieces

f. the flavours are made with a _____ company recipe

TIP

A useful method to practise answering flow-chart completion questions is listening to longer texts to complete short descriptions. Listen for the missing words and write them down exactly as you hear them.

12 Write the words you hear to complete the flow-chart. (These flow-chart notes are not exactly the same as the audio; first, read the notes and look at the key words.)

How raw sugar is made in Sucrose Factory:

sugar cane is **a.** _____ and taken to the factory

⬇

the cane is **b.** _____ to get juice

⬇

the juice is **c.** _____ and then thickened by boiling to make syrup

⬇

the **d.** _____ is boiled until sugar crystals grow

⬇

the sugar crystals are **e.** _____ to make raw sugar

TIP

Another useful skill when answering flow-chart completion questions is prediction. Before you listen, look at the flow chart and think about what the missing word might be. For example, do you think there will be a description? A process? A product name?

Getting ready to listen – Prediction

13 You will hear the introduction to Listening 1. First, try to answer the following questions.

a. What type of text do you think this will be?

A. a conversation between two people

B. a conversation between more than two people

C. a monologue (just one person talking)

b. What is the main topic?

A. factories

B. the soft drink manufacturing process

C. drinking soft drinks

14 Check your answers.

Listening 1

Complete the flow-chart below. Write ONE WORD for each answer.

Soft drink factory production line:

water is filtered and sterilised in a large tank, and then **1.** _____ for quality

⬇

the **2.** _____ flavours are made using a secret company recipe

⬇

these flavours are mixed with sugar to make **3.** _____ which is sterilised and then added to the water

⬇

4. _____ are added when the drink is mixed with carbon dioxide in a carbonator

⬇

the drink is **5.** _____ in bottles and cans

⬇

the bottles are labelled

⬇

the soft drinks are **6.** _____ around the country

Listening 1 – check

Check your answers.

Listening 2

Complete the flow-chart below. Write ONE WORD for each answer.

Chewing gum factory production line:

gum is **7.** _____ from trees

⬇

it is **8.** _____ and dried and the resulting product arrives at the factory

⬇

this is heated and **9.** _____, an important step to make sure the gum is clean

↓

sugar syrup, **10.** _____ and colours are added to the hot gum

↓

the gum is mixed until smooth in a round machine

↓

another machine **11.** _____ out the gum and then it is cooled before being cut into pieces

↓

foil-wrapped pieces of gum are **12.** _____ in packets

↓

the packets are **13.** _____ and boxed for distribution around the country

Final activity

A *Work together in groups of three or four.*

    a.   Decide on a product.

    b.   Plan a talk about how a product is made.

B *Take turns to give your talks.*

    a.   Don't say the name of the product.

    b.   Use the process verbs you have learned to explain the process.

    c.   Ask your partners what your product is.

C *Listen to your partners give their talks.*

    a.   See if you can identify the products they are talking about.

    b.   Check to see if you are correct.

Dieting

This Unit and IELTS

In Section 3 of the IELTS Listening test, you listen to a longer conversation and answer a variety of questions. In this unit, you will listen to conversations on dieting and answer **sentence completion** questions.

Introducing the topic

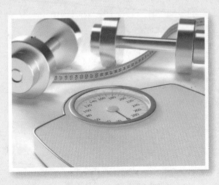 

Dieting is a common issue among young people, especially girls. In Western countries, as many as fifty or sixty percent of girls are unhappy with their body weight. Many of them try unhealthy forms of dieting in order to lose weight.

1   Discuss these questions with a partner.

    a.   Do you think young people should go on diets?

    b.   Do you or your friends ever go on diets?

    c.   What forms of dieting do you think are unhealthy?

    d.   What do you think is the best way to lose weight?

Vocabulary

2 *Pay attention to how these words sound.*

extreme	diet	invite	serious
avoid	concerned	weight	public
lose	obsessed	habits	gain
continue	fitness	realise	

Check the meaning of the words in your dictionary. If possible, check them in an English - English dictionary as well as a translation dictionary.

3 *Write a word from the box to complete each sentence (not all of the words in the box are used).*

habits	serious	fitness	extreme	weight
lose	realise	diet	avoid	obsessed

a. Your eating habits can affect your _____, and over time, your health.

b. Many girls go on diets to _____ weight and look slim.

c. It is important to watch what you eat, but also to have a high level of _____.

d. An _____ diet is one where you make many changes to your eating habits.

e. If you spend too much time thinking about something, you are _____.

f. It's important to _____ when you have unhealthy habits.

4 *Check your answers.*

5 *Write the words you hear in Exercise 2 to complete the sentences (each missing word is from the same word family as a vocabulary list word, but it may be in a different form).*

a. Many people don't know how much they _____.

b. Some girls get really obsessed about _____.

c. Extreme weight _____ can be bad for your health.

d. To be healthy, it's important to keep _____.

e. We _____ our friends around for a special dinner.

f. If you are training _____ for a sport, you may be on a special diet.

6 *Check your answers.*

7 Write the number of the phrase *1-3* that matches the phrases *a-e*.

    a.   worried about her weight

    b.   get bigger

    c.   go on dieting

    d.   obsessed with her weight

    e.   keep dieting

    f.   get fat

        1.   continue dieting
        2.   concerned about her weight
        3.   gain weight

TIP

In an IELTS Listening test, the words you hear may not be exactly the same as the words on the page. It is useful to know other words with the same meaning (synonyms), and to know which words go well together (collocations).

8 Write the phrase to complete each sentence.

    a.   I'm worried about Jane. She is _____.

    b.   I don't think she should _____.

    c.   I think she needs to _____ some _____.

9 Write prepositions to complete these sentences.

    a.   We always used to meet _____ coffee.

    b.   I don't like to eat _____ public. I don't want people to see me.

    c.   I often see people I know shopping _____ the supermarket.

    d.   I think it's important to listen _____ your friends when they talk to you.

Review: Identifying opinions

10 Write the words you hear to complete each sentence.

    a.   I don't really think it's a _____.

    b.   You could be _____.

    c.   It's not a nice thing to say, but it's _____ .

11 Do the speakers have the same opinion? Write **yes** or **no**.

    a. _____   b. _____   c. _____

Actions and possible consequences

12 Match the possible consequence to complete each sentence.

        i.   might pay attention
        ii.   probably wouldn't exercise as much
        iii.   may find it affects her health
        iv.   may stop gaining weight
        v.   may not listen to me
        vi.   may diet until she ends up in hospital

TIP

When discussing things, people often give explanations for their opinions. Often, these relate to things that may happen (possible consequences) as a result of certain actions. One way of expressing a possible consequence is to use a conditional statement with a modal verb.

a. If she keeps exercising, she _____.

b. If she stopped her gymnastics training, she _____.

c. If we don't do anything, she _____.

d. If I tell her to change her eating habits, she _____.

e. If you tell her what to do, she _____.

f. If she gains a lot of weight, she _____.

Present tense endings

In English, we use the present tense to talk about habits. It is useful to be able to hear the '-s' ending in the singular third person form of verbs, such as 'The sun rises …'. These look simple; however, you need to understand the three different ways of saying these endings. They can make listening difficult.

13 *Look at the list of verbs and try to classify them according to the way the '-s' ending is said.*

diet	exercise	gain	lose	tell
try	keep	change	invite	obsess
realise	weigh	need		

a. /s/	b. /z/	c. /iz/
		e.g. apologises

14 *Check your answers.*

15 *Write the word you hear to complete each sentence.*

a. I think she _____ about her weight.

b. If she _____ too much, she may get sick.

c. If she _____ weight too quickly, that isn't healthy.

d. He said he _____ her to dinner every week, but she never goes.

e. I hope she _____ that she needs to change her habits.

Task type: Sentence completion

In this task type, you must write *no more than three words* to complete each sentence. This means the answer could be one, two or three words long. You must write these words exactly as you hear them. To become good at this, try dictation practice exercises: listen to words and write them down exactly as you hear them.

The sentence you must complete may not contain exactly the same words as you hear. The words you see on the paper will have the same meaning, but they may be synonyms of what you hear.

Language focus – Reported speech

16 *Write the name of the speaker for each sentence: Sue, George, John. (Sue and George are talking about their friend John.)*

    a.   I thought it was very rude.   _____

    b.   Jane is getting fat.   _____

    c.   That was a terrible thing to say. _____

    d.   He should say sorry.   _____

    e.   I am going to apologise.   _____

17 *Write the words to complete the last sentence.*

Well, when I saw him, he said that he _____ apologise.

18 *Complete each sentence to report what you heard.*

    a.   Sue said that she _____.

    b.   George said that he _____.

    c.   John said that he _____.

    d.   Sue said that she _____.

    e.   John said that he _____.

    f.   George said that he _____.

Getting ready to listen – Prediction

19 *You will hear the introduction to Listening 1. First, try to answer the following questions.*

    a. What type of text do you think this will be?

        A. a conversation between three people

        B. a conversation between more than three people

        C. a monologue (just one person talking)

    b. The people speaking are:

        A. a man and a woman.

        B. two women and a man.

        C. three women and a man.

    c. What is the main topic?

        A. exercise

        B. a friend's problem

        C. supermarkets

20 *Check your answers.*

Listening 1

Complete the sentences below. Write NO MORE THAN THREE WORDS for each answer.

1. Sarah said she didn't _____ in reply to the three previous invitations for dinner.
2. Anna said that Sarah doesn't agree to meet her _____ these days.
3. Carolyn and Blair think that Sarah doesn't want to eat _____.
4. Anna saw Sarah in the supermarket and thought she _____.
5. Anna said that Sarah didn't buy any _____ .
6. Blair is worried that Sarah might diet until she has to spend time _____.
7. The friends decide to invite Sarah to a party and _____ about her dieting problem.

Listening 1 – check

Check your answers.

Listening 2

Complete the sentences below. Write NO MORE THAN THREE WORDS for each answer.

8. Helen says that Tina is _____ now, despite gaining weight.
9. Helen thinks that Tina's weight gain might be because she isn't _____ _____ as she was before.
10. Donna says that Tina stopped gymnastics training so that she can _____ _____.
11. Helen thinks that Tina will notice her weight gain is unhealthy and make changes to _____.
12. Donna says Tina doesn't need to be concerned about her weight if she _____ _____.
13. Peter suggests they give her an invitation to go with them for _____.

Final activity

A *Work together in groups of three or four.*

   a. Talk about your opinions of dieting and healthy eating.
   b. Talk about the possible consequences of different actions.

B *Listen carefully.*

   a. See if you have the same opinions as others in your group.
   b. Make notes on other people's opinions.
   c. Write sentences for each person, using reported speech.

This Unit and IELTS

In Section 4 of the IELTS Listening test, you listen to a monologue. There will not be any pauses for you to write your answers. In this unit, you will learn how to listen for detail, with a focus on dates and time phrases. You will complete some **classification** questions.

Introducing the topic

The most famous international sporting competition is the Olympic Games. There are actually two sets of Games, the Summer Olympics and the Winter Olympics. Each of these is held every four years, but with a two year gap between them. Thus the 2006 Winter Olympics were in Italy and the 2008 Summer Olympics were in Beijing.

1 Discuss these questions with a partner.

    a. Do you know when and where the Olympic Games were first held?

    b. How many sports were there in the early Games?

    c. When and where are the next Winter Olympics going to be held?

    d. What about the next Summer Olympics?

Vocabulary

🎵 *2 Listen to the sentences and write down the dates you hear.*

a.   *776 B.C.*

b.   _____

c.   _____

d.   _____

e.   _____

f.   _____

g.   _____

h.   _____

i.   _____

j.   _____

k.   _____

l.   _____

m.   _____

TIP

A key to successful listening is being able to understand the dates and numbers you are hearing. Understanding the pronunciation of dates and numbers is a very important part of IELTS Listening.

🎵 *3 Tick the number that you hear.*

Dates		
e.g 776	1776	✔
a. 654	1654	
b. 423	1423	
c. 992	1992	
d. 377	1377	
e. 532	1532	
f. 859	1859	
g. 229	1229	
h. 1010	2010	
i. 772	1772	

🎵 *4 Write the numbers that you hear.*

Dates
e.g 1910
a. ....
b. ....
c. ....
d. ....
e. ....
f. ....
g. ....
h. ....
i. ....

Task type: Classification

In Section 4 of IELTS listening, there may be **classification questions**. These focus on details such as relationships, rather than opinions. You need to match a numbered **list of items** from the listening text to a **set of criteria**. You must read the instructions carefully.

Remember to use the reading time to read the questions. This will introduce some of the vocabulary in the listening text. It will also help you think about the kind of answers to write.

Example of classification

5 In pairs, quickly discuss the following questions.

a.   What do you have to write—words, letters or numbers?

b.   How many items should you write for each answer?

c.   What do the letters A-C refer to?

6 *Complete the classification questions.*

Language focus – Past tense endings

In English, we use the simple past to talk about history. It is important for you to understand the difference between regular and irregular verbs.

- **Irregular** verbs are those such as 'make – made', 'fly – flew', 'is/are – was/were', 'hold – held', 'understand – understood'. You have to learn these one by one.
- **Regular** verbs, which have an '-ed' ending in the simple past, look easy. However, you need to understand the three different ways of saying these endings. They can make listening difficult.

7 *Classify the list of regular verbs according to the way the '-ed' ending is said.*

    Example: *devoted /id/*

included	added	allowed	founded	permitted
planned	offered	worked	relied	faced
lasted	managed	demonstrated		

/t/	/d/	/id/

8 *Check your answers.*

9 *Write the words to complete each sentence.*

a. In 708 B.C., wrestling was _____ as an Olympic sport for the first time.

b. Over time, other events such as boxing and horse racing were _____.

c. Women weren't _____ to watch or compete in the ancient Olympics.

d. The International Olympic Committee was _____ in 1894.

e. In 1896, 241 athletes _____ for medals.

f. In 1924, women were finally _____ to compete.

g. Organisers for the Beijing Olympics _____ for 302 different events.

h. The 2006 Winter Olympics _____ seven sports, with 84 separate events.

Time phrases – Interpreting meaning

We use a lot of different time phrases when we talk about the history of something. You need to know that B.C. (before Christ) and A.D. (Anno Domini) are used for dates in English. We also use phrases such as:

'during the 1830s' to mean the decade (10 years) from 1830—1839;

'by the end of the 1950s' to mean that something happened before 1960;

'not until the 1830s' to mean that something did not happen before 1830;

'the twentieth century' to mean the 100 years from 1900—1999.

10 *Tick the correct option.*

a. The first recorded Olympic Games were held:

before 776 B.C.   in 776 B.C.   after 776 B.C.

b. The first pentathlon was held:

before 708 B.C.   in 708 B.C.   after 708 B.C.

c. Women were permitted to compete in the Olympics

before 1924   in 1924   after 1924

d. The last Winter Games to be held in the same year as the Summer Games were held in:

1988   1992   1994

e. Two French brothers demonstrated their hot air balloon:

before June 1783   in June 1783   after June 1783

f. Many people were trying to be the first to fly a plane:

in the 1890s   between 1900 and 1909   between 1910 and 1920

g. The first jet plane flew:

before 1939   in 1939   in 1940

11 *Classify the statements about computers according to these time periods.*

	Before 1938	1939 – 1945 (World War II)	1946 – now
e.g.			✓
a			
b			
c			
d			
e			
f			
g			
h			
i			
j			
k			

Title: **History of Computers**

Getting ready to listen – Prediction

12 *You will hear the introduction to Listening 1. First, try to answer the following questions.*

a. What type of text do you think this will be?
   A. a conversation between two people
   B. a conversation between more than two people
   C. a monologue (just one person talking)

b. What is the Community Sports Officer likely to be discussing?
   A. great sporting moments in history
   B. great Olympic athletes
   C. the history of the Olympic Games

13 *Check your answers.*

Listening 1

Complete the classification questions.

Questions 1 – 7

When did the following take place?

A	before 394 A.D.
B	between 1830 and 1896
C	after 1896

*Write the correct letter, **A**, **B**, or **C** next to questions **1-7**.*

1	women permitted to compete	....
2	wrestling added as an Olympic sport	....
3	Winter Games first held	....
4	Seven sports with 84 separate events	....
5	International Olympic Committee founded	....
6	11,000 athletes from 202 nations	....
7	first Games held after revival campaign	....

Listening 1 – check

Check your answers.

Listening 2

Complete the classification questions.

Questions 8 – 14

When did the following events take place?

A	before 1900
B	between 1900 and 1910
C	after 1911

*Write the correct letter, **A**, **B**, or **C** next to questions **8-14**.*

8	Wright brothers flew 35 metres	....
9	first flight by jet plane	....
10	hot air balloon flew with animal 'passengers'	....
11	helicopter flew for 14 minutes	....
12	gliders were flown successfully	....
13	first manned helicopter flight	....
14	Cayley tried to solve the mystery of flight	....

Final activity

A *Make notes on the history of something, for example:*

  a. the mobile phone
  b. the digital camera
  c. the mp3 player
  d. the car navigation system
  e. the sewing machine

B *Work with a partner.*

  a. Give a 1 – 2 minute talk on your topic.
  b. Answer your partner's questions.
  c. Listen to your partner's talk.
  d. Ask 3 – 4 questions.

Online Safety

This Unit and IELTS

In Section 3 of the IELTS Listening test, you listen to a longer conversation and answer a variety of questions. In this unit, you will listen to conversations on online safety and answer **short answer** questions.

Introducing the topic

All kinds of people access the internet. You can publish information online, by putting photos on your website, or writing notes on your friends' websites. Sometimes strangers, people who you do not even know, try to look at your information. Making sure that strangers cannot see your private information is an important part of online safety. It is also important to understand that people can pretend to be someone else online, and lie about their age and other personal information.

1 Discuss these questions with a partner.

    a.   Do you have a website, or a place online where you talk with friends?
    b.   Have you met any strangers on the internet?
    c.   Have any of your friends met anyone in person after meeting them online?
    d.   Do you think the internet is safe for young people?

Vocabulary

2 Pay attention to how these words sound.

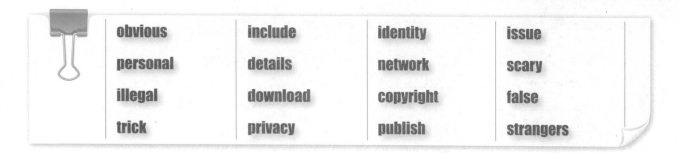

obvious	include	identity	issue
personal	details	network	scary
illegal	download	copyright	false
trick	privacy	publish	strangers

Check the meaning of the words in your dictionary. If possible, check them in an English - English dictionary as well as a translation dictionary.

3 Write the word from the box to complete each sentence (*not all of the words in the box are used*).

| personal | include | false | details | network |
| trick | strangers | publish | privacy | |

a. It's important to protect your _____ when using the internet.

b. It may not be a good idea to _____ your address and phone number on your webpage.

c. Check that your _____ information cannot be viewed by the public.

d. To _____ to the internet means to put something on a website.

e. _____ are members of the public who you don't know.

f. Some websites contain _____ information to try and _____ you.

4 Check your answers.

5 Write the number of each definition next to the matching word.

a. ____ to network   d. ____ illegal

b. ____ identity   e. ____ obvious

c. ____ issue   f. ____ to download

Collocations

6 Write the pairs of words to complete each sentence.

a. It's a bad idea to give your _____ to strangers.

b. When someone takes your personal information and pretends to be you, it is called _____.

c. There are many _____ sites, where people can meet new friends.

d. Music companies are trying to stop _____ of their songs.

e. _____ is when people use the internet to make someone feel bad.

TIP

In an IELTS Listening test, you may have to write words exactly as you hear them. It is useful to know which words go well together (collocations).

7 *Write the phrase you hear to complete each sentence.*

a. Check the _____ on your social networking site.

b. It can be easy to _____ online.

c. A _____ is your personal site or the first page of your website.

d. Many people can access their _____ online.

e. _____ is a term for all your personal information on the internet.

8 *Write the prepositions that you hear to complete each sentence.*

a. Never give _____ information to strangers.

b. Information that is published _____ the internet is public information.

c. Be careful when you meet _____ with new friends.

d. Some people prefer talking face _____ face, rather than online.

e. If you are going to meet someone, get some friends to go along _____ you.

Question tags

9 *Choose whether the speaker is sure or unsure.*

a. sure   unsure
b. sure   unsure
c. sure   unsure
d. sure   unsure
e. sure   unsure

TIP

Question tags are used when you want to confirm something you say. The intonation of question tags shows whether you are sure about the information or not. Question tags with falling intonation show certainty, and rising intonation shows uncertainty.

Task type: Revision – Short answer questions

10 *Complete the short-answer questions. Write NO MORE THAN THREE WORDS for each answer.*

a. What is Jodi trying to add to her web page?

_____

b. Why does Deb say Jodi should not add them to her web page?

_____

c. What other things has Jodi got on her web page that Deb says is unsafe?

her _____ and _____

Sentence completion

11 *Complete the sentences below. Write NO MORE THAN THREE WORDS for each answer.*

TIP

Another useful skill when answering sentence completion questions is prediction. Before you listen, look at the sentence and think about what the missing words might be. Remember, there may be one, two or three words in each space.

a. Karl is not interested in the new site because he doesn't _____ things on the internet.

b. According to James, modern online shopping sites are not as _____ as they used to be.

c. Karl worries that these websites might _____ and then not send you the product you ordered.

d. Karl thinks auction websites are unsafe, because _____ items on these sites.

Language focus – Inferring information

12 *Answer the questions below.*

a.	Does she believe what she was told?	yes	no
b.	Did she already know what she was told?	yes	no
c.	Is she agreeing with what she was told?	yes	no
d.	Is she saying that she thinks it is safe?	yes	no

TIP

Sometimes people say things indirectly. You may be asked a question where you need to infer information or opinions. Listen and think about what the person is trying to say.

Getting ready to listen – Prediction

13 *You will hear the introduction to Listening 1. First, try to answer the following questions.*

a. What type of text do you think this will be?

   A. a conversation between three people

   B. a conversation between more than three people

   C. a monologue (just one person talking)

b. The people speaking are:

   A. students who are friends.

   B. a teacher and students.

   C. students who don't know each other.

c. What is the main topic?

   A. how to use a computer

   B. the dangers of the internet

   C. how to use the internet safely

14 *Check your answers.*

Questions 1 – 4

Complete the short-answer questions. Write NO MORE THAN TWO WORDS AND / OR A NUMBER for each answer.

1. What is the theme of the group's assignment?
   _____

2. What topic do the students say is a problem in other countries?
   _____

3. What may thieves be able to get into if they have your personal information?
   your _____

4. How long is each part of the presentation?
   _____

Questions 5 – 9

Complete the sentences below. Write NO MORE THAN THREE WORDS for each answer.

5. Ryan wants to present information on downloading unlawfully, because he did _____ _____ on it earlier.

6. Jason thinks _____ is an interesting topic because young people don't know how dangerous their internet activities can be.

7. Liz suggests that details about the _____ of using the internet should be part of their project.

8. Some people publish false work information on the internet to _____ so they give away their personal details.

9. Liz suggests that everyone checks the _____ on their internet sites, so they can access their information.

Listening 1 – check

Check your answers.

Listening 2

Questions 10 – 12

Complete the short-answer questions below. Write NO MORE THAN TWO WORDS AND / OR A NUMBER for each answer.

10. Where has Susie just added images?

    her _____ on Teenspace

11. Why does Mike say information on the internet can be used by other people?

    _____

12. The site that was shown on television gave the girl's name and what other information?

    _____

Questions 13 – 17

Complete the sentences below. Write NO MORE THAN THREE WORDS for each answer.

13. Pete says he prefers talking to his friends _____ rather than online.

14. Susie plans to _____ through her social networking page.

15. Mike says it is dangerous _____ personal details to people you don't know.

16. Many young people frequently _____ on the internet.

17. Susie asked her friends to come with her if she goes to _____ someone she met online.

Final activity

A *Work together in groups of three or four.*

   a. Talk about your opinions on publishing personal information online.
   b. Talk about the safety issues, especially for young people.
   c. Give any examples of risky behaviour that you have heard of.

B *As you listen:*

   a. See if you have the same opinions as others in your group.
   b. Make notes on other people's opinions.
   c. Note down their reasons and decide if you agree.

Environment

This Unit and IELTS

In Section 4 of the IELTS Listening test, you listen to a monologue. There will not be any pauses for you to write your answers. In this unit, you will learn how to listen for main ideas, with a focus on pronoun reference and paraphrase. You will complete some **multiple choice** and **classification** questions, as well as a **summary**.

Introducing the topic

The environment is an important global issue. A key problem is the question of how to manage tourism so that it is good for a country. This means making sure that the local area benefits from the tourist industry and reducing the negative effects of having so many extra visitors.

1 *Discuss these questions with a partner.*

  a. Do a lot of tourists visit your country?
  b. Can you list at least three advantages a country gains from tourism?
  c. What are some of the disadvantages?
  d. What are some possible solutions for the problems you have listed?

Vocabulary

2 *Tick the word you hear.*

	Target vocabulary	
	to affect (v) /	an effect (n)
a.	affects	effects
b.	affects	effects
c.	affects	effects
d.	affect	effect
e.	affects	effects
f.	affect	effect
g.	affect	effect
h.	affects	effects
i.	affect	effect

TIP
A key to successful listening is being able to understand whether you are hearing the noun or the verb when they are similar.

3 *Write the word to complete each sentence.*

a. First, think about the global _____ of tourism.

b. Tourism certainly _____ the world as a whole.

c. One positive _____ is the increased awareness that tourists have of people in poorer countries.

d. The loss of wildlife habitat is a negative _____ of the tourist industry.

e. Next, consider how tourism _____ the local economy.

f. The noise of helicopters _____ people walking the Inca Trail.

g. Tourism has a positive _____ on the number of jobs available for local people.

h. Tourism _____ local supplies of food, water and energy in a negative way.

4 *Tick the words that you hear.*

	Word families	
a.	reduction	reduce
b.	expansion	expand
c.	destruction	destroy
d.	improvement	improve
e.	creation	create
f.	provision	provide

5 *Write the word to complete each sentence.*

    a. The _____ of tourism in poor areas can cause problems such as water shortages.

    b. One positive effect of tourism is the _____ of new jobs.

    c. Another is the _____ of money to look after wildlife in those areas.

    d. The income generated by tourism should be used to _____ local roads and rubbish disposal systems.

    e. People are trying to _____ the impact of tourists in popular areas.

    f. The _____ of habitat affects animals and birds.

    g. Tourism income can be used to _____ for conservation of animals and plants.

    h. Tourist facilities often _____ over good farm land, which puts pressure on food supplies.

6 *Tick the correct column, to classify the words you hear.*

	Buildings and facilities	Methods of transport
a.	……………..	……………..
b.	……………..	……………..
c.	……………..	……………..
d.	……………..	……………..
e.	……………..	……………..
f.	……………..	……………..
g.	……………..	……………..
i.	……………..	……………..
j.	……………..	……………..
k.	……………..	……………..
l.	……………..	……………..
m.	……………..	……………..

Task type: Multiple choice, classification, summary

In Section 4 there may be **multiple choice** questions, **classification** questions and / or a summary. You must read the instructions carefully. Also remember to use the reading time to read the questions. This will introduce some of the vocabulary in the listening text. It will also help you think about the kind of answers to write.

7 *Match the events **1-3** to the time periods, **A-E**.*

> **Questions 1 – 3**
>
> When did the following events in the history of the computer take place?
>
> > A   1600 - 1800
> > B   1800 - 1900
> > C   1900 - 1938
> > D   1939 - 1945 (World War II)
> > E   1946 till now
>
> *Write the correct letters **A-E** next to questions **1-3**.*
>
> > 1   a. First computers built with silicon chips   ....
> > 2   b. Colossus used to decode language   ....
> > 3   c. First mechanical calculators developed   ....

Language focus: Pronoun reference – use of 'it', 'this', 'these' and 'that'

In English, we use pronouns to refer to a word or phrase that was stated earlier. The most common ones are 'it', 'this', 'these' and 'that'. Understanding what these words refer to is an important listening skill.

8 *Tick the correct option.*

a.	it	=	tourism	the area and its economy
b.	it	=	local people	experience of other cultures
c.	These	=	problems	tourists
d.	this	=	increased population	peak season
e.	This	=	major tourist area	pollution
f.	These	=	many forms of pollution	chemicals
g.	this	=	a passenger	rubbish
h.	This	=	tourism	destruction of reefs and beaches

9 *Complete the sentences with **it**, **this**, **these** or **that**.*

a. I think both tourists and local people can benefit from the experience of other cultures; _____ increases understanding of how and why people have different customs.

b. Finally, there are other physical effects of tourism such as the destruction of coral reefs and beaches to use the coral and sand as building materials. _____ has happened in the Philippines.

c. As population numbers may increase by as much as 10 times at peak season, _____ can lead to shortages of food for local people.

d. Now, sadly, there are also a variety of problems that go with tourism. _____ can be broadly grouped in three categories …

e. Next, another significant issue for any major tourist area is pollution. _____ takes many forms.

f. Pollution takes many forms, such as air pollution, noise pollution, littering problems, rubbish disposal, the amount of chemicals used for golf courses and swimming pools and the disposal of human waste. _____ all have to be managed.

g. What are some advantages that tourism brings to an area and its economy? Well, _____ is certainly a way a region can make money.

h. Each cruise ship passenger generates about 3.5 kgs of rubbish daily. Quite a lot of _____ ends up in the sea and along the shorelines.

Paraphrase

10 *Match the sentences you hear, **1-4**, to the sentences **a-d** below.*

TIP
Paraphrasing means understanding words with similar meanings.

Paraphrases
a. ____ It's important to think about the global effects of tourism.
b. ____ There are several advantages that tourism brings to an area and its economy.
c. ____ Unfortunately, tourism also involves a number of negative effects.
d. ____ In many tourist places, there are water shortages because of the large numbers of tourists.

Reading the question paper

11 *Read the summary below and choose the correct options.*

Questions 1 – 5

It's also important to consider the effects of tourism on a (**1.** *noun / adjective*) region and its people and economy. (**2.** *noun / adjective*) creates a variety of jobs for all sorts of people. It also enables people to learn new skills and start their own small businesses. An additional benefit is that both tourists and local people can gain an (**3.** *noun / adjective*) of other cultures and customs. Ideally, the money that is earned by tourism in a particular area will be used to improve (**4.** *noun / adjective*) and health services for people in that area. Such income can also be used to build better (**5.** *noun / adjective*) and rubbish disposal systems and to protect wildlife in the region.

Getting ready to listen – Prediction

12 *You will hear the introduction to Listening 1. First, try to answer the following questions.*

a. What type of text do you think this will be?

    A. a conversation between two people

    B. a conversation between more than two people

    C. a monologue (just one person talking)

b. Who is the speaker likely to be?

    A. a museum Education Officer

    B. a tourist

    C. a tourist guide

c. What is the speaker likely to be talking about?

    A. some advantages and disadvantages of tourism

    B. how much money tourists spend

    C. the best accommodation for tourists

13 *Check your answers.*

Listening 1

Complete the questions.

Questions 1 – 2

*Choose the correct answer, **A**, **B** or **C**.*

1   What are the two levels of tourism that are talked about?
   A   environmental and social
   B   positive and negative
   C   global and local

2   How much air travel is a result of tourism?
   A   16%
   B   60%
   C   66%

Questions 3 – 7

Write NO MORE THAN THREE WORDS for each answer.

It's also important to consider the effects of tourism on a **3.** _____ region and its people and economy. **4.** _____ creates a variety of jobs for all sorts of people. It also enables people to learn new skills and start their own small businesses. An additional benefit is that both tourists and local people can gain an **5.** _____ of other cultures and customs. Ideally, the money that is earned by tourism in a particular area will be used to improve **6.** _____ and health services for people in that area. Such income can also be used to build better **7.** _____ and rubbish disposal systems and to protect wildlife in the region.

Listening 1 – check

Check your answers.

Listening 2

Complete the questions.

Questions 8 – 10

*Choose the correct answer, **A**, **B** or **C**.*

8 How much water does a tropical golf course use?

A   the same amount as 60,000 villagers

B   more than 60,000 villagers

C   less than 60,000 villagers

9 What is a typical 'peak season' population increase?

A   twenty times

B   seven times

C   ten times

10 What happens if pollution is not well managed?

A   There are too many swimming pools.

B   Fewer tourists visit.

C   Poor countries need modern facilities.

Questions 11–14

Which kind of pollution affects these places?

A   Taj Mahal

B   Yellowstone Park

C   the Caribbean

D   the Philippines

*Write the correct letter, **A**, **B**, **C** or **D** next to questions **11-14**.*

11 Destruction of reefs and beaches   ....

12 Rubbish problems   ....

13 Air pollution and acid rain   ....

14 Noise pollution   ....

Final activity

A *Make notes on tourism issues in your country. For example:*

a. How does tourism affect the Great Wall of China?

b. How does tourism affect the Terracotta Warriors?

c. How does tourism affect the Summer Palace?

B *Work with a partner.*

a. Give a 1–2 minute talk on your topic.

b. Answer your partner's questions.

c. Listen to your partner's talk.

d. Ask 3–4 questions.

Answer Key

1. no answers

2. no answers

3. Write the words to complete each sentence.
   - a. primary school
   - b. prefer
   - c. sit
   - d. fee
   - e. instruments
   - f. surname
   - g. practise

4. Write the numbers as words and numbers.
   - a. 12 / twelve
   - b. 16 / sixteen
   - c. 30 / thirty
   - d. 67 / sixty-seven
   - e. 90 / ninety
   - f. 189 / one hundred and eighty-nine
   - g. 1,345 / one thousand, three hundred and forty-five
   - h. 7,894 / seven thousand, eight hundred and ninety-four
   - i. 520,000 / five hundred and twenty thousand
   - j. 1,000,000 / a million

5. Predict the type of answers required.
   - a. number
   - b. word
   - c. number
   - d. word
   - e. 2 + words

6. Write the names, numbers and dates that you hear.
   - a. 8 / eight
   - b. Banks
   - c. 30th / the 30th / 30
   - d. Fairview
   - e. in the afternoon

7. Match the words in the box to the homonyms below.
   - a. aloud—allowed
   - b. band—banned
   - c. bass—base
   - d. fourth—forth
   - e. grade—greyed
   - f. higher—hire
   - g. I'll—aisle
   - h. pair—pear
   - i. reed—read
   - j. sight—site—cite
   - k. their—there
   - l. he'll—heal—heel
   - m. wait—weight
   - n. you're—your

8. no answers

9. Check your answers.
   - a. two / 2
   - b. exam
   - c. phone / telephone

Listening 1
   1. 7 / seven
   2. 6 / six
   3. viola
   4. (the) 17th / 17 / seventeen / (the) seventeenth
   5. 2 pm / 2:00 pm / 2:00 / two o'clock
   6. 205 / two hundred and five
   7. 26 / twenty-six
   8. D
   9. 13 / thirteen
   10. 5 / five

Listening 2
   11. (the) Hillcrest
   12. 1:30 pm / half past one / one thirty
   13. D
   14. pencil
   15. stand
   16. 3 / three, scales (in this order, both required for 1 mark)
   17. 20 / twenty
   18. accuracy
   19. website / web site
   20. eight / 8

1. no audio

2. Pay attention to how the words sound.

practical	exam	sit an exam	surname
primary school	prefer	reception	fee
assume	practice	mistake	examiner

3. Write the words to complete each sentence.
   - a. In most countries, children go to **primary school** at the age of five or six.
   - b. I don't like coffee very much. I **prefer** tea.
   - c. When you enrol at a language school, you may have to **sit** a placement test.
   - d. At my son's music club, the **fee** for a year is $400.
   - e. The double bass and cello are stringed **instruments**.
   - f. My given name is Irene. My **surname** is Wilson.
   - g. I try to **practise** on the viola for at least 30 minutes each day.

4. Write the numbers as words and numbers.
   - a. 12
   - b. 16
   - c. 30
   - d. 67
   - e. 90
   - f. 189
   - g. 1,345
   - h. 7,894
   - i. 520,000
   - j. A million

5. no audio

6. Write the names, numbers and dates that you hear.
   - a. He passed Grade 8 on the piano last year.
   - b. I live in Banks Rd, that's B-A-N-K-S.
   - c. I'll sit the exam on July the 30th.
   - d. The exams will be held at Fairview School. That's F-A-I-R-V-I-E-W...
   - e. We're not sure of the exact time but the meeting will be held in the afternoon.

7. no audio

8. no audio

9. Check your answers.
   Narrator: *You will now hear a conversation between a music exam candidate and the receptionist at a music school. Listen to the*

conversation and fill in the form as you hear the information.

Irene: Hello, this is the Woodlands School of Music. Irene speaking.

John: Hello. My name's John Kepler. I want to sit my Grade 7 viola exam this weekend...

Listening 1

Narrator: *You will now hear a conversation between a music exam candidate and the receptionist at a music school. Listen to the conversation and fill in the form.*

Irene: Hello, this is the Woodlands School of Music. Irene speaking.

John: Hello. My name's John Kepler. I want to sit my Grade 7 viola exam this weekend... the practical exam... Can you help me?

Irene: Certainly, John. How do you spell your surname please?

John: Kepler... that's K...E...P...L...E...R.

Irene: Thanks... yes, I can see your name here on my class list on the computer...that's Grade 7 you want to sit?

John: Yes, Grade 7...

Irene: Yes, I see you passed Grade 6 in 2007. Now, you play the violin, John, is that right?

John: No... not the violin...I play the viola.

Irene: Oh yes, sorry. Now the piano exams are in the morning and the exams for other instruments are in the afternoon.

John: So my exam will be this Saturday afternoon, July the 17th?

Irene: That's right, yes...this Saturday... July the 17th. We've only got one other viola student sitting an exam, so you can choose whether you'd like to sit at two o'clock or three o'clock. Which time would you prefer?

John: Two o'clock would be good, thanks.

Irene: That's fine. Two o'clock, then. You'll need to pay the fee at the reception desk before you sit the exam...the fee for all Grade 7 practical exams is $205.

John: Did you say $205?

Irene: That's correct, yes. Your exam room will be Room 26. Room 26 is in D Block.

John: OK, thanks.

Irene: Can you tell me the three pieces you'll be playing? If you tell me now it'll save time on Saturday.

John: Yes... From List A... I'll play the first piece... by Bach. From List B... I'll play the Glazunov... that's number 13... And from List C... I'll play number 6... that's the piece by Minsky.

Irene: So that's ... List A, number 1...List B, number 15...sorry ... number 13, and from List C...number 6.

John: That's right.

Irene: And John, I assume you know you'll be asked to play five scales from the list of 14 scales...

John: Yes, I have to play five scales.

Irene: Well, good luck. I'll be at the desk on Saturday, so I'll see you then.

John: Thank you very much. Goodbye.

Irene: Goodbye.

Listening 2

Narrator: *You will now hear a conversation between the music exam candidate and a school music tutor. Listen to the conversation and fill in the form.*

Tutor: Hello John.

John: Oh...hello Ms Richardson!

Tutor: Tell me, John, where are the music exams being held this year? At the Hillcrest Primary School again?

John: Yes, the same place as last year. The Hillcrest Primary School ... Ms Richardson, do you have any advice for me?...for the exam day...?

Tutor: Well, I think it's good to get there early...at least half an hour before the exam. What time's your exam?

John: Two o'clock.

Tutor: Well, I'd get there around 1:30pm ... you want to practise for a little while... you want to warm up your viola and make sure it's in tune...just remind yourself of the tuning of each string ...C...G...D...A ...

John: Of course...C...G...D...A... I can't believe I'll forget but I'll write them down.

Tutor: Good idea. It's best to be sure.

John: What should I take with me, apart from my viola and music, of course?

Tutor: Well...let me see...three things, I think...A spare bow would be a good idea, in case you have an accident with your good one. Take a cleaning cloth to wipe the strings before you start. Oh, and take a pencil...so you can make notes you want...any notes you want to, on your music.

John: Shall I take my own music stand?

Tutor: That's a good idea. They could lend you one but you might not be able to put it up quickly. So, yes, take your own music stand.

John: OK.

Tutor: Do you know the order of the exam?

John: I think so. I'd better make sure, though.

Tutor: There are three parts to the exam. Remember that first you have the sight-reading. You should be fine with that. We've done a lot of sight-reading practice. Secondly, they'll ask you to play your three prepared pieces of music, and the third part is the scales.

John: I've got that. Thanks...Ms Richardson, how do they mark the exam?

Tutor: Well, it's marked out of 100%. The prepared pieces are the most important part. They're worth 60%. The other two parts, the sight-reading and scales, are marked out of 20% . The examiner is looking mainly for accuracy and fluency. Accuracy means the right notes, in perfect tune, held for the right length, good timing. Fluency is more a matter of your style—the way you interpret the piece and play each phrase...

John: After the exam, how can I find out my mark?

Tutor: You can go to the Woodlands website a week after the exam and you can see your result there. And you'll get an official letter in the mail as well.

John: Oh, that's right. I remember that from last year.

Tutor: If you pass Grade 7, you can go on to do your final grade, Grade 8, in 2009.

John: Yes, that's my aim. Thanks, Ms Richardson. Bye for now.

Tutor: Goodbye, John, and good luck!

ANSWERS   Unit 2   Eating Healthily

1. no answers

2. Write the word or words to complete each sentence.
   a. wholesome
   b. obese
   c. responsible for
   d. education
   e. lifestyle
   f. physical education
   g. nutritionist
   h. active
   i. moderation
   j. Traditional
   k. tuck shop
   l. expert
   m. youth

3. no answers

4. Classify the words you hear.
   Types of fruit: pear, banana
   Types of vegetables: celery, carrot
   Grains: rice, wheat
   Prepared food (healthy): filled roll, salad
   Prepared food (unhealthy): fried chicken, meat pie
   Food preparation (verbs): to stir-fry, to boil
   Adjectives to describe food: low-fat, sugary

5. Discuss the questions.
   a. There are three answer options.
   b. The letters A, B, C are written beside the answer options.

6. Can you hear the answer to question 1?
   A—selling more healthy food

7. Write the words you hear next to their synonyms.
   a. great
   b. headmaster
   c. more
   d. sleepy
   e. publicity
   f. obese
   g. to select
   h. food kiosk
   i. junk food
   j. physical education
   k. wholesome
   l. encourage
   m. to recommend
   n. raw
   o. expert
   p. portion

8. no answers

9. Check your answers.
   a. C   b. B   c. A

Listening 1
   1. A   2. B   3. C
   4. B   5. C   6. C
   7. B

Listening 2
   8. B   9. C   10. C
   11. A   12. C   13. B
   14. A   15. B

SCRIPTS   Unit 2   Eating Healthily

1. no audio

2. Write the word or words to complete each sentence.
   a. In order to stay healthy, we should eat **wholesome** foods, such as fruit, vegetables and whole grains.— "wholesome"—W-H-O-L-E-S-O-M-E
   b. A person who is **obese** is extremely overweight, and in danger of becoming ill because of it.—"obese"—O-B-E-S-E
   c. Schools are **responsible for** teaching pupils subjects such as maths, science and geography.—"responsible for"—R-E-S-P-O-N-S-I-B-L-E F-O-R
   d. We go to school and university in order to gain a good **education**.—"education"—E-D-U-C-A-T-I-O-N
   e. People who have an unhealthy **lifestyle** are generally unfit and get sick more often.—"lifestyle"—L-I-F-E-S-T-Y-L-E
   f. At school we have **physical education** classes outside, where we run and learn to play different kinds of sports.—"physical education"—P-H-Y-S-I-C-A-L E-D-U-C-A-T-I-O-N
   g. A **nutritionist** is someone who specialises in the areas of food and diet.—"nutritionist"—N-U-T-R-I-T-I-O-N-I-S-T
   h. People who are **active** spend a lot more time moving around and doing things than people who are not.— "active"—A-C-T-I-V-E
   i. Doing something in **moderation** means not doing it too much.—"moderation"—M-O-D-E-R-A-T-I-O-N
   j. **Traditional** methods are methods that have been used for a long time and passed from one generation to another.—"traditional"—T-R-A-D-I-T-I-O-N-A-L
   k. The school **tuck shop** is the place where you can go to buy snacks and light meals.—"tuck shop"—T-U-C-K S-H-O-P
   l. An **expert** is someone who knows a lot about a particular subject area.—"expert"—E-X-P-E-R-T
   m. The term **youth** refers to young people—usually children and teenagers.—"youth"—Y-O-U-T-H

3. Pay attention to how these words sound.
   1. high-fat
   2. high-sugar
   3. low-fat
   4. meat pie
   5. sausage roll
   6. cream doughnut
   7. fruit
   8. salad
   9. sandwich
   10. wholegrain
   11. bread
   12. junk food
   13. chips
   14. fried chicken
   15. filled roll
   16. yoghurt
   17. vegetables
   18. grain
   19. serving
   20. portion
   21. banana
   22. cereal
   23. sugary
   24. apple

25. pear	26. kiwi fruit
27. carrot	28. celery
29. rice	30. to steam
31. to boil	32. to bake
33. to stir-fry	34. oil
35. raw	36. dressing

4. Classify the words you hear.

Types of fruit: **pear, banana**

Types of vegetables: **celery, carrot**

Grains: **rice, wheat**

Prepared food (healthy): **filled roll, salad**

Prepared food (unhealthy): **fried chicken, meat pie**

Food preparation (verbs): **to stir-fry, to boil**

Adjectives to describe food: **low-fat, sugary**

5. no audio

6. Can you hear the answer to question 1?

Narrator: *You are now going to hear a radio broadcast about the changes happening in school food kiosks.*

Radio broadcaster: In view of current concerns about increasing numbers of obese children and teenagers, it comes as no surprise that school tuck shops are beginning to replace high-fat, high-sugar foods with healthy, low-fat options. Instead of the traditional unhealthy meat pies, sausage rolls and cream doughnuts, kids are being offered more wholesome options, such as fruit, salads, and sandwiches made with wholegrain bread.

7. Write the words you hear next to their synonyms.
   a. good *and* great; great; G-R-E-A-T
   b. principal *and* headmaster; headmaster; H-E-A-D-M-A-S-T-E-R
   c. greater amounts *and* more; more; M-O-R-E
   d. tired *and* sleepy; sleepy; S-L-E-E-P-Y
   e. advertisements *and* publicity; publicity; P-U-B-L-I-C-I-T-Y
   f. overweight *and* obese; obese; O-B-E-S-E
   g. to choose *and* to select; to select; S-E-L-E-C-T
   h. tuck shop *and* food kiosk; food kiosk; F-O-O-D (space) K-I-O-S-K
   i. fast food *and* junk food; junk food; J-U-N-K (space) F-O-O-D
   j. sport *and* physical education; physical education; P-H-Y-S-I-C-A-L (space) E-D-U-C-A-T-I-O-N
   k. healthy *and* wholesome; wholesome; W-H-O-L-E-S-O-M-E
   l. help *and* encourage; encourage; E-N-C-O-U-R-A-G-E
   m. to suggest *and* to recommend; to recommend; R-E-C-O-M-M-E-N-D
   n. uncooked *and* raw; raw; R-A-W
   o. specialist *and* expert; expert; E-X-P-E-R-T
   p. serving *and* portion; portion; P-O-R-T-I-O-N

8. no audio

9. Check your answers.

Narrator: *You are now going to hear a radio broadcast about the changes happening in school food kiosks.*

Radio broadcaster: In view of current concerns about increasing numbers of obese children and teenagers, it comes as no surprise that school tuck shops are beginning to replace high-fat, high-sugar foods with healthy, low-fat options. Instead of the traditional unhealthy meat pies, sausage rolls and cream doughnuts, kids are being offered more wholesome options, such as fruit, salads, and sandwiches made with wholegrain bread.

Listening 1

Narrator: *You are now going to hear a radio broadcast about the changes happening in school food kiosks.*

Radio broadcaster: In view of current concerns about increasing numbers of obese children and teenagers, it comes as no surprise that school tuck shops are beginning to replace high-fat, high-sugar foods with healthy, low-fat options. Instead of the traditional unhealthy meat pies, sausage rolls and cream doughnuts, <u>kids are being offered more wholesome options</u>, such as fruit, salads, and sandwiches made with wholegrain bread.

But what is the view of the general public and parents of school-aged children and teenagers on this issue? <u>Many think it's a great idea</u>, saying that schools will encourage kids to develop healthy eating habits by providing healthy food options. Some, however, argue that schools should not be telling children what they can and can't eat, and that children should be free to choose for themselves. Others argue that the reason for the increasing rate of obesity among youth is not enough exercise. These people suggest that schools spend more time teaching physical education. Finally, there are those who believe that the <u>parents, and not the school, are responsible for teaching a healthy attitude towards food and eating</u>. The claim is that overweight kids come from overweight homes.

And what of the kids themselves? What do they think about this debate? Some of them say that if their favourite snacks are not available at school, they will simply <u>stop at the corner store on the way</u> to buy them. Others say that the junk food options still available at school—such as chips and fried chicken—are cheaper than the healthier options, and, therefore, they'd be more likely to choose these. For example, in one school tuck shop we visited, one portion of deep-fried chips and chicken cost <u>$2.50</u>, while a filled roll and a pot of low-fat yoghurt together cost $4.

As with many of these types of issues, education and moderation are probably a good place to start. First, it would help to ensure that parents know enough about healthy eating practices to be able to teach these to their children. This could include <u>television publicity</u>, newspaper inserts and brochures delivered to mailboxes. Secondly, schools can encourage children to eat more fruit and vegetables, and fewer pies and chips by making sure that the <u>majority of snacks and other food items for sale are healthy</u>, while allowing a few unhealthy favourites to remain.

Listening 2

Narrator: *You are going to hear a talk to school children about how to have a healthy lifestyle.*

Nutritionist: Good morning, everyone. My name is Claire Higgins. I'm a nutritionist from the Department of Health.

Your <u>headmaster</u>, Mr White, has invited me here to talk to you today about healthy eating and active lifestyles.

Now, as you'll all be well aware, the school tuck shop has started to replace some of the junk food options on its menu with much healthier fruit, salads and sandwiches. I realise that not all of you are happy with this change, but <u>by introducing more fruit, vegetables</u> and whole grains to your diet, you will be healthier and happier in the long run.

You may or may not already know that health experts recommend at least five servings of fresh fruit and vegetables per day—and more if you can manage it. This means at least <u>three</u> portions of vegetables and at least two pieces of fruit every day to stay healthy.

As an example menu, you could consider cutting up a banana on your cereal for breakfast in the morning. Remember that breakfast is the most important meal of the day. Those who decide to miss breakfast are usually very hungry by late morning, and often resort to unhealthy, sugary snacks. <u>Missing breakfast can also make you sleepy</u>, and prevent you from concentrating in class—so make sure you always eat a good breakfast.

To continue with our menu, morning tea could be a piece of fruit, such as an apple, pear or kiwifruit, or a vegetable—such as a carrot or piece of celery—cut into sticks. For lunch, you could have a salad sandwich on wholegrain bread, or some kind of cooked grain, like rice, with steamed or boiled vegetables. At dinner time, be sure to include servings of several different vegetables. Try to take advantage of what's in season, and choose a variety of colours—green, orange and white. Again, make sure that you use a low-fat cooking method—steaming, boiling, baking or stir-frying in a small amount of oil. Additionally, in summer, <u>fresh vegetables can be washed and served raw in a salad</u> with a low-fat dressing.

You will also know that as part of a healthy lifestyle, you need to be active and include some kind of physical exercise in your daily programme. For children and teenagers, we recommend at least <u>30 minutes</u> of exercise per day. This could mean, for example, walking or biking to school instead of going in the car or catching the bus or train. Where this isn't possible, you could spend your evenings kicking a ball around in your backyard, or <u>having a game of basketball or tennis with friends</u> at the local court. You could also consider joining a sports club or doing another kind of physical activity, such as dancing or horse-riding.

And the next time you go to your school tuck shop, pick one of the healthier foods on offer. You'll be surprised at how much better it'll make you feel.

ANSWERS   Unit 3   Sport

1. no answers

2. no answers

3. Write the word or words to complete each sentence.
   a. speed   b. 400; 100
   c. runners; long   d. start line

e. challenging   f. hurdles
g. starting gun   h. registration

4. Choose the words from the box that match the meanings you hear.
   a. E   b. B   c. C
   d. F   e. D   f. A

5. Write the letters, A-F, in the order that you hear the words in the box.
   a. D   b. C   c. E
   d. F   e. B   f. A

6. Write the names you hear next to questions a-h.
   a. Ashgrove   b. Dave
   c. Lancaster   d. Andy
   e. Woodlands   f. Pete
   g. Thomas   h. Robbie

7. Write the correct letters A-G next to questions a-g.
   a. C   b. G   c. D
   d. E   e. A   f. B
   g. F

8. no answers

9. Check your answers.
   a. B   b. C   c. D
   d. A

Listening 1
   1. D   2. C   3. A
   4. B   5. B   6. C
   7. A   8. B   9. E
   10. D   11. A   12. C

Listening 2
   13. F   14. C   15. G
   16. D   17. E   18. A
   19. D   20. A   21. F
   22. J   23. H   24. C

Final activity
   Answer: You are second. Not first.

SCRIPTS   Unit 3   Sport

1. no audio

2. Pay attention to how these words sound.
   ready   favourite   ankle   schedule
   successful   organise   challenging   turn up
   registration   First Aid   question   accident

   Sport-related vocabulary
   runners   100 metres sprint   400 metres relay
   team speed   baton   long jump
   hurdles   high jump   cross country
   course   timekeeper   start line
   starting gun   water jump

3. Write the word or words to complete each sentence.

a. In a sprint race, **speed** is important.

b. In the **400** metre relay, four people in a team run **100** metres each.

c. In an athletics event, **runners** may also try out other sports, such as the **long** jump.

d. All the runners must be ready at the **start line** before the race begins.

e. Some cross-country races are very **challenging**.

f. The **hurdles** event is a sprint race with jumps.

g. A race starts when the **starting gun** is fired.

h. Runners and teams must go to the **registration** table to enter a race or to find out their time.

4. Choose the words from the box that match the meanings you hear.

a. the person who controls the time-keeping at a race

b. to plan and arrange an event

c. an event in which athletes jump over a bar

d. a small wooden bar used in relay races

e. to arrive at an event

f. an area of land marked out for a race

5. Write the letters, A-F, in the order that you hear the words in the box.

Narrator: *You will hear a text about a runner who is injured before a race.*

Jill hoped to be **successful** in the 100 metres. She was the **favourite**. But shortly before the race she had an **accident** while training. She tripped on a bar and hurt her **ankle**. They couldn't change the **schedule** just because of her, so sadly she had to withdraw. She went to the **First Aid** tent where they put some ice on the ankle and told her not to run for a day or two.

6. Write the names you hear next to questions a-h.
   a. A-S-H-G-R-O-V-E   b. D-A-V-E
   c. L-A-N-C-A-S-T-E-R   d. A-N-D-Y
   e. W-O-O-D-L-A-N-D-S   f. P-E-T-E
   g. T-H-O-M-A-S   h. R-O-B-B-I-E

7. Write the correct letters A-G next to questions a-g.
Competitors in the 800 metre event are asked to come to the track now. Your race starts at 11 am. There will be a delay in the 400 metre relay, the time for this event is now 2 pm. Competitors for the high jump, please be ready at the jump at 12 pm. The long jump will follow at 1 pm. The results for the 100 metre sprint races at 9 am and the 10 am hurdles are available at the registration table. Competitors in the cross country, please register by 1 pm for your race at 1:30 pm.

8. no audio

9. Check your answers.

Narrator: *You will hear two athletes at a track and field meet talking about their relay race, and about teams, colours and events.*

Listening 1

Narrator: *You will hear two athletes at a track and field meeting talking about their relay race, and about teams, colours and events.*

Andy: Hi Dave.

Dave: Hi Andy.

Andy: Are you ready for the 400 metres relay, <u>Dave? You're running first</u>. We need your speed at the start! <u>I'll be running third</u>. I like third.

Dave: Who's running fourth for us? Is it Pete? Is he OK? He had a sore ankle, didn't he?

Andy: <u>Pete's fine now. So he'll be fourth</u> as usual. <u>Robbie will run second</u>. So I'll take the baton from Robbie and pass it on to Pete.

Narrator: *Listen to section 2 of the audio.*

Dave: I hear that we're going to wear <u>white</u> today. Is that right?

Andy: Yes, that's right.

Dave: Who are the favourites for this race?

Andy: I think we are! Go, <u>Lancaster College</u>!

Dave: Who are the team in the <u>green</u>?

Andy: That's <u>Ashgrove College</u>.

Dave: And the runners in red? Where are they from?

Andy: They're from <u>Highland Park</u>.

Narrator: *Listen to section 3 of the audio.*

Dave: We should do well. What time's our relay?

Andy: Let me see. I've got the schedule here. Um...the <u>400 metres relay is at 1:30 pm</u>.

Dave: I'm also in the long jump and the hurdles. What time are they? They're later in the afternoon, aren't they?

Andy: Yes, the <u>long jump's at 3 pm</u> and the <u>hurdles are at 4:30 pm</u>. It's a big day for you!

Dave: Yes, it's fun, though. You're in other events yourself, aren't you?

Andy: Yes, I'm in the <u>high jump</u>. That's at <u>1 pm</u>. And I'm in the <u>100 metres sprint at 5 pm</u>.

Dave: Good luck Andy!

Andy: Thanks Dave. See you at the relay. Go Lancaster College!

Listening 2

Narrator: *You'll hear two organisers of a cross country running race explaining the event to volunteers and telling them where to stand.*

Penny: Hello everyone. Thank you for getting here early. I'm sure the cross country race today will be very successful. John and I have organised a challenging course. We expect runners to start turning up in about 30 minutes so we need to work fast. I'll hand you over to John to describe the course and the different jobs we have to do.

John: OK, listen everyone please. We need people at different points on the course.
<u>Felicity, we need you on the start line</u>. I'll wave when we're all ready and you can fire the starting gun. Now, <u>Thomas</u>, would you please stand <u>beside the first jump</u>. That's the fence in front of the pine trees over there. Oh, by the way, we need someone at the <u>registration table</u> right here. Who can do that? You can, <u>Matt</u>? That's great. So we've got Felicity at the start line, Thomas at the fence and Matt on the registration table. What else? Oh, yes, a timekeeper? We thought you would be good at that, <u>Jeremy</u>! Great, thanks. You've done that before so you know what to

do, don't you? You can sit <u>in the timekeeper's tent</u> over there when you're not too busy. Who else do we need?

Penny: <u>Tony</u>, would you please stand <u>beside the water jump</u>. Just keep an eye on people.

Help anyone who falls over. If someone gets injured, we've always got <u>Catherine</u>, who's done First Aid training. She's got a <u>First Aid tent</u> over near the finish line. So if you see anyone get hurt, get them to Catherine as quickly as you can.

John: Thanks, Penny. OK everyone. Any questions? No. OK then. Penny and I will be walking around the whole time. Let's know if you need anything.

Narrator: *Listen to section 2 of the audio.*

Gather round everyone. This won't take long. First of all, I would like to congratulate Mick and Sarah, who <u>won</u> the Open Men's and Open Women's Races respectively. What an extraordinary effort and personal best times for them both! A round of applause for them please. Actually, looking at the results board, I can see that you've <u>all</u> done well. There have been quite a few really good times posted today. Now...the shower block's over near the car park, so feel free to freshen up but don't take too long. Our team of volunteers has been working hard in the kitchen and they've produced a very nice spread in the <u>clubrooms</u>. They've made tea and coffee, as well as several cold drinks, and there's a lot <u>to eat</u>—sandwiches, savouries, fruit, biscuits and I'm sure I saw some chocolate cake. So just come on over back to the clubrooms as soon as you can. At this stage I would like to thank <u>all of those who have helped</u> make today's events a success. Please give them a hand! I'm sure the organising committee would like to see you all—athletes and helpers—again at <u>next year's</u> cross country championships.

ANSWERS   Unit 4   Media

1. no answers

2. no answers

3. no answers

4. Check your answers.
   a. recommend   b. comfortable
   c. operate   d. inspect
   e. focus

5. Write the base form of the verbs you hear as past participles to complete the sentences.
   a. designed   b. packed away
   c. carried   d. folded
   e. set   f. operated
   g. inspected

6. Write the word beside each number according to the order in which you hear them.
   a. F   b. E   c. D

d. B   e. A   f. C

7. What is a label?
   B. a word or name that identifies something

8. Which type of visual do the following items probably belong to?
   a. B   b. C   c. A

9. Label the diagram.
   a. C   b. G   c. A
   d. F   e. I

10. Choose the correct adverbs to complete the sentences.

	correct letter	position in sentence
a.	B	(ii)
b.	A	(i)
c.	C	(ii)
d.	E	(ii)
e.	D	(ii)

11. Write the letters A-H to show the order in which you hear these words or phrases.
    a. C   b. F   c. A
    d. B   e. G   f. H
    g. E   h. D

12. Write the correct letter for the position in relation to the tent.
    a. C   b. A   c. B
    d. E   e. D

13. Write the passive verbs correctly.
    1. are designed   2. are fitted
    3. is designed   4. be carried
    5. be packed

14. Tick the sentence you hear.
    C

15. no answers

16. Check your answers.
    a. C   b. B

Listening 1
   1. B   2. D   3. F   4. G
Listening 2
   5. B   6. C   7. F   8. G

SCRIPTS   Unit 4   Media

1. no audio

2. Pay attention to how these words sound.

recommend	comfortable	operate	inspect
extremely	easily	carefully	neatly
thoroughly	on the side of	beside	in front of
behind	above	carry	design
pack away	inspect		

3. no audio

4. Check your answers.
   a. I **recommend** that you buy a video camera with the international guarantee.
   b. A rubber hand grip makes the camera very **comfortable** to hold.
   c. You **operate** the camera by looking through the lens and pushing the 'Record' button.
   d. Quality control workers in the factory will **inspect** your camera carefully before it is boxed ready for sale.
   e. The camera will **focus** on the subject automatically.

5. Write the base form of the verbs you hear as past participles to complete the sentences.
   a. design
   b. pack away
   c. carry
   d. fold
   e. set
   f. operate
   g. inspect

6. Write the word beside each number according to the order in which you hear them.
   a. thoroughly
   b. especially
   c. neatly
   d. easily
   e. extremely
   f. carefully

7. What is a label?
   A label is:
   A. a collar
   B. a word or name that identifies something or
   C. a type of camera

8. no audio

9. Label the diagram of a television.
   This portable television is nearly twenty years old. It has a **handle** on the top for carrying it. There is a silver **dial** on the front at the top; I think it turns the television on and off. The **screen** is on the front, that's still the same! There is a **speaker** under the dials. The television comes with a small **remote**.

10. Choose the correct adverbs to complete the sentences.
    1. The computer bag is roomy, so the computer fits into it **easily**.
    2. This camera is very good, but it's **extremely** expensive.
    3. You should take the lens off **carefully**.
    4. The manufacturers inspect each new lens **thoroughly**.
    5. The camera bag has special pockets, so everything can be packed away **neatly**.

11. Write the letters A-H to show the order in which you hear these words or phrases.
    a. Now, **underneath** the camera is the hand grip.
    b. That's this thing **here**, on top of the camera.
    c. This is the microphone, **on top of** the camera.
    d. Buy a protective glass that fits **on the front of** the lens when you're not using the camera.
    e. The rubber cup is there so you can hold the camera **against** your eye.
    f. You can store the microphone **on the right-hand side of** the carry bag.
    g. You can move the microphone **around** to face the person who is talking.
    h. The battery is stored **on the left-hand side of** the carry bag.

12. no audio

13. Write the passive verbs correctly.
    1. These cameras **are designed** for easy handling.
    2. Nearly all cameras today **are fitted** with automatic focusing.
    3. The bag **is designed** to allow all the parts to fit in neatly.
    4. The camera is light and can **be carried** easily.
    5. The cord and battery can **be packed** away neatly.

14. Tick the sentence you hear.
    In the IELTS Listening test, you often need to label parts of a diagram correctly.

15. no audio

16. Check your answers
Narrator: *You are going to hear a description of the parts of a video camera and an explanation of the way it works.*

Listening 1
Narrator: *You are going to hear a description of the parts of a video camera and an explanation of the way it works.*

Hello everyone! Welcome to our first class in movie-making. The essence of making movies is in your own creativity. But the camera itself is important, so I'll start by describing the camera and how it works. Of course, movie cameras vary but basically they have the same parts.

This is my camera. It's designed for ease of use. Look carefully and I'll describe three of the parts of the camera. One of the most important parts is the lens, on the front here. Nearly all cameras today are fitted with a zoom lens, so you can zoom in and out easily if you want to.

In the manual that came with your camera, you can read about how to clean the lens, how to change it and how to protect it by buying a protective glass that fits on the front of the lens when you're not using the camera.

You must look after the lens carefully. It can be damaged easily.

Now, underneath the camera is the hand grip. It's designed for easy handling, so you can hold the camera steady while you're filming. When you're not using the camera you can fold the grip up and then the camera can be packed away neatly into the carry bag.

If you're right-handed like me, you probably hold the camera in your right hand and use your left hand for turning the camera on and for manual focusing.

The last thing I want to point out just now is the microphone. That's this thing here, on top of the camera. It means you have audio as well as video, or moving pictures. The microphone is quite sensitive, so be careful with it. It comes right off easily, so you can pack it away in the bag.

You need to turn the mic towards the person who is talking. Generally, the person will be straight ahead but sometimes you'll want to move it. So—lens, hand grip and microphone. And the last thing I'll mention at this point is the rubber cup... that's where you put the camera up against your eye...Well, that's enough for now. Next, I'd like you to pick up your own cameras.

Listening 2

Hello everyone. You all did very well last week! You seem to be getting used to your cameras and I think you now know all the parts of the camera and what they do.

This week I'll talk about caring for your camera. Most cameras will last you a long time if you look after them.

Make sure you have a strong carry case. Let's look at mine. You can see that the different parts fit in neatly. This part shaped like a circle in the top left hand corner is for the cord that connects the camera with the electrical supply when you need to charge the battery.

On the top right hand side you can store the microphone. It has to fit neatly, so it doesn't move around and get damaged. I keep it there all the time, except when I'm actually going to do some audio recording.

Now, on the bottom left-hand side I can store the battery. It's a good idea to take the battery out if you're not using the camera for a long time... I always do. Batteries today stay charged up for a long time, but they are better out of the camera. Most cameras today, like this, come with a rechargeable battery.

Finally, you can see where I store the camera itself, here in the bottom right. The camera can't move and the case is made of hard material, so you can knock the case or even drop it and the camera won't be damaged.

If you haven't got a camera case, I recommend that you buy one as soon as you can... Well, that's about all I have to say on storage. Now, let's move on to some practical work.

ANSWERS   Unit 5   Giving Directions

1. no answers

2. no answers

3. Complete the table by writing the words you hear in the correct columns.

    Verbs for asking / giving directions: to get to, to reach, to cross

    Nouns related to roads and streets: corner, intersection, traffic lights

    Names of shops and buildings in town: restaurant, bank, main square

    Nouns referring to parts of a street or building: front, side, end

    Direction words: left, right, east

4. In pairs, quickly discuss the following questions.
    a. 2 answers
    b. 2 letters, from **B-G**
    c. **A** (has already been used for the example), a word or a number
    d. No (some of the letters on the map are given as distracters)

5. Can you hear the answer to the example question?
    example = A (because Brenda's house is on the corner of Anne and Queen Streets, across the road from the corner store)

6. Write the prepositional phrases next to the correct pictures below.
    a. on the corner of
    b. across the road from; on the opposite side to
    c. close to   d. far from
    e. next to   f. on the right of
    g. on the left of   h. at the end of

7. Write the phrases next to the correct pictures below.
    a. go east   b. go west
    c. go north   d. go south
    e. go along   f. turn left
    g. turn right   h. go straight ahead
    i. go up   j. go down
    k. go past

8. no answers

9. Check your answers.
    a. A   b. C   c. B

Listening 1
    1. E   2. G

Listening 2
    3. D   4. H   5. E
    6. F   7. C

SCRIPTS   Unit 5   Giving Directions

1. no audio

2. Pay attention to how these words sound.

to get to	service station	to miss
corner	to reach	front
across	public library	town hall
close to	opposite	main square
next to	right (adv.)	to cross
east	left (adv.)	bank
past	right (adj.)	traffic lights
intersection	end	restaurant
until	side	chemist

3. Complete the table by writing the words you hear in the correct columns.

    Verbs for asking / giving directions: **to get to, to reach, to cross**

    Nouns related to roads and streets: **corner, intersection, traffic lights**

    Names of shops and buildings in town: **restaurant, bank, main square**

    Nouns referring to parts of a street or building: **front, side, end**

    Direction words: **left, east, right**

4. no audio

5. Can you hear the answer to the example question?

Narrator: *You are now going to hear two friends talking on the telephone. One friend is asking the other for directions to someone's house.*

Katie: Hello. Katie speaking.

Brenda: Hi, Katie. It's Brenda here. How are you?

Katie: I'm fine, thanks.

Brenda: Look, Katie, are you going to Helen's party tonight? I've decided to go, but I'm not sure how to get to her house.

Katie: Oh, yes, sure. I'm not going because I have to work, but I know how to get there. Where do you live?

Brenda: I live on the corner of Anne and Queen Streets, across the road from the corner store.

6. Write the prepositional phrases next to the correct pictures below.

   a. on the corner of

   b. across the road from *or* on the opposite side to

   c. close to   d. far from

   e. next to   f. on the right of

   g. on the left of   h. at the end of

7. Write the phrases next to the correct pictures below.

   a. go east   b. go west

   c. go north   d. go south

   e. go along   f. turn left

   g. turn right   h. go straight ahead

   i. go up   j. go down

   k. go past

8. no audio

9. Check your answers.

Narrator: *You are now going to hear two friends talking on the telephone. One friend is asking the other for directions to someone's house.*

Katie: Hello. Katie speaking.

Brenda: Hi, Katie. It's Brenda here. How are you?

Katie: I'm fine, thanks.

Brenda: Look, Katie, are you going to Helen's party tonight? I've decided to go, but I'm not sure how to get to her house.

Listening 1

Narrator: *You are now going to hear two friends talking on the telephone. One friend is asking the other for directions to someone's house.*

Katie: Hello. Katie speaking.

Brenda: Hi, Katie. It's Brenda here. How are you?

Katie: I'm fine, thanks.

Brenda: Look, Katie, are you going to Helen's party tonight? I've decided to go, but I'm not sure how to get to her house.

Katie: Oh, yes, sure. I'm not going because I have to work, but I know how to get there. Where do you live?

Brenda: I live on the corner of Anne and Queen Streets, across the road from the corner store.

Katie: Oh, right. Well, I live quite close to you—on the corner of Queen Street and Tramway Road, next to Bob's house.

Brenda: Oh, really! I didn't know that.

Katie: Anyway, to get to Helen's house, you need to go east along Queen Street, and past the intersection with Tramway Road, until you get to a service station on the corner.

Brenda: Okay, a service station on the corner.

Katie: Now, if you reach the public library on the opposite corner, you'll know you've gone too far.

Brenda: Right. Got that.

Katie: You need to turn right at the service station into Bettina Road.

Brenda: Bettina Road?

Katie: Yeah, that's right. And Helen's house is at the end of the road, on the opposite side to the service station. You won't miss it. It's a big white house with a purple letter box in front.

Brenda: Okay. Well, that doesn't sound too difficult. I'm sure I'll be able to find it. Thanks, Katie.

Katie: No worries. Enjoy the party. Bye.

Brenda: Bye.

Listening 2

Narrator: *You are going to hear a conversation between a man, Mike, and a passer-by on the street.*

Mike: Excuse me. I'm trying to get to the dance party in Bryce Street.

Passer-by: Dance party?

Mike: Yeah. There's a whole lot of Latin American dance bands playing tonight. I think it's in the main hall.

Passer-by: Oh, yes. I suppose that'll be the town hall. Well, right now, as you can see, we're in the main square, at the corner of Brooklyn Road and Victoria Street. You can see the Central Bank across the road on the opposite corner.

Mike: Okay.

Passer-by: Now, the best way is probably for you to stay on this side of Victoria Street. You don't need to cross the road.

Mike: Right.

Passer-by: Go east along Victoria Street. You'll see the traffic lights where Park Road crosses Victoria Street.

Mike: Right.

Passer-by: Don't turn there. Go straight ahead. You'll pass a restaurant on your left, and a chemist on your right.

Mike: Okay.

Passer-by: The next road is Knox Street. There's a public library on the corner. Turn left at the library and go straight ahead until you see a service station on the corner on your right. You'll now be at Claudelands Street.

Mike: Okay. Claudelands Street.

Passer-by: Turn right at the intersection and go east. The town hall is at the end of the road on the left, just past the corner store.

Mike: At the end of the road?
Passer-by: Yes. That's right.
Mike: Great. Okay, thanks for your help.
Passer-by: No problem.

a. Geoff Beck	
b. Luna Mobiles	
c. The radio programme, 'Technology and You'...	✓
d. Another radio programme	

ANSWERS Unit 6 Advertising

1. no answers

2. Write the word or words you hear to complete each sentence.
   a. advertising   b. customers
   c. product   d. value
   e. cell phone   f. discount
   g. quality   h. salesperson
   i. coverage

3. Write how many syllables each word has.
   a. company   3
   b. technology   4
   c. comfortably   3
   d. convenient   4
   e. coverage   3
   f. fashionable   3
   g. feature   2
   h. purchase   2
   i. service   2
   j. value   2

4. no answers

5. Check your answers.
   a. service   b. value
   c. cell phone

6. Choose a synonym.
   a. purchase   b. convenient

7. Match the key vocabulary.
   a. value   b. fashionable
   c. brand   d. customer

8. Write 'word' or 'number' beside each symbol or abbreviation below.
   a. number   b. word
   c. number   d. number
   e. word   f. word
   g. number   h. word
   i. number   j. number

9. Cross out the answers that would not be acceptable.
   b. ~~quality products and happy customers~~
   e. ~~the day before yesterday~~
   f. ~~green, blue and pink~~

10. Tick one box to answer the question.

11. Read the following text and underline the 'this', 'that' or 'it' reference words.

    Let me tell you about four new products. First, the Luna 500. <u>It's</u> one of my favourites! <u>This little beauty</u> has some great games, a camera, the internet and a voice recorder. <u>It's</u> fashionable, too! <u>It</u> comes in red, green, blue and pink. The price of <u>this</u> beauty is $849. Now, <u>that's</u> not cheap but you'll love <u>it</u>. <u>It's</u> very good value for money. Secondly, the Aquila 50. My daughter loves <u>this one</u>. Not as many features as the Luna but <u>it's</u> slimmer and lighter. <u>It</u> has excellent games and a 5 megapixel camera, so you get really sharp shots.

12. Write the correct letter, A or B, to show what 'this' and 'it' refer to.
    a. A   b. B
    c. A   d. A

13. Write 'this', 'that' or 'it' in the following sentences.
    a. this   b. it   c. that
    d. It   e. That

14. Discuss these questions with a partner.
    a. **One**—a monologue means 'one' voice.
    b. **Four**—games, camera, internet connectivity and voice recorder.
    c. **No**—not all the phones will have all four features; the table is necessary to include varying information.

Listening 1
(1 point each)

	Games	Camera	Internet connectivity	Voice recorder
LUNA	Y	Y	Y	Y
AQUILA 50	Y	Y		
HERMES	Y	Y		
RIVA	Y			

Listening 2
1. $27   2. $29.50
3. 26c / 26 cents   4. 20c / 20 cents
5. 27c / 27 cents   6. all main cities
7. nationwide and islands

1. no audio

2. Write the word or words you hear to complete each sentence.
   a. Many companies spend a lot of money on television **advertising**.
   b. They want you to become one of their **customers**.
   c. Advertisers want you to buy a certain **product**.
   d. They often claim that they offer the best **value** for money.
   e. In many countries nearly everyone owns a **cell phone**.
   f. Companies may offer a **discount** to get you to buy something.
   g. If you want it to last a long time, you should buy a **quality** phone.
   h. If you are not sure which phone to buy, you can ask a **salesperson** to help you.
   i. Choose a phone with nationwide **coverage** if you travel a lot.

3. Write how many syllables each word has.
   a. company [3]   b. technology [4]
   c. comfortably [3]   d. convenient [4]
   e. coverage [3]   f. fashionable [3]
   g. feature [2]   h. purchase [2]
   i. service [2]   j. value [2]

4. no audio

5. Check your answers.
   a. sales and **service**
   b. **value** for money
   c. **cell phone** coverage

6. no audio

7. no audio

8. no audio

9. no audio

10. Tick one box to answer the question.
    Good afternoon listeners. Geoff Beck from Luna Mobiles here with the 'Technology and You' slot this afternoon. This is a radio advertising programme in which I bring you up to date with the best buys in the world of technology.

11. no audio

12. no audio

13. Write 'this', 'that' or 'it' in the following sentences.
    a. We have a discount on the Luna 500. Don't miss **this** opportunity.
    b. The Luna 500 is slim and fashionable. You'll love **it**.
    c. This one is expensive, but **that** one over there is being sold at a discount today.
    d. The battery is reliable. **It** will keep going for up to 48 hours of use.
    e. The first Aquila was made in 2003. **That** model sold well, but today's Aquila is even more popular.

14. no audio

Listening 1

Narrator: *In the Listening text monologue, you will hear advertising and information about cell phones.*

Good afternoon listeners. Geoff Beck from Luna Mobiles here with the 'Technology and You' slot this afternoon. This is a radio advertising programme in which I bring you up to date with the best buys in the world of technology. Today—cell phones! Where we would be without them? I'll tell you about the latest innovations, the best features, and the best value for money in the exciting world of cell phones. Let me tell you about four new products! First, the Luna 500. It's one of my favourites! This little beauty has some great games, a camera, the internet and a voice recorder. It's fashionable, too! It comes in red, green, blue and pink. The price of this beauty is $849.00. Now, that's not cheap but you'll love it. It's very good value for money. Secondly, the Aquila 50. My daughter loves this one. Not so many features as the Luna but it's slimmer and lighter. It has excellent games and a 5 megapixel camera, so you get really sharp shots. The Aquila costs $749.00. Not cheap but good value, especially with that camera. Now, moving on, if you don't want to pay a lot of money but you need a good phone, the Hermes 580 could be the phone for you. This little gem sits comfortably in the palm of your hand. It has some good games and a camera. You can buy this one for just $395.00. Compare it with the one you've got now. Isn't it time you got a new one? At that price you can't lose. A similar phone, but even less expensive, is the Riva A65. You'll love this one. This is the one for people who say to me, "If I want a camera, I'll buy a camera! I want a cell phone!" This is the phone for you. It doesn't have expensive features. But as a phone it's great. Slim. Fashionable. Convenient. Good quality. It has some games but that's all.

Remember, for all these products you get fantastic sales and service. Look out for discounts next week on all these products.

Listening 2

Narrator: *In the listening text monologue, you will hear information on some mobile phone companies and the services they offer.*

Good afternoon listeners. Linda Harris from Luna Mobiles here with the 'Technology and You' slot this afternoon, taking over from Geoff Beck, who's on holiday this week. Today we're looking at your mobile phone companies. Fortunately we have a choice! I'm going to preview five major companies in the market. Let's say you've bought your phone and now you're free to join up with a company. You'll want to find a company and then decide the best plan. Let's talk prices. We're going to look at the top five companies in the market— Commix, Phontic, Pluto, World and Dialog. For the basic service, Commix charges $24 per month, Phontic $27 and Pluto is the same. World is a little more expensive at $28 and Dialog comes in at $29.50. A little more expensive, but they maintain you get value for money! The peak hour charges are very similar, too. Commix, Phontic and Pluto all charge 26c per hour, World charges 28c and Dialog is again the most expensive, at 32 cents per hour. Off peak charges might interest you. These are the night hours between 8 pm and 8 am. Good times for phoning relatives in other countries.

Commix, Phontic and Pluto charge the same amount for off-peak services, at just 20 cents per hour, while World and Dialog are more expensive, both at 27 cents per hour.

Now coverage is very important. Coverage means how far the phone signal goes. In other words, the areas in which you can actually use your phone. Now, Commix has good coverage nationwide but Phontic only covers all main cities. Pluto and World are nationwide. No trouble there. And Dialog's coverage is nationwide and islands. That's why it's more expensive. 'Nationwide and Islands' means you can use Dialog right across our country and also on the all the Western and Northern Islands, where they have phone towers and access.

Well, you can see you have lots of choice. Don't forget to pick up a copy of 'Mobile Memorandum', our company's newsletter, to see these figures again and make your choice. You can read our recommendations, too.

OK. Let's go back to Sandy Little for the 4 o'clock news.

ANSWERS   Unit 7   Education

1. no answers

2. no answers

3. Write the adjectives that describe people.

positive	negative
nice	grumpy
friendly	boring
easy-going	horrible
interesting	strict

4. Circle the underlined word you hear in each sentence.
   a. horrible   b. easy-going
   c. interesting   d. friendly
   e. compulsory

5. no answers

6. no answers

7. Check your answers.
   a. English (iv)   b. science (x)
   c. German (vi)   d. maths (ix)
   e. history (viii)   f. art (i)
   g. drama (iii)   h. French (v)
   i. art history (ii) j. geography (vii)

8. Circle the subject that the person is talking about.
   a. maths   b. German
   c. art   d. geography
   e. art history   f. French
   g. science   h. drama

9. Look at the instructions and matching questions.
   a. 6   b. 4   c. No
   d. Yes   e. Letters, A-F
   f. F (because that has been given as the example)

10. no answers

11. no answers

12. Tick the surnames you hear.

Andrews	Campbell	Davis
Ford	Harris	King
Oliver	Patterson	Stevens
Turner		

13. Circle the surname you hear.
   a. Evans   b. Brown   c. King
   d. Palmer   e. Dawson   f. Campbell
   g. Taylor   h. Edwards   i. Lewis

14. no answers

15. Circle the title you hear.
   a. Mr   b. Ms   c. Dr
   d. Mrs   e. Miss

16. Circle the surname you hear.
   a. Jones   b. Ford   c. Hill
   d. Granger   e. Black

17. no answers

18. Check your answers.
   a. A   b. B   c. B

Listening 1
   1. D   2. B
   3. A   4. C

Listening 2
   5. A   6. C
   7. D   8. B

SCRIPTS   Unit 7   Education

1. no audio

2. Pay attention to how these words sound.

compulsory	nice	friendly
elective (adj)	grumpy	really (adv.)
elective (noun)	easy-going	boring
horrible	interesting	strict

3. no audio

4. Circle the underlined word you hear in each sentence.
   a. Ms Taylor can be really **horrible** sometimes.
   b. Mr Harris is a really **easy-going** teacher.
   c. Miss Williams teaches really **interesting** classes.
   d. Mr Smith seems to be quite **friendly**, doesn't he?
   e. Maths and science are **compulsory** subjects at our school.

5. Pay attention to how these words sound.

maths	science	history
English	art	French
geography	German	drama
art history		

6. no audio

7. Check your answers.

a. language, travel	English
b. laboratory, experiments	science
c. language, Germany	German
d. numbers, equations	maths
e. past, events	history
f. drawing, painting	art
g. acting, actor	drama
h. language, France	French
i. paintings, styles	art history
j. countries, map	geography

8. Circle the subject that the person is talking about.

a. I've never been very good at doing equations and working with numbers.

b. I think it'd be a very useful language to learn.

c. I love drawing and painting pictures.

d. We learn all about different countries and see where they are on the map.

e. We look at famous paintings and learn about the different styles and when they were popular.

f. We have to learn a lot of verbs and it's difficult to pronounce.

g. I like going to the laboratory to do experiments.

h. I think it might be fun learning how to act.

9. no audio

10. Can you hear the answer to the example question?

Narrator: You are going to hear two friends, Bill and Sarah, discussing what school subjects they are going to take.

Bill: Hi, Sarah. How are you?

Sarah: Oh, okay. But I'm having trouble deciding which classes to take this term.

Bill: Well, I'm guessing you already know that maths, science, history and English are compulsory?

Sarah: Yeah, I know. It's just that I'm not really sure which of the electives to do. Last term I had a really horrible teacher for art history—Ms Taylor—and I want to make sure I end up with someone a bit nicer this time.

11. Pay attention to how these common English surnames sound.

Anderson, Andrews, Brown, Black, Campbell, Collins, Davis, Dawson, Edwards, Evans, Fisher, Ford, Granger, Green, Harris, Hill, Johnson, Jones, King, Lewis, Marshall, Oliver, Palmer, Patterson, Reed, Robinson, Stevens, Smith, Taylor, Turner, Watson, Williams

12. Tick the surnames you hear.

Andrews	Campbell	Davis	Ford	Harris
King	Oliver	Patterson	Stevens	Turner

13. Circle the surname you hear.

a. Evans	b. Brown	c. King
d. Palmer	e. Dawson	f. Campbell ·
g. Taylor	h. Edwards	i. Lewis

14. Pay attention to how the titles sound.

a. Miss Brown	b. Ms Brown	c. Mrs Brown
d. Mr Brown	e. Dr Brown	

15. Circle the title you hear.

a. **Mr** Smith	b. **Ms** Smith	c. **Dr** Smith
d. **Mrs** Smith	e. **Miss** Smith	

16. Circle the surname you hear.

a. The new science teacher's called Mr **Jones**.

b. Ms **Ford** takes the first year Spanish classes.

c. If you're looking for Mrs **Hill**, she's in room 7A.

d. Miss **Granger**'s taking the art classes this term.

e. If you want to change classes, you'll need to speak to Mr **Black**.

17. no audio

18. Check your answers.

Narrator: *You are going to hear two friends, Bill and Sarah, discussing what school subjects they are going to take.*

Bill: Hi, Sarah. How are you?

Sarah: Oh, okay. But I'm having trouble deciding which classes to take this term.

Bill: Well, I'm guessing you already know that maths, science, history and English are compulsory?

Sarah: Yeah, I know. It's just that I'm not really sure which of the electives to do. Last term I had a really horrible teacher for art history—Ms Taylor—and I want to make sure I end up with someone a bit nicer this time.

Listening 1

Narrator: *You are going to hear two friends, Bill and Sarah, discussing what school subjects they are going to take.*

Bill: Hi, Sarah. How are you?

Sarah: Oh, okay. But I'm having trouble deciding which classes to take this term.

Bill: Well, I'm guessing you already know that maths, science, geography and English are compulsory?

Sarah: Yeah, I know. It's just that I'm not really sure which of the electives to do. Last term I had a really horrible teacher for art history—Ms Taylor—and I want to make sure I end up with someone a bit nicer this time.

Bill: Yeah, Ms Taylor can be a bit grumpy sometimes, and she always sets a lot of homework ... I know! If you like art history, why don't you do art? Mr Harris teaches that, and he's really easy-going.

Sarah: Yeah, but I'm hopeless at drawing and painting. I like looking at it more than actually doing it...Maybe a foreign language? I've always wanted to learn French.

Bill: Well, there's a <u>new teacher</u> for French this term—Mrs Brown. I can't tell you what she's like, but she looks okay.

Sarah: I don't really want to risk it ... How about Miss <u>Williams</u>? I've had her for <u>geography</u> before, and she's really interesting. She's been all over the world, and she always used to talk to us about the different countries she's visited.

Bill: Yeah, but that's the thing—she only teaches geography; none of the elective subjects.

Sarah: Oh, well then, I guess that really just leaves German. Doesn't Mr <u>Smith</u> teach that? He seems friendly enough.

Bill: Yeah, he's okay. But he <u>only teaches the upper classes</u>. If you wanted to do level one German, you'd end up with Mr <u>Jones</u>, and he's <u>usually away sick</u>.

Sarah: Oh dear. I guess I'll just stick with art history. At least the subject's okay.

Listening 2

Narrator: *You are going to hear two friends, Mary and Fred, discussing what school subjects they are going to take.*

Mary: Hi Fred. Have you decided which electives you're going to do this term?

Fred: Well, I'm definitely doing German again, with Mr Green. I want to travel to Europe at the end of the year, and maybe try and work in Germany. I'm not sure about my second subject though.

Mary: What about art? I'm starting art classes this term with that new teacher ... What's her name?

Fred: Oh, that'll be Ms <u>Palmer</u>. I think she's going to be teaching <u>art history</u> too now that Dr <u>Reed's left</u>.

Mary: Oh, has he? What a shame! He was a really good teacher. Where's he gone?

Fred: I think he's gone to lecture up at the university. Anyway, art's not really my thing. I've never been into drawing and painting in a big way.

Mary: Oh...Well, you could do another language. If you do French, you'll be well prepared for going to Europe.

Fred: French? No way! That's Mrs <u>Fisher's</u> class, and she's really <u>strict</u>. If you don't do your homework, she makes you stay after school and copy out French verb tables.

Mary: Oh. Does she? Well, what about something a bit different? I know they're starting <u>drama</u> classes this term. That could be fun. I'm half thinking about doing that one myself.

Fred: Oh, really? Who's teaching those? I've always wanted to have a try at acting.

Mary: It's Mr <u>Turner</u>. I think he spent a bit of time working as an actor in London, so the classes should be quite good.

Fred: Oh well, in that case, I think I'll have a go at drama.

ANSWERS   Unit 8   Recycling

1. no answers

2. no answers

3. Write the word or words you hear to match each meaning.

a. landfill	b. recycling	c. soapy
d. (the) general public	e. plant	f. (to) melt
g. furnace	h. mould	i. (to) roll

4. no answers

5. Check your answers.

a. Recycling	b. landfill	c. plant
d. furnace	e. roll	f. mould

6. Write the words next to their synonyms below.

a. container	b. to sort	c. to crush
d. to put	e. to clean	f. to collect
g. liquid	h. to transport	

7. In pairs, quickly discuss the following questions.
   a. words
   b. No more than two—this means either *one or two* words.

8. Write the words and phrases that you hear.

a. glass recycling	b. jars (and) bottles
c. wash (the) items	d. bottle banks
e. brown (or) green	f. glass collection
g. drink cans	h. saves energy
i. recycling process	j. hot furnace
k. aluminium cans	l. drink machines

9. Complete the phrases.

a. jars (and) bottles	b. bottle banks
c. different colours	d. drink cans
e. recycling process	f. hot furnace
g. plant	

10. Complete the phrases.

a. drink (or) food	b. bottle banks
c. glass plant	d. landfills
e. small pieces	f. heated (and) rolled

11. no answers

12. Order these steps in a process.
    The order is: e, c, f, a, d, b

13. Complete the sentences.

a. are collected	b. is crushed
c. is melted	d. are sterilized
e. is rolled	f. are transported

14. Complete the flow-chart notes.

a. collected	b. crushed
c. melted	d. poured

15. no answers

16. Check your answers.
    a. C   b. C   c. A

Listening 1

1. warm, soapy	2. bottle banks
3. glass collection	4. glass plant
5. (are) sterilized	6. (is) broken
7. sand, ash	8. furnace
9. bottles; jars	10. fibreglass

Listening 2

11. can banks / recycling bins

12. liquid, paper	13. recycling plant
14. small pieces	15. melted
16. (large) moulds	17. rolled
18. new cans	19. washed
20. gas (and) liquid	

SCRIPTS Unit 8 Recycling

1. no audio

2. Pay attention to how these words sound.

aluminium   ash   chemical   fibreglass
gas   limestone   sand   glass
metal

3. Write the word or words you hear to match each meaning.
   a. landfill; L-A-N-D-F-I-L-L; landfill
   b. recycling; R-E-C-Y-C-L-I-N-G; recycling
   c. soapy; S-O-A-P-Y; soapy
   d. the general public; the G-E-N-E-R-A-L (space) P-U-B-L-I-C; the general public
   e. plant; P-L-A-N-T; plant
   f. melt; M-E-L-T; melt
   g. furnace; F-U-R-N-A-C-E; furnace
   h. mould; M-O-U-L-D; mould
   i. roll; R-O-L-L; roll

4. no audio

5. Check your answers.
   a. **Recycling** products uses less energy than making them new.
   b. If you recycle, you are helping to reduce the waste at your local **landfill**.
   c. Bottles and cans are collected and taken to a recycling **plant**, where they are made into new products.
   d. Glass or metal can be heated in a **furnace** until it melts.
   e. A machine can **roll** out the metal to make it thin.
   f. Hot glass can be poured into a **mould** to make it into a shape.

6. Write the words next to their synonyms below.
   a. bin; container; C-O-N-T-A-I-N-E-R
   b. to separate; to sort; S-O-R-T
   c. to break; to crush; C-R-U-S-H
   d. to place; to put; P-U-T
   e. to sterilize; to clean; C-L-E-A-N
   f. to pick up; to collect; C-O-L-L-E-C-T
   g. drink; liquid; L-I-Q-U-I-D
   h. to take; to transport; T-R-A-N-S-P-O-R-T

7. no audio

8. Write the words and phrases that you hear.
   a. glass recycling; glass recycling
   b. jars and bottles; jars and bottles
   c. wash the items; wash the items
   d. bottle banks; bottle banks
   e. brown or green; brown or green
   f. glass collection; glass collection
   g. drink cans; drink cans
   h. saves energy; saves energy
   i. recycling process; recycling process
   j. hot furnace; hot furnace
   k. aluminium cans; aluminium cans
   l. drink machines; drink machines

9. Complete the phrases.
   a. **jars** and **bottles** are collected
   b. taken by the general public to **bottle banks**
   c. sorted into **different colours** by glass collection companies
   d. millions and millions of **drink cans**
   e. first step in the **recycling process**
   f. melted in a very **hot furnace**
   g. taken to another **plant** for further processing

10. Complete the phrases.
   a. This is to ensure that there isn't any **drink** or **food** left on the glass.
   b. Bottles and jars are taken by the general public to **bottle banks**.
   c. The glass is taken to a **glass plant** where the actual recycling takes place.
   d. The process of recycling these cans is very important, because it saves energy and reduces the amount of waste in **landfills**.
   e. The cans are then transported to a recycling plant where they are cut into **small pieces**.
   f. First, the aluminium is **heated** and then **rolled** by a machine to make it thin.

11. no audio

12. Order these steps in a process.
First, the glass bottles and jars are washed. Secondly, they are collected from outside people's homes. Thirdly, they are taken to a recycling plant. After that, the glass is broken into small pieces. Next, it's mixed with sand and melted in a furnace. Finally, the melted glass is poured to make new bottles and jars.

13. Complete the sentences.
   a. The bottles and jars **are collected** in recycling bins.
   b. The glass **is crushed** into small pieces.
   c. The aluminium **is melted** in a hot furnace.
   d. The bottles **are sterilized** at the recycling plant.
   e. The aluminium **is rolled** to make it thin.
   f. The drinks **are transported** to shops and supermarkets for sale.

14. Complete the flow-chart notes.
First, the glass bottles and jars are **collected** in recycling bins. Then they are sterilized and **crushed** at the plant. After that, the glass is **melted**, and in the final stages, **poured** to make new bottles.

15. no audio

16. Check your answers.
Narrator 1: *You are now going to hear a talk about glass recycling.*
Narrator 2:
Glass recycling is now a standard process in many towns and cities of the world. Millions of glass items are used every day, with bottles, jars and light bulbs being among the most common. The process of recycling glass rather than making it new saves energy and reduces the amount of waste at landfills.

Listing 1

Narrator 1: *You are now going to hear a talk about glass recycling.*

Narrator 2:

Glass recycling is now a standard process in many towns and cities of the world. Millions of glass items are used every day, with bottles, jars and light bulbs being among the most common. The process of recycling glass rather than making it new saves energy and reduces the amount of waste at landfills.

The first step in the process of recycling household glass is to wash the items in <u>warm, soapy</u> water. This is to ensure that there isn't any drink or food left on the glass. Secondly, the jars and bottles are collected by one of two systems, depending on the town or city. In some places, bottles and jars are taken by the general public to <u>bottle banks</u>. Bottle banks are large recycling bins, usually with three holes that enable the glass to be separated by colour—clear, brown or green. In other cities, people put their bottles and jars in a container which they leave outside their house on a set day of the week. A truck then comes past, and the glass is collected and sorted into different colours by <u>glass collection</u> companies.

Thirdly, the glass is taken to a <u>glass plant</u>, where the actual recycling process takes place. At the glass plant, one of two things can happen. In the first case, the bottles <u>are sterilized</u> and then reused for their original purpose—that is, soft drink bottles are refilled with soft drinks, or jam jars are refilled with jam, and so on. Reusing bottles as they are saves money, and saves more energy than the second process. In the second case, the glass is melted down and made into new bottles or other products entirely. First, all of the glass of one colour is placed into a big crushing machine and <u>broken</u> into small pieces. It is important to separate the different types and colours of glass, because they have different chemical properties. Then, the crushed glass is mixed with amounts of <u>sand, ash</u> and limestone and placed in a <u>furnace</u> to be melted.

Finally, most of the melted glass is poured to make new <u>bottles and jars</u>. However, depending on the quality, it can be used to make other products, including floor tiles and <u>fibreglass</u>.

Listening 2

Narrator 1: *You are going to hear a talk about the recycling process for aluminium cans.*

Narrator 2:

Every year, millions and millions of drink cans are sold around the world. Approximately 75 per cent of these drink cans are made of aluminium. The process of recycling these cans is very important because it saves energy and reduces the amount of waste in landfills.

In the first step in the recycling process, the used cans are collected. As with glass bottles and jars, this means that the cans are either taken by the general public to large <u>recycling bins</u>—known as 'can banks'—outside supermarkets and other shops, or picked up from outside people's houses by can collection companies. Secondly, the cans are taken to special centres, where they are checked for any <u>liquid, paper</u> or other materials that could be a problem for the recycling process. Thirdly, the cans are then transported to a <u>recycling plant</u>, where a machine cuts them into <u>small pieces</u>. Then the pieces of aluminium are <u>melted</u> in a very hot furnace, before being poured into huge <u>moulds</u> and left to go cold.

In the next stage, the big blocks of aluminium are taken to another plant for rolling. First, they are heated and then <u>rolled</u> by a machine to make them thin. Next, they are left to cool, before being rolled a second time until they are thin enough to make <u>new</u> aluminium <u>cans</u>. The thin pieces of aluminium are then put into another machine where they are cut up and made into new cans. After this, the new cans are painted with the colours and the logo of the drink company.

In the final stages, the cans are placed in an oven to dry, before being <u>washed</u>. Lastly, the new, clean aluminium cans are filled with <u>gas and liquid</u>. They are now ready to be transported to shops, supermarkets and drink machines for people to buy. Then, the recycling process begins all over again.

ANSWERS Unit 9 Food

1. no answers

2. no answers

3. Complete the names of the items on the menu.

a. garlic bread	b. tomato soup
c. seafood chowder	d. chicken wings
e. green salad	f. spaghetti bolognaise
g. fish and chips	h. steak and vegetables
i. roast lamb with potatoes	j. bacon and egg pie
k. carrot cake	l. apple pie
m. ice-cream sundae	n. fruit salad
o. chocolate mousse	p. red wine

4. Complete the questions.

a. order	b. starter	c. salad
d. main	e. dessert	f. drinks

5. Choose the one you hear.

a. C	b. B	c. A
d. B	e. C	f. C

6. Complete the menus.
   a. Starter: garlic bread
      Main: spaghetti bolognaise
      Dessert: ice-cream sundae
      Drink: beer
   b. Starter: chicken wings
      Main: steak and vegetables
      Dessert: fruit salad
      Drink: red wine
   c. Starter: seafood chowder
      Main: bacon and egg pie
      Dessert: carrot cake
      Drink: coffee
   d. Starter: green salad
      Main: fish and chips
      Dessert: chocolate mousse
      Drink: white wine

7. Answer the multiple choice questions.

a. B	b. C
c. B	d. A

8. Complete the form.
   a. chicken wings   b. spaghetti bolognaise
   c. fruit salad   d. white wine

9. no answers

10. Check your answers.
   a. A   b. B   c. C

Listening 1

Part A
   1. A   2. C   3. A

Part B
   4. garlic bread   5. steak and vegetables
   6. chocolate mousse

Listening 2

Part A
   7. B   8. A   9. B

Part B
   10. tomato soup   11. roast lamb
   12. steak (and/with) vegetables
   13. ice-cream sundae   14. red wine

SCRIPTS Unit 9 Food

1. no audio

2. Pay attention to how these words sound.

bread	tomato	steak	potato
ice-cream	soup	lettuce	carrot
bacon	mousse	seafood	spaghetti
peas	egg	wine	chicken
fish	broccoli	pie	beer
salad	chips	lamb	cake
coffee			

3. Complete the names of the items on the menu.
   a. garlic **bread**; garlic **bread**
   b. **tomato** soup; **tomato** soup
   c. **seafood** chowder; **seafood** chowder
   d. **chicken** wings; **chicken** wings
   e. green **salad**; green **salad**
   f. **spaghetti** bolognaise; **spaghetti** bolognaise
   g. fish and **chips**; fish and **chips**
   h. **steak** and vegetables; **steak** and vegetables
   i. roast **lamb** with potatoes; roast **lamb** with potatoes
   j. **bacon** and **egg** pie; **bacon** and **egg** pie
   k. carrot **cake**; carrot **cake**
   l. **apple** pie; **apple** pie
   m. **ice-cream** sundae; **ice-cream** sundae
   n. **fruit** salad; **fruit** salad
   o. chocolate **mousse**; chocolate **mousse**
   p. red **wine**; red **wine**

4. Complete the questions.
   a. What would you like to **order**?
   b. Will you be having a **starter**?
   c. Would you like a green **salad**?
   d. What will you have for your **main** course?
   e. Would you like to order a **dessert**?
   f. Would you like any **drinks** with your meal?

5. Choose the one you hear.
   a. bacon and egg pie   b. chocolate cake
   c. fish and chips   d. roast lamb with broccoli
   e. seafood salad   f. chicken wings

6. Complete the menus.
   a. Starter: garlic bread; garlic bread
      Main: spaghetti bolognaise; spaghetti bolognaise
      Dessert: ice-cream sundae; ice-cream sundae
      Drink: beer; beer
   b. Starter: chicken wings; chicken wings
      Main: steak and vegetables; steak and vegetables
      Dessert: fruit salad; fruit salad
      Drink: red wine; red wine
   c. Starter: seafood chowder; seafood chowder
      Main: bacon and egg pie; bacon and egg pie
      Dessert: carrot cake; carrot cake
      Drink: coffee; coffee
   d. Starter: green salad; green salad
      Main: fish and chips; fish and chips
      Dessert: chocolate mousse; chocolate mousse
      Drink: white wine; white wine

7. Answer the multiple choice questions.
Narrator: *You are going to hear two friends, Michelle and Paul, discussing the food on a menu.*
Paul: Have you decided what you're going to order yet?
Michelle: Yeah. I think I'll have the garlic bread to start, and for the main course I'm going to order the steak and vegetables.
Paul: Do you know what the vegetables are?
Michelle: No. It doesn't say.
Paul: Then I think I'll have something different in case they are green vegetables. I don't really like green vegetables.
Michelle: Well, what about roast lamb with potatoes? That doesn't have green vegetables.
Paul: Yeah, that's a good idea. I'll have the lamb.
Michelle: Are you going to have dessert?
Paul: Definitely! I've already decided to get the ice-cream sundae.
Michelle: Hm...I like ice-cream, but I'm trying to eat more healthily, so I think I'll skip dessert.
Paul: Okay. Let's order, then.

8. Complete the form.
Narrator: *You are going to hear a conversation between a woman, Jill, and a waiter.*
Waiter: Are you ready to order?
Jill: Yes, we are. My husband's just gone to the bathroom, so I'll order for both of us.
Waiter: Right.
Jill: Let's see...I'll have the green salad to start, and my husband will have the chicken wings.
Waiter: And for your main course?
Jill: I'll have the fish and chips, and my husband will have the spaghetti bolognaise.

Waiter:	And will you be ordering any desserts?
Jill:	Yes. I'll have the carrot cake, and my husband will have the fruit salad.
Waiter:	And would you like anything to drink with your meals?
Jill:	Yes. I'll have a white wine, and my husband will have a beer.
Waiter:	Certainly, madam.

9. no audio

10. Check your answers.

Narrator: *You are going to hear two friends, Lucy and Dan, discussing the food on a menu.*

Lucy:	Hi, Dan. Sorry I'm late. Wow! You've managed to get a pretty good table.
Dan:	Yeah. When I booked, I asked for one by the window. The view's great, isn't it?
Lucy:	Yeah, it is. Have you had a chance to look at the menu yet? I'm starving.
Dan:	Well, I've had a quick look at the starters, but I'm not that hungry, so I might just have a main.
Lucy:	Oh, well, I'm definitely having a starter. I haven't eaten since this morning. Let's see...

Listening 1

Part A

Narrator: *Part A. You are going to hear two friends, Lucy and Dan, discussing the food on a menu.*

Lucy:	Hi, Dan. Sorry I'm late. Wow! You've managed to get a pretty good table.
Dan:	Yeah. When I booked, I asked for one <u>by the window</u>. The view's great, isn't it?
Lucy:	Yeah, it is. You can see the river from here...and the university. Have you been to this restaurant before?
Dan:	No, I haven't, but I've had some good recommendations, so I thought I'd try it out... Where have you been, anyway?
Lucy:	Oh, I had to go and see Professor Oliver about an assignment I'm doing, and ended up talking for ages...Have you had a chance to look at the menu yet? I'm starving.
Dan:	Well, I've had a quick look at the starters, but <u>I'm not that hungry, so I might just have a main</u>.
Lucy:	Oh, well, I'm definitely having a starter. I haven't eaten <u>since this morning</u>. I've been so busy all day! Let's see...

Part B

Narrator: *Part B. You will now hear the rest of the conversation.*

Dan:	I saw they have tomato soup on the starter menu. I know you always like that.
Lucy:	Mm, yes, I do, but I feel like something different this time. Maybe seafood...Yeah, I think I'll have the seafood chowder and some <u>garlic bread</u>.
Dan:	I didn't think you liked seafood.
Lucy:	Well, I haven't tried it for ages. I might like it now. Anyway, it's just chowder, so it should be mostly liquid.

Dan:	Oh, well. It's your dinner. What do you think you'll have for a main?
Lucy:	I'm not sure. I haven't decided yet.
Dan:	I was going to order the roast lamb with potatoes, but then I saw they have bacon and egg pie. It's my favourite, so I'll probably go with that.
Lucy:	Hm...I don't really like bacon. The flavour's too strong. Maybe something with more vegetables in it...There is <u>steak and vegetables</u>, but I don't really like steak ... Let's see ... um ... I think I'll have the spaghetti bolognaise ... What are you going to have for dessert?
Dan:	I wasn't going to have dessert, but if you are, I'll get one...
Lucy:	I'm really hungry, so I'll definitely get something. Um ... I think I'll have the apple pie. That sounds good.
Dan:	Okay. The <u>chocolate mousse</u> sounds good too. I think I'll have that.
Lucy:	Alright. I'll see if I can get the waiter's attention and we can order.

Listening 2

Part A

Narrator: *Part A. You are going to hear a conversation between a man, Bob, and a waiter.*

Waiter:	Good evening.
Bob:	Good evening. We have a reservation. <u>Mr and Mrs Williams.</u>
Waiter:	Certainly. Let's see ... Mr and Mrs Wilson...
Bob:	No, it's not Wilson. It's Williams.
Waiter:	Oh. I'm very sorry, sir. Of course, Williams ... Let's see ... We have a table by the door or one by the window. Which would you prefer?
Bob:	We'll take the table <u>by the window</u>. It's a bit cold by the door.
Waiter:	Certainly. That'll be table number <u>24</u>. Follow me. Here are the menus. Let's know when you're ready to order.
Bob:	Thanks.

Part B

Narrator: *Part B. You will now hear the rest of the conversation.*

Waiter:	Are you ready to order?
Bob:	Yes, we are. My wife's just gone to the bathroom, but I can order for both of us.
Waiter:	Right.
Bob:	Let's see ... What comes with the green salad?
Waiter:	Lettuce and tomatoes with a dressing, sir.
Bob:	Is it possible to have that without the dressing?
Waiter:	Yes, certainly, sir.
Bob:	In that case, I'll have the green salad.
Waiter:	Okay...green salad without the dressing. And for your wife?
Bob:	She'll have the <u>tomato soup</u>.
Waiter:	Right. And would she like any garlic bread with that?
Bob:	No, that's alright. The soup will be fine.
Waiter:	And for your main course?

Bob:	I'd like the <u>roast lamb</u> with potatoes. And my wife wanted to know what vegetables come with the steak.
Waiter:	The steak comes with broccoli, carrots and peas.
Bob:	Okay. I think that should be alright. She doesn't like peas very much, but broccoli and carrots are fine.
Waiter:	I could ask the chef to prepare it without the peas if she'd prefer.
Bob:	Oh, yes. That might be better.
Waiter:	Right. The <u>steak and vegetables</u>, minus the peas... And would you like any desserts?
Bob:	Ah, I think I'll just have a coffee.
Waiter:	And anything for your wife?
Bob:	Yes. She'll have the <u>ice-cream sundae</u>.
Waiter:	Chocolate or caramel for the topping?
Bob:	What? Oh, chocolate would be alright, I imagine.
Waiter:	And would you like any other drinks with your meals?
Bob:	Yes, <u>red wine</u>, please.
Waiter:	Certainly, sir. I'll send the wine waiter over right away.

ANSWERS Unit 10 Technology

1. no answers

2. no answers

3. Write the word or words to complete each sentence.

a. digital camera	b. model	c. screen
d. resolution	e. megapixels	f. zoom
g. features	h. specifications	i. warranty
j. upgrade	k. notebook	l. hard drive
m. processor	n. antivirus software	
o. graphic card	p. gigabyte	q. megabytes

4. no answers

5. Write the word or words to complete each sentence.

a. reasonable	b. convenient	c. expensive
d. clear	e. small	f. long
g. wide	h. reliable	i. cheap
j. slow	k. large	l. short
m. high	n. low	o. big
p. fast		

6. Write the words and phrases you hear.

a. the cheapest	b. more convenient than
c. the least expensive	d. smaller than
e. less reliable than	f. the biggest
g. clearer than	h. the widest
i. the fastest	j. higher than
k. lower than	l. the largest
m. the longest	n. more reasonable than
o. shorter	p. the slowest

7. Complete the sentences.

a. cheaper	b. more reliable
c. the widest	d. a larger
e. the most expensive	f. a slower
g. a lower	h. more convenient
i. the biggest	j. a longer
k. the fastest	l. clearer
m. a higher	n. the shortest
o. more reasonable	p. the smallest

8. In pairs, consider the table below.
    a. words and/or numbers
    b. One, two or three items, but no more.
    c. The words and numbers from the box.
    d. n/a (students try to guess some of the answers)

9. Complete the notes above.

1. (the) largest	2. (the) highest
3. (the) most	4. cheaper than
5. (a) 30-inch	6. (a) shorter
7. (the) best	8. (a) smaller
9. (the) lowest	10. (a) 2-year

10. no answers

11. Check your answers.
    a. C   b. C   c. B

Listening 1

Part A

1. (the) widest	2. (the) largest
3. (the) most expensive	4. (a) (slightly) lower
5. (a) convenient	6. shorter than
7. (the) cheapest	8. (the) lowest
9. (a) reasonable	

Part B

10. 8 / eight	11. 5x / 5 times / five times
12. 2.5 inches	13. 2-year / two-year
14. 6-month / six-month	

Listening 2

Part A

15. (the) fastest	16. (the) best
17. antivirus software	18. (a) (slightly) smaller
19. (the) largest	20. (the) lower
21. (the) smallest	22. (the) longest
23. (the) most reliable	

Part B
24. B   25. E   26. G

SCRIPTS Unit 10 Technology

1. no audio

2. Pay attention to how these words sound.

model	digital camera	specifications
graphic card	screen	megapixels
notebook (computer)	antivirus software	warranty

152

zoom	hard drive	megabyte (MB)
resolution	to upgrade	processor
gigabyte (GB)	features	

3. Write the word or words to complete each sentence.

   a. I'm looking to buy a **digital camera**.
   b. Do you know which **model** you'd prefer?
   c. This one here has a large **screen**.
   d. The **resolution** is excellent.
   e. It's 8.4 **megapixels**.
   f. It also has a 5x optical **zoom**.
   g. This one certainly has a lot of **features** for the money.
   h. If you'd like to see the exact **specifications**, just let me know.
   i. We offer a very comprehensive 2-year **warranty**.
   j. You can also **upgrade** this to 5 years by paying an extra $150.
   k. This **notebook** is very light and easy to carry.
   l. The **hard drive** has a lot of space for storing files.
   m. This one here has quite a fast **processor**.
   n. They all come with free **antivirus software**.
   o. The **graphic card** enables you to deal with a lot of images.
   p. It has a 2 **gigabyte** hard drive.
   q. The upgrade will give you an extra 500 **megabytes**.

4. no audio

5. Write the word or words to complete each sentence.

   a. The price for this one is very **reasonable**.
   b. The screen size makes it very **convenient** for viewing photos and movies.
   c. This model is quite **expensive**.
   d. This television has a very **clear** picture.
   e. The screen on this one is a bit too **small**.
   f. These all come with a **long** warranty.
   g. This camera has a nice **wide** zoom.
   h. This model here is very **reliable**.
   i. If you want a **cheap** model, you can't expect as many features.
   j. The processor on this computer is quite **slow**.
   k. This one has quite a **large** capacity.
   l. This one here only comes with a **short** warranty.
   m. This digital camera has a **high** megapixel count.
   n. This one offers a lot of features for a **low** price.
   o. The hard drive on this computer isn't **big** enough.
   p. I need one with a **fast** processor.

6. Write the words and phrases you hear.

a. the cheapest	b. more convenient than
c. the least expensive	d. smaller than
e. less reliable than	f. the biggest
g. clearer than	h. the widest
i. the fastest	j. higher than
k. lower than	l. the largest
m. the longest	n. more reasonable than

o. shorter   p. the slowest

7. Complete the sentences.

   a. This model is **cheaper** than that one.
   b. This computer is **more reliable** than the other one.
   c. This camera has **the widest** zoom.
   d. This one has **a larger** screen.
   e. This television is **the most expensive** of the three.
   f. This one here has **a slower** processor than that one.
   g. This notebook comes at **a lower** price than the other one.
   h. You'll find that this screen size is **more convenient** for viewing photos.
   i. This model has **the biggest** hard drive.
   j. This one comes with **a longer** warranty.
   k. This model definitely has **the fastest** processor.
   l. This screen gives you **a clearer** picture.
   m. This one comes at **a higher** price because of all the features.
   n. This notebook has **the shortest** warranty.
   o. The price of this television here is **more reasonable**.
   p. The one here definitely has **the smallest** screen.

8. no audio

9. Complete the notes above.

Narrator: *You are going to hear a salesman describing three different television sets to a customer.*

Salesman: If you're looking to buy a flat-screen TV, then we have three very good models at different prices. Now, you'll see over here the Movie Max Series 2. It's a very good model, and of the three, it has the largest screen—a 40-inch screen—and the longest warranty—a 5-year warranty—and the highest resolution. Of course, this also means that it's the most expensive, at $2,500, but it's certainly worth it with all the features. Plus, we'll throw in a free Movie Max DVD player if you buy this week.

If you're looking for something a little cheaper, the Teleview XT is ideal. Now, the screen is a little smaller than the Movie Max—at 30 inches—and the resolution is a little lower, but you still get a very good picture. Obviously, the warranty is shorter, but three years is still very reasonable, given the price—at only $1,900, I would say the Teleview XT offers the best value for money of the three options.

Now, finally, if you're really concerned about budget, the Vistotron comes in at only $1,500. However, you still get some great features with this one, so you won't be wasting your money. Of course, the screen is slightly smaller again—it has a 25-inch screen—and it does have the lowest resolution, but if you look, you'll see that the picture is very clear, and the colours are very good. And of course, we offer a very comprehensive 2-year warranty on this model—and remember that while this is the shortest one we offer, the service is excellent, and I shouldn't expect any problems with the Vistatron. It's a reliable model.

10. no audio

11. Check your answers.

Narrator: *You are going to hear a saleswoman describing three different digital cameras to a customer.*

Saleswoman: If you're looking to buy a digital camera, then we have three very good models at different prices. If you'd like to come this way, you'll see that the CF Superzoom has the largest range of features. With the highest megapixel count, it'll allow you to print clearer pictures at larger sizes. It also has the widest zoom, so that you can bring those far away objects closer to you. And having the largest screen size makes viewing photos and movies very easy on the eye. This model is the most expensive, but it does offer the best warranty.

Listening 1

Part A

Narrator: *Part A. You are going to hear a saleswoman describing three different digital cameras to a customer.*

Saleswoman: If you're looking to buy a digital camera, then we have three very good models at different prices. If you'd like to come this way, you'll see that the CF Superzoom has the largest range of features. With the highest megapixel count, it'll allow you to print clearer pictures at larger sizes. It also has the <u>widest</u> zoom, so that you can bring those far away objects closer to you. And having the <u>largest</u> screen size makes viewing photos and movies very easy on the eye. This model is the <u>most expensive</u>, but it does offer the best warranty.

Now, if you're looking for something a little cheaper, the Photo-Pal A23 is an excellent option. While the megapixel count and the zoom range are <u>slightly lower</u> than the CF Superzoom, they still offer amazing quality and value for money. Again, the screen is a little smaller, but it's still a <u>convenient</u> size for viewing photos and movies. And perhaps the best thing about it is the low price. The warranty is obviously <u>shorter than</u> what you'd get with the Superzoom, but for a small price, you can upgrade the warranty to the same one.

And, finally, if you'd just like to come round here, you'll see the <u>cheapest</u> model of the three—the QT Easishot. While it obviously doesn't have all of the features of the Superzoom or the Photo-Pal, it dòes take very good pictures, and I'm certain you won't be disappointed if you go for this option. The megapixel count and the zoom range are the <u>lowest</u>, but they're still not bad if you consider the price. The screen is a <u>reasonable</u> size for viewing those photos and movies, and as with all of our cameras, it comes with a full warranty on parts and manufacturing.

So feel free now just to browse, and if you have any more questions, I'll be right over there at the sales desk.

Part B

Narrator: *Part B. You will now hear the rest of the conversation.*

Saleswoman: Right. Now, if you'd like to know all of the specifications for each model, we have them right here on our computer system. Let's see ... Okay. The CF Superzoom is 12 megapixels, which is quite a lot more than the other two models. The Photo-Pal A23 is <u>8</u> megapixels and the QT Easishot is 7. Again, the Superzoom has the best zoom—a <u>5x</u> optical zoom—although the Photo-Pal is excellent as well, with a 4x optical zoom. The Easishot offers the standard 3x optical zoom, which I think you'll find is the case for most of our cameras in the lower price range. And, as for screen size, the Superzoom has a 3.5-inch screen, which is a little larger than the 3-inch s creen on the Photo-Pal, but not really too much difference there. The Easishot screen is just that bit

smaller at <u>2.5 inches</u>.

Finally, you need to consider the warranties. The Superzoom has a standard <u>2-year</u> warranty, but by paying only $75 more, you can upgrade that to five years full service and parts. The Photo-Pal comes with a standard 1-year warranty, and an extra one-year upgrade for $50, while the Easishot comes with a <u>6-month</u> warranty, which can be upgraded to one year for only $25.

There, now, I hope that answers all of your questions. If you'd like to know anything about any of the other models on display, please just ask.

Listening 2

Part A

Narrator: *Part A. You are going to hear a salesman describing three different notebook computers to a customer.*

Salesman: If you're interested in buying a notebook, then we have three very good models at different prices. I'll explain the features of each one in general terms, and then if you'd like to know anything else, I can get you the exact specifications.

Right. Now, if you'd like to come this way, I'll show you our best model. This is the Speedy Z notebook, which should have all of the features you need and more. It has the biggest hard drive, and the <u>fastest</u> processor of the three, so for running your applications and downloading images and video files, it's certainly the fastest. It also comes with the <u>best</u> graphic card, so if image capability is what you're after, then it's definitely your first choice. It also comes with free <u>antivirus software</u>, a free flash drive and a free carry bag, so if you want my opinion, it's the best deal in store.

And just over here, we have the Maestro Supalite notebook. It is a cheaper model than the Speedy Z, but still comes with a lot of features, so you won't be disappointed. The hard drive is only slightly <u>smaller</u> than the Speedy Z, although not by much, and the processor is a tiny bit slower, but again, you shouldn't really notice the difference unless you're dealing with a whole lot of images. However, you will notice that the Maestro does come with the <u>largest</u> screen, which has excellent resolution, I might add. Plus, I'll throw in some free extras, including the antivirus software, and a free carry bag. So for the <u>lower</u> price, you're still getting an excellent deal.

And finally, if you'd just like to come over this way, we have the Genius XT. Now, it is the cheapest model, but it certainly does have some great features for a small machine. Of course, it doesn't have the fastest processor or the biggest hard drive, but it does have the capacity to run most of the applications you've mentioned. The only thing is, it does come with the <u>smallest</u> graphic card, so if you were particularly concerned about its capacity for dealing with images, then you might want to be thinking about one of the two other models. One thing that might surprise you is that it comes with our <u>longest</u> warranty. Yes, the Genius XT is one of the <u>most reliable</u> models we've ever dealt with, so we're more than happy to extend that privilege to our customers.

Part B

Narrator: *Part B. You will now hear the rest of the conversation.*

Salesman: If you'd just like to wait a moment, I'll get all of the specifications up here on my screen. Right. Now, the Speedy Z has a 2 GB hard drive and a 256 MB graphic card. And the screen size is ... just let me scroll down a bit ... yes, here we go. It's a 15-inch screen, while, I think you'll remember, the Maestro Supalite has the largest screen, at 17 inches. Okay. Now, for the Speedy Z, you get a 2-year warranty, but that can easily be upgraded to 5 years for an extra $150, which I think is definitely worth the money. And the price for that model— that's without the extra warranty—is $1,750.

Now, let me just bring up the details for the Maestro ... Ah, here we are. Yes. The Maestro Supalite comes with a 2 GB hard drive and a 128 MB graphic card. We already know the screen size ... And, let me see ... For the warranty, you get the standard one year, but you can upgrade that to two years for an extra $75 ... but of course, if price is an issue, that's entirely optional. The price for this model—again, that's with the standard warranty—is $1,295.

And, finally, I'll just find the Genius XT ... Okay. The Genius comes with a 1 GB hard drive and the graphic card is 64 MB. The screen is not too much smaller than the Speedy Z—it's a 12-inch screen —and it includes free McGinty antivirus software if you're keen on that brand. Plus, there's the extended warranty, which is five years. That can't be upgraded, unfortunately, but I'm sure you'll agree that it's very generous at the price, in any case—only $899.

Alright. If you'd like to look at any of our other models, or if you have any other queries, I'd be happy to answer your questions.

ANSWERS   Unit 11   Censorship

1. no answers

2. no answers

3. Write the word or phrase from the box to complete each sentence.
   a. commit   b. nightmare   c. in real life
   d. responsibility e. rating   f. appropriate

4. Match the vocabulary list words.
   a. behaviour   b. allow   c. suitable
   d. battle   e. restrictions   f. right
   g. disturbing   h. fair

5. Write the synonym you hear to complete the sentences.
   a. behaviour   b. let   c. appropriate
   d. fight   e. unsuitable   f. right
   g. upsetting   h. reasonable

6. Write the noun form of these adjectives and verbs.
   a. violence   b. crime   c. action / act
   d. restriction   e. protection   f. behaviour

7. Identify the word you hear.
   a. violent   b. criminal   c. action
   d. restricting   e. protective   f. behave

8. Consider which type of word is missing from each space—circle your choice.

a. adverb   b. noun   c. verb
d. verb   e. verb   f. noun

9. Write the words you hear in the gaps above.
   a. violently   b. crimes   c. acting
   d. restrict   e. protected   f. behaviour

10. Write the opinion words you hear.
    a. I suppose so   b. It makes sense c. I disagree
    d. That's right   e. I guess   f. I don't think so

11. Work in pairs / Alternatively, use the audio.
    Examples of possible responses:
    a. I don't think they should be allowed to (see violent television shows).
    b. That's right, I agree.
    c. I disagree (don't agree) with that. (I think the government has a responsibility to control what is available.)
    d. You're right. / I agree with you.
    e. I don't agree with that. (There needs to be some censorship.)

12. Write the words that are missing from these sentences.
    a. Ratings   b. copy   c. young children
    d. allowed to   e. Violent shows   f. frighten
    g. act violently

13. no answers

14. Complete the sentence with the words you hear.
    a. protect   b. disturbed   c. nightmares
    d. criminals   e. scenes   f. commit crimes
    g. responsibility

15. no answers

16. Check your answers.
    a. B   b. B   c. A

Listening 1
   1. old enough   2. violent battle   3. real life
   4. age restriction 5. parents
   6. movies, DVDs / movies / DVDs

Listening 2
   7. criminals   8. young children
   9. anyone / children, adults
   10. crime   11. adults   12. disagree

SCRIPTS   Unit 11   Censorship

1. no audio

2. Pay attention to how these words sound.

in real life	fair	protect
violent	disturbing	battle
appropriate	scene	responsibility
suitable	frighten	nightmare
behaviour	right	commit
fighting	be allowed to	rating

3. Write the word or phrase from the box to complete each sentence.
   a. Some people worry that television crime shows or violent computer games may show how to **commit** a crime.
   b. If you have a bad dream, it's called a **nightmare**.
   c. Sometimes it is necessary to distinguish between what can happen on television or in a game and what happens **in real life**.
   d. Who should take **responsibility** for what children see on television?
   e. The **rating** of a movie is the score it receives, either to say how good it is, or to show who it is suitable for, and whether it contains anything offensive.
   f. Parents want to be sure that their children are watching television that is **appropriate** for their age.

4. no audio

5. Write the synonym you hear to complete the sentences.
   a. Do violent computer games affect children's **behaviour**?
   b. Some parents may **let** their children watch violent movies.
   c. Ratings tell parents if a movie is **appropriate** for their children.
   d. A computer game may have graphic **fight** scenes.
   e. Age restrictions can prevent children from seeing **unsuitable** material.
   f. There may be more than one **right** way to restrict movies and games.
   g. Some television shows may be **upsetting** to small children.
   h. Any rules about censorship need to be **reasonable**.

6. no audio

7. Identify the word you hear.
   a. violent   b. criminal   c. action
   d. restricting   e. protective   f. behave

8. no audio

9. Write the words you hear in the gaps above.
   a. Some parents worry their children will behave **violently** after playing computer games.
   b. Some movies and television shows show how to commit **crimes**.
   c. Do you ever try **acting** like a character from a movie?
   d. Some countries have laws to **restrict** the content of computer games.
   e. Children need to be **protected** from some of the sites on the internet.
   f. Some people say that watching violent movies doesn't affect their **behaviour**.

10. Write the opinion words you hear.
    a. **I suppose so.** I'd never thought of it like that before.
    b. **It makes sense** that there are the same rules for everyone.
    c. **I disagree** with the idea that computer games are

dangerous.
    d. **That's right.** Those games are not suitable for children.
    e. **I guess** we'll have to make a decision tomorrow.
    f. **I don't think so.** It isn't fair to have different rules for games than movies.

11. Work in pairs / Alternatively, use the audio.
    a. What do you think about children viewing violent television shows? (*state opinion*)
    b. Some computer games are designed for adults, so they should have an age restriction. (*agree*)
    c. Only parents should be responsible for what computer games their children play. (*disagree*)
    d. Violent television shows should not be shown on television at all. (*agree*)
    e. Adults should be able to choose what they can watch on television. (*disagree*)

12. Write the words that are missing from these sentences.
    a. **Ratings** show if a game is suitable for parents to buy.
    b. Children might try and **copy** a game when playing with their friends.
    c. That game is not suitable for **young children**.
    d. People younger than sixteen are not **allowed to** buy this game.
    e. **Violent shows** on television should be banned.
    f. These kinds of shows might **frighten** children.
    g. Even worse, young people might **act violently** after playing violent computer games.

13. no audio

14. Complete the sentence with the words you hear.
    a. Ratings on games mean that we can **protect** children.
    b. If children see fighting on TV, they may feel **disturbed**.
    c. Seeing violent actions may give young people **nightmares**.
    d. People could turn into **criminals** as a result of watching violence on TV.
    e. Some games show violent battle **scenes**.
    f. People could learn how to **commit crimes** by watching TV.
    g. I think it should be the **responsibility** of young peoples' families to decide what movies they can see.

15. no audio

16. Check your answers.
Narrator: *You are going to hear a conversation between two friends, Bob and Jane, and Paul, Jane's younger brother. They're talking about the age restriction on a new computer game.*

Listening 1
Narrator: *You are going to hear a conversation between two friends, Bob and Jane, and Paul, Jane's younger brother. They're talking about the age restrictions on a new computer game.*
Bob: Hey, have you seen the new *Crazy Attacks* computer game? It's great!
Jane: Yeah, it's amazing! It's my new favourite game. I've been playing it all weekend.

Paul: It looks really good, but it has an age restriction, so I want to play it but I'm not <u>old enough</u> to buy it!

Jane: Really? How old do you have to be to buy it Paul?

Paul: Sixteen. It's not fair!

Jane: Well, it does have some <u>violent battle</u> scenes. I guess they don't want young children to see these. And I have to agree. I don't think that game is suitable for children.

Bob: That's right...I think it might give them nightmares!

Jane: Or even worse, they might try and copy the fighting in the game when they are playing with their friends. If they fight like that in <u>real life</u>, they could easily get hurt.

Paul: I think I should be allowed to buy it. I'm not going to do anything stupid like that just because I saw it in a game.

Bob: Well maybe you won't, Paul, but the ratings might help protect others. This game isn't so disturbing, but some games are designed for adults, and aren't appropriate for children, so they have to have an <u>age restriction</u>.

Paul: I don't think we need ratings on computer games because it should be the <u>parents'</u> responsibility to make sure their children don't see things that will frighten them.

Jane: I agree, but parents need to know the age restriction ratings to know what is safe to give to their children. Otherwise they might buy something that isn't suitable.

Bob: And anyway, <u>movies and DVDs</u> have ratings and age restrictions, so I think games should too.

Jane: I agree. You can't go to see a movie rated R16, Paul, so it makes sense that you can't play R16 games.

Paul: I guess that's true, but I still don't think it's fair!

Listening 2

Narrator: *You are going to hear a conversation between three friends, Carla, Jack and Sally, about their opinions on television restrictions.*

Carla: Ugh. Did you see that? I don't think they should be allowed to show things like that on television.

Jack: Really? What are you watching, Carla?

Carla: Well, it's a documentary about <u>criminals</u>, and, as part of the show, they just showed how a man was murdered! It's violent and upsetting, and I don't want to see that kind of thing on TV.

Sally: I know what you mean. I don't think they should show that kind of violence at this time of day. Young children might see it!

Jack: You're right Sally. I don't think that show is suitable for <u>young children</u>. I suppose there should be stronger restrictions about what they can show on television during the day.

Sally: Yes, I agree. I don't think it's right to show killing and other violence at times when children can watch. If they see it, they might be disturbed by it and then start to behave violently. What do you think, Carla?

Carla: Yes, but not just children. I don't think <u>anyone</u> should watch this kind of television. If adults see how to commit a <u>crime</u> on television, they might try to copy it in real life.

Jack: No, I disagree. In my opinion <u>adults</u> should be able to

choose what they watch on television. Crime shows are always very popular, so I think this kind of show might be okay late at night when children won't see it.

Sally: I think that restrictions should protect children, but I agree with Jack. Because these shows are so popular, maybe they shouldn't restrict them completely, just put them on at a later time.

Carla: Well, that would be better, but I don't think it's enough. I still think they should stop these shows altogether.

Jack: I'm afraid I don't agree with you there Carla, I really like crime shows so I don't want them stopped.

Sally: Well, I guess we'll have to agree to <u>disagree</u> on this subject.

Carla: I guess we will.

ANSWERS   Unit 12   Leisure Activities

1. no answers

2. no answers

3. Check your answers.

Words	No. of syllables	Words	No. of syllables
dangerous	3	techniques	2
fatal	2	protective	3
experienced	4	vital	2
certified	3	hazard	2
launch	1	forecast	2
emergency	4	proportion	3

4. Choose the letter of the word you hear which best matches the meaning of the word in the table.

   a. fatal   i) causing death
   b. experienced   i) competent
   c. vital   i) essential
   d. proportion   ii) ratio
   e. dangerous   i) unsafe
   f. have a go   ii) try (to do...)
   g. techniques   ii) methods or ways
   h. emergency   i) crisis
   i. certified   ii) qualified
   j. hazards   i) dangers

5. Write the word or words to complete each sentence.

   1. experienced   2. proportion   3. Emergency
   4. dangerous   5. certified   6. hazards
   7. have a go   8. vital   9. fatal

6. no answers

7. Complete the sentences using the vocabulary for clothing and equipment.

   a. wetsuit   b. life jacket   c. helmet
   d. Gloves   e. first aid kit   f. harness
   g. waterproof

8. no answers

9. Check your answers.
    a. waterproof   b. life jacket   c. gloves
    d. wetsuit   e. first aid kit f. helmet
    g. ropes

10. Choose the options that you hear.
    a. Look out   b. You shouldn't c. Get
    d. go   e. sailing   f. Make sure
    g. check   h. choose   i. Make sure

11. Match the sentences you hear.
    a. iii   b. iv
    c. i   d. ii

12. Read the summary below and choose.
    a. verb—present continuous form
    b. adjective   c. adjective   d. adjective
    e. adjective   f. noun—plural   g. noun—singular
    h. noun—singular

13. no answers

14. Check your answers.
    a. C   b. C

Listening 1

    1. kite-surfing 2. fatal   3. emergency
    4. protective   5. vital   6. hazards
    7. weather   8. lofting

Listening 2

    9. rock   10. fatal   11. techniques
    12. harness / ropes / shoes   13. training
    14. natural   15. weather   16. fall

SCRIPTS   Unit 12   Leisure Activities

1. no audio

2. no audio

3. Check your answers.
    *The example is '*popular*'. It has three syllables.*
    a. dangerous   b. fatal   c. experienced
    d. certified   e. launch   f. emergency
    g. techniques   h. protective   i. vital
    j. hazard   k. forecast   l. proportion

4. Choose the letter of the word you hear which best matches the meaning of the word in the table.
    Example:

focus:	i) ratio	ii) centre of attention
a. fatal	i) causing death	ii) unsafe
b. experienced	i) competent	ii) essential
c. vital	i) essential	ii) causing death
d. proportion	i) competent	ii) ratio
e. dangerous	i) unsafe	ii) crisis
f. have a go	i) avoid (doing)	ii) try (to do)
g. techniques	i) dangers	ii) methods or ways
h. emergency	i) crisis	ii) fatal
i. certified	i) essential	ii) qualified
j. hazards	i) dangers	ii) unsafe

5. Write the word or words to complete each sentence.
    1. Even **experienced** kite-surfers sometimes have serious accidents.
    2. Bad weather causes a significant **proportion** of rock climbing accidents.
    3. **Emergency** techniques are things you need to do to protect yourself in a crisis.
    4. Going kite-surfing in stormy weather is very **dangerous**.
    5. If you have training with a **certified** instructor, you are less likely to hurt yourself.
    6. Natural **hazards** are things like rocks that are not man-made but occur naturally.
    7. If you **have a go** at kite-surfing, it means you try to do it.
    8. It is **vital** to check the weather before going rock climbing.
    9. There are a number of **fatal** accidents every year in sports such as kite-surfing and rock climbing.

6. no audio

7. Complete the sentences using the vocabulary for clothing and equipment.
    a. A **wetsuit** is used to keep people warm in the water.
    b. A **life jacket** is used to keep you afloat if you fall in the water.
    c. A **helmet** is used to protect your head.
    d. **Gloves** are important for keeping your hands warm.
    e. It is wise to have a **first aid kit** if there is any chance of injury in your sport.
    f. A **harness** is an important piece of equipment for a climber who uses ropes.
    g. Take **waterproof** clothing if it looks like rain.

8. no audio

9. Check your answers.
    a. It looks like it's going to rain. Take your **waterproof** jacket.
    b. Kayakers wear a **life jacket** in case they fall out of the kayak and into the water.
    c. Wear **gloves** in cold weather so your hands don't get too cold.
    d. If you're going out surfing today, it's cold, so wear your **wetsuit!**
    e. Your guide will have a **first aid kit** to use if you get injured.
    f. Wear a **helmet** when climbing to protect your head from falling rocks.
    g. Make sure all your **ropes** are correctly fastened before starting to climb.

10. Choose the options that you hear.
    a. **Look out** for natural hazards such as loose rocks.
    b. **You shouldn't** try kayaking if you don't know how to swim.
    c. **Get** specialized climbing shoes. You'll really notice the

difference!

d. Never **go** climbing in the mountains if storms are forecast.

e. You shouldn't try **sailing** if you don't know how to swim.

f. **Make sure** you take extra food and clothes in case you get caught in a storm.

g. You need to **check** wind speed and direction before you launch your kite.

h. Always **choose** a location that suits your level of skill.

i. **Make sure** there is a safety release system for your kite.

11. Match the sentences you hear.

a. I'm going to talk about skate-boarding, and some of the safety rules involved.

b. You need to take a skate-boarding course with a certified trainer. That way you can learn essential skills.

c. Always check the weather. You need to avoid skate-boarding if it's stormy as you might get injured.

d. If you want to try skate-boarding, you need to get the proper safety equipment, and learn how to use it.

12. no audio

13. no audio

14. Check your answers.

Narrator 1: *You will hear a Community Education lecturer introducing some safety issues that are essential for beginner kite-surfers.*

Narrator 2: Good morning everyone. Today, as part of our focus on safety in sport, I'm going to talk about kite-surfing, and some of the safety rules you should follow.

Listening 1

Narrator 1: *You will hear a Community Education lecturer introducing some safety issues that are essential for beginner kite-surfers.*

Narrator 2: Good morning everyone. Today, as part of our focus on safety in sport, I'm going to talk about kite-surfing, and some of the safety rules you should follow.

Now, kite-surfing's become a very popular sport in many parts of the world, and the number of kite-surfers is growing rapidly. However, people often don't observe proper safety rules. This means it can be dangerous and there've been some nasty accidents. In fact, about 14% of accidents last year were fatal. Those deaths included some experienced kite-surfers.

So, to start with, get proper training! Kite-surfing isn't something you can just learn by having a go. You should take a course with a certified kite-surfing instructor. That way you can learn how to set up your kite, use safety equipment and launch the kite. There are emergency techniques you need to learn. Also, you shouldn't try kite-surfing if you don't know how to swim.

Next, get proper protective clothing such as a helmet, a life jacket and a wetsuit. You also need a safety release system, so you can get free of the kite at any time. Remember to check all your equipment every time you go out. If it's winter, you'll need extra clothing and gloves.

Right ... so you've got your equipment and done some guided training, and you're really keen to go out and practise your new sport. At this point, there're two vital bits of advice I should give you.

First of all, choose the right location. Make sure there isn't much activity on the water or the beach. It's really important to avoid collisions with other people or boats. There'll often be people practising other water sports, such as surfing, swimming and kayaking. There may also be people just having fun on the beach! And you really need to think about natural hazards such as rocks. Look out for any notices restricting kite-surfing—some places have a total ban on the sport.

Second, always check the weather. In particular, never go out if a storm is forecast. Also, you must check the speed and direction of the wind. Never go out in gusty weather as there is a risk of being pulled high into the air by the wind. This is called 'lofting'. Actually, lofting causes a big proportion of serious accidents, so this is a real concern.

Ok. Now I'd like you all to watch this video and note any hazards that you observe [fade]...

Listening 2

Narrator1: *You will hear a Community Education lecturer discussing some of the safety features to be considered for free climbers.*

Narrator2: Good morning everyone. Today, as part of our overall focus on safety in sport, I'm going to talk about rock climbing, and some of the safety rules you should follow.

Now, rock climbing's become a very popular sport in many parts of the world, and the number of rock climbers has grown rapidly over the past 40 years. However, falls are often fatal and these deaths include some experienced climbers.

So, to start with, get proper training! Rock climbing isn't something you can just learn by having a go. You should take a course with a qualified instructor. That way you can learn basic skills, such as how to tie special knots and set up your climbing ropes for climbing with a partner. There are emergency techniques you need to learn. Also, you shouldn't try rock climbing if you haven't first practised on a climbing wall with safety equipment.

Next, get proper protective equipment such as a safety helmet, a harness, ropes and climbing shoes. You also need to carry chalk as it will give you a better grip. It is essential to carry waterproof clothing, energy food (such as dried fruit and chocolate) and a basic first aid kit. Remember to check all your equipment every time you set out to climb. If it's winter, you'll need extra layers of clothing.

Right ... so you've got your equipment and done some guided training, and you're really keen to go out and practise your new sport. At this point, there're two vital bits of advice I should give you.

First of all, choose the right location. It's really important to keep clear of other people in the same area, to avoid getting in the way. And you really need to think about natural hazards such as crumbly rocks. Look out for any notices restricting rock-climbing—some places have a ban because of dangerous conditions.

Second, always check the weather. Never go out if storms are forecast. Climbers need dry handholds, so rain and snow are dangerous. Also strong winds can cause climbers to fall.

Actually, accident statistics show that bad weather conditions cause a significant proportion of serious accidents.

Ok. Now I'd like you all to watch this video and note any hazards you can observe [fade]...

ANSWERS   Unit 13   Social Issues

1. no answers

2. no answers

3. Write the word or words from the box to complete each sentence.
   a. security conscious   b. stored; racks
   c. tickets; machine   d. Lockers; baggage
   e. leave; cover; roof

4. Choose the option that you hear.
   a. exit   b. baggage   c. parking
   d. surveillance   e. mall

5. Number these expressions in the order that you hear them.
   1. __d__ just inside the door
   2. __c__ outside the door
   3. __f__ in the far corner
   4. __e__ to your right
   5. __a__ between two people
   6. __b__ opposite the door

6. no answers

7. Write the store names into the plan.
   a. supermarket   b. food court
   c. ice cream parlour   d. menswear store
   e. department store

   Answers as shown on plan:
   You are here: X

supermarket			electronics store
food court	ice cream parlour	menswear store	department store

8. Decide whether these are questions or statements.
   a. statement   b. question   c. statement
   d. question   e. question

9. Choose check, confirm or change.
   a. check   b. change
   c. check   d. confirm

10. Decide if the speaker is checking, confirming or changing information.
    a. changing   b. checking   c. changing
    d. confirming   e. checking

11. no answers

12. Check your answers.
    a. B   b. C   c. B

Listening 1
   1. F   2. B   3. A
   4. H   5. C   6. E

Listening 2
   7. D   8. G   9. F
   10. C   11. I   12. B

SCRIPTS   Unit 13   Social Issues

1. no audio

2. Pay attention to how these words sound.

leave	cover	conscious	ticket
entrance	roof	store	machine
upgrade	surveillance	locker	mall
racks	security	baggage	exit

3. Write the word or words from the box to complete each sentence.
   a. If you worry about safety, you are **security conscious**.
   b. Bikes are often **stored** on bike **racks**, which are metal bars that hold bikes upright.
   c. You can buy train **tickets** from a ticket office or **machine**.
   d. **Lockers** are locked cupboards used to store **baggage** or maybe bikes.
   e. It's a good idea to **leave** your bike under **cover**, which means leaving it in a place with a **roof**.

4. Choose the option that you hear.
   a. He is waiting by the **exit** to the International Centre.
   b. These lockers are for storing **baggage**.
   c. She wants to know if there is a safe **parking** area for her bike.
   d. The station has video **surveillance**.
   e. I'm going to park my bike outside that **mall**.

5. Number these expressions in the order that you hear them.
   a. between two people   b. opposite the door
   c. outside the door   d. just inside the door
   e. to your right   f. in the far corner

6. Pay attention to how these words sound.

clothes store	food court
menswear store	department store
art supplies shop	ice cream parlour
electronics store	jewellery store
supermarket	

7. Write the store names into the plan.
   a. Where is the department store?
      It's in the far corner, next to the electronics store.
   b. Where is the supermarket?
      We're standing outside the supermarket.
   c. Where is the food court?
      It's in the corner, next to the supermarket.
   d. Where is the menswear store?
      It's next to the department store.

e. Where is the ice cream parlour?

It's between the menswear store and the food court.

8. Decide whether these are questions or statements.

a. There's a bike parking area next to the station door.

b. There's no ticket office?

c. There are ticket machines just inside the door.

d. There are bike lockers in the station?

e. The information desk is in the corner?

9. Choose check, confirm or change.

Kelly: Where can I buy a ticket at the station?

Ben: Well, there's no ticket office, so use the ticket machines just outside the door.

Kelly: The ticket machines are just outside the door?

Ben: Oh no, sorry, they are just inside the door.

Kelly: Just inside the station door?

Ben: That's right.

10. Decide if the speaker is checking, confirming or changing information.

a. Oh sorry, what I meant to say was, go straight ahead and then turn left.

b. So ... the cafe is in the far corner?

c. Oh, actually, don't go that way. Instead, take the second right.

d. Yes, the exit is on the right.

e. The entrance to the department store is on the left?

11. no audio

12. Check your answers.

Narrator: *You will hear a conversation between three friends, Lisa, Richard and Michelle, about the best place to park their bicycles at a train station.*

Listening 1

Narrator: *You will hear a conversation between three friends, Lisa, Richard and Michelle, about the best place to park their bicycles at a train station.*

R: Oh look, there's Lisa!

M: Hi Lisa, what are you doing today?

L: I'm going to ride my bike to Jones Street station and catch a train to visit my auntie.

M: That sounds like fun.

L: Yes, but I was wondering...do you know if there's a safe place at the station for me to leave my bike?

R: Jones Street station? I haven't been there in a while but I think there is a fairly large bike parking area.

L: Really? I have a plan of the station here. Can you show me where I should put my bike?

R: Well, there's a big outside parking area to the left of the station entrance.

M: Wait. Did you know they've just upgraded that station? There are new bike racks, all under cover.

R: Wow, that's great news. Much better than just parking your bike outside.

L: Wait, can I just make sure? That's a bike park with a roof, to the left of the station door?

M: Yes, and they have video surveillance now, so someone is watching the bikes all the time. But, if you want to be really security-conscious, they have bike lockers now too.

R: So you can store your bike in a locker? Just like a baggage locker?

L: That sounds perfect, just what I wanted. Where are they?

R: Aren't they over by the platform? I mean, opposite the station entrance, where the ticket office used to be.

M: No, that's the information desk now. The ticket office has gone.

L: Wait a minute, did you just say there's no ticket office? How am I going to buy my train ticket?

M: Don't worry, there are ticket machines just inside the entrance, to your right.

L: OK. So, where are the bike lockers?

M: They're easy to find. Just on your right, just before you go into the main entrance.

L: Cool. What about the baggage lockers? Where are they, then?

M: They're behind the ticket machines. It's quite hard to get to them...I mean, you can't see the door from the station entrance—you have to go through the cafe to find them.

R: Is the cafe in the corner? I mean, is it in the far right corner of the station?

M: Yes, it's by the platform. So what I meant was, go through the cafe and you'll find the baggage lockers.

L: Great, thank you both. I'd better go now, or I'll miss my train!

Listening 2

Narrator: *You will hear a conversation between Mary and someone who is giving her directions at a large underground train station.*

M: Excuse me, can you help me?

SO: Sure, what do you need to know?

M: I'm looking for the exit to the International Centre, but this place is so big, I just can't seem to find it.

SO: I know what you mean; I had trouble the first time I came here too. Right, we're standing outside Music Music, so the International Centre is at the other end of the mall. Just go straight ahead.

M: Straight ahead to the other end of the mall?

SO: Oh no, if you keep going straight ahead to the end, then you'll be at the supermarket, won't you? Sorry, what I meant to say was go straight ahead and take the first left, between the art supplies shop and the food court.

M: So, I go straight ahead and take the first left?

SO: Oh wait ... sorry, that's the entrance to the department store. Can you see the bookstore, just after the art supplies shop, next to the supermarket?

M: Yes, I see where that is.

SO: Well, what I meant was go straight ahead from where we're standing and take the second left, between the art shop and the bookstore.

M: OK, so I'm going to walk past the food court and the entrance to the department store, and then turn left before the bookstore?

SO: That's right. You'll see an electronics store on your left. And then you'll see the exit for the International Centre between the bookstore and a small shop—I forget what it sells. Umm ...Oh yes, a <u>menswear store</u>. That's what it is.

M: OK, I've got it. Thanks for all your help.

SO: You're welcome!

ANSWERS   Unit 14   Money

1. no answers

2. Choose the word that matches the meaning.
   a. i) a combination   b. ii) a bargain
   c. i) to notify   d. i) a reputation
   e. i) visible   f. ii) thieves
   g. i) valuables   h. i) to distract
   i. ii) to be suspicious   j. ii) campus

3. no answers

4. Check your answers.
   a. distract
   b. bargain, campus
   c. documents, notify, visible, valuables
   d. transaction, suspicious
   e. traditional
   f. combination, reputation

5. Dictation: write the words to complete each sentence.
   a. keep your money   b. lot of cash
   c. leave them visible   d. in a handbag
   e. you must notify

6. no answers

7. Check your answers.
   1. suspicious   2. transaction   3. reputation
   4. documents   5. campus   6. distract
   7. combination   8. visible   9. valuables

8. Answer the short answer questions
   1. plans   2. market   3. footwear

9. Write the letter for each statement you hear in the correct column to complete the table.

Imperatives	Suggestions
b	e
c	h
d	j
f	l
g	
i	
k	

10. Write the word /words to complete each sentence.
   a. Don't use   b. Be careful
   c. Keep most   d. Never get
   e. should be left   f. Don't carry
   g. must notify   h. should always check

   i. always lock it   j. should probably consider
   k. Never leave   l. may be

11. no answers

12. Check your answers.
   a. C   b. C   c. B

Listening 1
   1. crowds   2. passport   3. tickets
   4. tissues   5. eye drops   6. too high
   7. 50% / fifty per cent

Listening 2
   8. obvious PIN   9. (the) police
   10. (the) bank / (your) bank   11. internet / email
   12. telephone / phone   13. laptops
   14. game cubes   15. steering lock
   16. car alarm

SCRIPTS   Unit 14   Money

1. no audio

2. Choose the word that matches the meaning.
   The example is: i) footwear   ii) clothing
   The correct answer is: i) footwear
   a. i) a combination   ii) a proportion
   b. i) a document   ii) a bargain
   c. i) to notify   ii) to avoid
   d. i) a reputation   ii) a proportion
   e. i) visible   ii) valuable
   f. i) crowds   ii) thieves
   g. i) valuables   ii) visible
   h. i) to distract   ii) to be wary
   i. i) distracted   ii) to be suspicious
   j. i) reputation   ii) campus

3. Classify these words according to the stress patterns in the table. Listen to the examples.
   a. advise   b. focus   c. realise
   d. proportion   e. experienced   f. celebration

4. Check your answers.

combination	visible	bargain
reputation	valuables	campus
documents	suspicious	notify
traditional	distract	transaction

5. Dictation: write the words to complete each sentence.
   a. It is important to **keep your money** and possessions safe, wherever you are.
   b. Don't carry a **lot of cash** or give out your bank account details to strangers on the telephone.
   c. Your passport, sunglasses, laptop and wallet are all valuable, so don't **leave them visible** in your car.
   d. Tissues, pens, eye drops or make-up are not as valuable and can be carried **in a handbag** or a waist bag.
   e. If things go missing from your hotel room, **you must notify** the tour leader and the police.

6. no audio

7. Check your answers.

1. To be **suspicious** means you think there is something wrong or dishonest.
2. Your bank statement will list all your **transaction**. Always check that there are no errors.
3. Some markets have a **reputation** for theft. You have to be very careful.
4. Essential travel **documents** include your passport and air tickets.
5. Accommodation for the first year students is usually available on a university **campus**.
6. The tour guide says that a group of people may try to **distract** you so they can take something such as your camera.
7. Thieves in crowded places often use a **combination** of crowds and distractions to take cameras and other valuables.
8. Make sure your money isn't **visible** and easy to take without you noticing.
9. It is important that you know where your **valuables** are at all times.

8. Answer the short answer questions.

Narrator: *You will hear a tour guide giving advice to a tour group on how to avoid theft.*

Hello everyone. Welcome to Kizani. Before you go off to your rooms, I'll just quickly discuss tomorrow's plans. We're going to visit the market in the old part of the city in the morning, and look around the palace after lunch. So there's quite a lot of walking. I hope you all have comfortable footwear!

9. Write the letter for each statement you hear in the correct column to complete the table.

Decide whether each statement you hear is an **imperative** or a **suggestion**.

Example: a. Don't use a waist bag for valuables; it's not safe.
*This is an **imperative**.*

Now, listen to the statements.

b. **Be careful** of local people who promise to help you find a bargain.
c. **Keep most** of your money in a money belt that is hidden under your clothes.
d. **Never get** money out of your money belt in a crowded place unless some of your tour group members are there with you.
e. Your passport, tickets and other essential documents **should be left** in the hotel.
f. **Don't carry** a lot of cash or keep cash in your hotel room.
g. If you lose your card, you **must notify** the bank and the police at once.
h. You **should always check** your bank statements to ensure that all the transactions are correct.
i. If you own a car, **always lock it**.
j. You **should probably consider** buying a steering lock or car alarm.
k. **Never leave** valuables such as CDs or mp3 players in view on the seats.

l. People here use debit cards. It **may be** a good idea for you to get one too.

10. See Exercise 9.

11. no audio

12. Check your answers.

Narrator: *You will hear a tour guide giving advice to a tour group on how to avoid theft.*

Listening 1

Narrator: *You will hear a tour guide giving advice to a tour group on how to avoid theft.*

Hello everyone. Welcome to Kizani. Before you go off to your rooms, I'll just quickly discuss tomorrow's plans. We're going to visit the market in the old part of the city in the morning, and look around the palace after lunch. So there's quite a lot of walking. I hope you all have comfortable footwear!

More importantly, though, we need to talk about how you can protect yourselves against theft, as the market is very crowded. Thieves love the combination of crowds and tourists and the Kizani market has a reputation for theft.

First of all, leave your passport, tickets and other essential documents in the hotel safe. You won't need them tomorrow and it's not worth the risk of having them stolen.

Second, you should carry enough cash for the day in a couple of buttoned or zipped pockets, for minor purchases. Keep any other money in a money bag or belt which you wear under your clothes, so it is not visible and doesn't attract attention. Never get money out unless some of your tour members are with you.

Third, don't use a waist bag for valuables, as it is too obvious! It's OK to have one for carrying minor items like tissues, eye drops and cheap reading glasses, but you mustn't keep your passport or money in it. In a crowded market, it is easy for a pair of thieves to bump and push you; you won't realise the waist bag has been taken till it's too late.

Next, hold equipment such as a camera all the time. Never put it on a table or on the ground, even if you are sitting right beside it. And always be suspicious of a group of young people crowding around you, as they may distract you while one of them takes something.

Finally, there is the issue of bargaining. The first price you will hear will, of course, be too high. The locals see you as rich tourists and hope to get a good deal. A fair price is about 50% of the initial price. Be wary of friendly locals who want to 'help' you get the 'best' bargain. It's likely that they will get some money for anything you buy, which of course pushes the price up. So while meeting people is one of the pleasures of travelling, you should be careful!

Right, now the bus will leave at 9 tomorrow morning, so please don't be late.

Listening 2

Narrator: *You will hear the accommodation officer advising a group of new international students on how to protect themselves against theft.*

Hi everyone. This morning I'm going to talk about some safety issues for you here at College Hall. After that, I'll take you on a tour of the campus, so you can find your way around when classes start tomorrow.

First of all, don't carry much cash or keep it in your room. You can easily get more from the campus bank. Actually it may be a good idea to get a debit card, which is used to take money from your account. If you get one, you need to set a PIN, or personal identification number. Now, don't use an obvious PIN, such as your birth year, don't tell anyone what your PIN is, even good friends, and be sure to sign your card as soon as you get it. Notify the police and your bank immediately if you lose your card.

Right ... ah ... there are several ATMs here on campus. An ATM is a money machine where you can use your card to get money. You should cover your PIN as you enter it so others can't see it. Also, always stand back from anyone using their card, or they may suspect you of noting their PIN.

Second, beware of internet or telephone scams. A 'scam' means people try to trick you into giving your PIN or banking password over the phone or in response to an email, so that they can access your bank account. Note that your bank will never ask you to do that. You should always check your statements to ensure that your transactions are correct.

Next, possessions such as laptops, mp3 players and game cubes are obviously attractive to thieves. There are special locks on the doors of College Hall, but other students can bring in visitors, so you need to take care. Be sure to lock your room when you go off to the shower, the dining room or to watch TV.

Finally, some of you may buy cars or bicycles. If you have a car, always lock it up. And don't leave any valuables such as sunglasses or a wallet where they may be seen. In fact, you should probably consider buying a steering lock or car alarm.

If you get a bicycle, you need to buy a lock and chain. Always secure your bike to something solid and take your helmet into lectures or your room.

Ok. That's enough for now. Let's go to the enrolment centre so you can collect your ID cards.

ANSWERS   Unit 15   Youth Issues

1. no answers

2. no answers

3. Number the nouns.

i. seminar	ii. references
iii. participation	iv. assignment
v. presentation	vi. schedule
vii. assessment	viii. research

4. no answers

5. Check your answers.
   a. presentation
   b. Participation; seminar
   c. research
   d. assessment schedule
   e. assignment; references

6. Choose the word (i or ii) that best matches the meaning.

   a. i: field trip   b. ii: overview
   c. i: continuous   d. ii: specific
   e. i: schedule   f. ii: seminar
   g. i: proportion   h. ii: bibliography
   i. i: participation   j. ii: framework

7. no answers

8. Check your answers.
   a. assignment   b. quiz   c. time management
   d. field trip   e. baseline   f. lecture
   g. research   h. assessment   i. article
   j. spreadsheet

9. Predict which kind of word you need.
   a. adverb   b. modal   c. modal
   d. verb; modal e. adverb   f. verb
   g. modal   h. adverb

10. Complete each sentence with the words you hear.
   a. Perhaps   b. would   c. may
   d. think; should e. definitely   f. believe
   g. could   h. probably

11. no answers

12. Check your answers.
   a. postgraduate studies   b. research topic
   c. thesis   d. theory
   e. equipment; surveys   f. government; relevant

13. no answers

14. Check your answers.
   a. Cook   b. Games People Play
   c. New York   d. Body Language
   e. 1948

15. no answers

16. Check your answers.
   a. A   b. B

Listening 1
1. B   2. A   3. C
4. (A) quiz   5. (A) poster   6. Oral presentation
7. quizzes   8. 5,000 word essay   9. Research projects
10. (A) seminar

Listening 2
1. homework   2. on-line discussion group
3. seminar
4. sixteen / 16; six / 6 [both answers necessary for one mark]
5. zero / 0   6. five / 5
7. five / 5   8. fifteen / 15
9. twenty / 20   10. ten / 10

SCRIPTS   Unit 15   Youth Issues

1. no audio

2. Pay attention to how these words sound.

| assessment | schedule | overview |
| spreadsheet | framework | exam |

assignment	quiz	continuous
specific	baseline	knowledge
field trip	presentation	research
in-depth	visual aid	project
participation	seminar	proportion
percentage	time management	discussion
article	references	bibliography
lecture		

3. Number the nouns below in the order you hear them in the sentences.

  i. What time is the **seminar** tomorrow?
  ii. I just need to add one more book title to my list of **references** and then I'm finished.
  iii. Thank you for your **participation** in the project.
  iv. Have you handed in your **assignment** yet?
  v. Jeff was so nervous when he gave his oral **presentation** to the class.
  vi. I have looked at the **schedule** for next semester and it seems fine to me.
  vii. Continuous **assessment** means a lot more work for the teachers—so much marking!
  viii. The latest **research** indicates sea temperatures are rising.

4. no audio

5. Check your answers.
  a. I have to give an oral **presentation** next week. I'll have to stand up in front of everybody and talk on this topic for three to five minutes.
  b. **Participation** in the **seminar** is important. Our lecturer says we must take part in the discussion.
  c. Over the next few weeks I need to gather a lot of information from various sources for my **research** project.
  d. Look at this timetable with all the dates of the essays and tests. It's a very busy **assessment schedule**.
  e. I've just received a terrible grade for my last **assignment**. I forgot to make a list of all the books, articles and websites I used to get information for the essay. The lecturer said a list of **references** is essential!

6. Listen and choose the word (i or ii) that best matches the meaning.
  a. One: field trip   Two: framework
  b. One: assignment   Two: overview
  c. One: continuous   Two: references
  d. One: spreadsheet   Two: specific
  e. One: schedule   Two: research
  f. One: lecture   Two: seminar
  g. One: proportion   Two: presentation
  h. One: baseline   Two: bibliography
  i. One: participation   Two: discussion
  j. One: article   Two: framework

7. Decide which of the words or phrases from the vocabulary list best fits each description.
  a. They have to complete one set task every two weeks.
  b. Yesterday we had a quick, short-answer, knowledge test.

  c. I organise my time carefully and keep up-to-date with my work.
  d. Next week the whole class is going to the mountains to study alpine plants.
  e. We need to work out a standard or starting point by which to measure student progress.
  f. Professor Brown gave an hour-long talk on that topic.
  g. They're finding out facts and collecting information and data for their project.
  h. They talked about how many marks to give for each essay, assignment and test.
  i. Professor Knox had a piece of writing published in a well-known journal.
  j. Accountancy students use a particular computer program to show the figures they're working with.

8. Check your answers.
  a. They have to complete an **assignment** every two weeks. Assignment: A-S-S-I-G-N-M-E-N-T
  b. We had a **quiz**. Quiz: Q-U-I-Z
  c. I have good **time management**. Time management: T-I-M-E M-A-N-A-G-E-M-E-N-T
  d. The class is going on a **field trip**. Field trip: F-I-E-L-D T-R-I-P
  e. We need to establish a **baseline**. Baseline: B-A-S-E-L-I-N-E
  f. Professor Brown gave a **lecture**. Lecture: L-E-C-T-U-R-E
  g. They are doing some **research**. Research: R-E-S-E-A-R-C-H
  h. They discussed **assessment**. Assessment: A-S-S-E-S-S-M-E-N-T
  i. Professor Knox published an **article**. Article: A-R-T-I-C-L-E
  j. Accountancy students often use a **spreadsheet** to display numbers. Spreadsheet: S-P-R-E-A-D-S-H-E-E-T

9. no audio

10. Complete each sentence with the words you hear.
  a. **Perhaps** there is a particular theory you'd like to challenge.
  b. This research project **would** involve costly equipment.
  c. There **may** be government funding that you can apply for.
  d. I **think** we **should** look at this book.
  e. That should **definitely** be the second choice.
  f. I **believe** a good system is important.
  g. We **could** display the posters in the hall.
  h. August is **probably** the best month for handing in the research project.

11. You will hear part of a discussion between a student and her academic advisor.

AA: Good morning, Emma. Now you wanted to see me to talk about your **postgraduate studies**, is that right?

Emma: Yes, I graduated last year and I want to continue my studies but I'm not sure what **research topic** to choose.

AA: Lots of students have difficulty finding a research

topic. One thing is certain—writing your **thesis** will be much easier if you make the right choice now. Of course you have some idea of the general subject area that you're interested in?

Emma: Yes, but...

AA: And you have read widely in this topic area?

Emma: Yes, I have but I don't always agree with some of the theories that are put forward.

AA: Aha! That's a good place to start. Perhaps there is a particular **theory** you would like to challenge. This could be the focus of your research. Another thing you should consider before you decide on your area of specialisation, though, is your finances. If your financial resources are limited, perhaps you shouldn't commit to a research project which would involve costly **equipment** or expensive **surveys**.

Emma: I hadn't thought about that.

AA: Well, there may be **government** funding you can apply for, or a local business or industry might be willing to provide funding if your research is **relevant** to what they are doing.

12. Listen again.

13. You will hear three students discussing the reading list for their assignment.

Duncan: Which books on the reading list do you think will be most useful for our assignment?

Kate: Well, to start with, I think we should look at Argyle and **Cook**, 'Gaze and Mutual Gaze', Cambridge University Press, 1976.

Cara: What a funny title! Okay, number one, Argyle and Cook.

Duncan: How about '**Games People Play**'?

Kate: I've heard that title before. Sounds interesting. 'Games People Play'. Who wrote it?

Duncan: Berne, Grove Press, **New York**.

Cara: That's number two then. And number three?

Kate: That should definitely be Lambert's '**Body Language**', 1996.

Duncan: All right. 'Body Language'. What's next?

Kate: What about 'Body Language of Children' by Szasz?

Duncan: I think our assignment focuses on adult behaviour.

Kate: The fourth could be 'A Psychology of Gesture' by Wolfe. It's a very old title—it was published by Methuen in London long before we were born—in **1948** actually.

Cara: 1948—that is old, but if it's been around that long, and it's on our reading list, it must be a classic. Yes, I think we should include that.

14. Listen again.

15. no audio

16. Check your answers.

Narrator: *You will hear a senior teacher, Ms Potts, discussing an assessment schedule for the next academic year with a new teacher, John.*

Listening 1

Narrator: *You will hear a senior teacher, Ms Potts, discussing an assessment schedule for the next academic year with a new teacher, John. Listen carefully and answer questions 1-3.*

J: Thank you, Ms Potts, for offering to help me with this assessment schedule.

Ms P: Well, John, let's get started, shall we?

J: Uh-huh. My computer's over there.

Ms P: Actually, I prefer to work with a pencil and a big piece of paper to start with. I can get a better overview that way. You can do a spreadsheet when we've finished.

J: That's fine with me.

Ms P: Okay, you need to create a schedule of assessments to use next year, is that right?

J: Yes. I need to develop some kind of framework for assessing student performance over the course of the whole academic year.

Ms P: I think a good system is important to ensure that you do collect enough evidence for each student. You know, in the good old days, there used to be one major assessment and that was the final exam. There was a mid-year test and the occasional quiz in class but the only thing that counted was the final exam mark.

J: Continuous assessment is fairer though, don't you agree? Imagine if you got sick or felt terribly nervous on exam day and didn't perform well.

Ms P: Well, continuous assessment is just that, continuous, so you'll need to begin by listing the months of the school year.

J: Right, February to November.

Narrator: *Before you hear the rest of the conversation, you have some time to look at questions 4-10.* [*Pause*]. *Now listen to the dialogue and answer questions 4-10.*

Ms P: Now, next to each month allow space to include information on what to assess and how much to assess, as well as the specific assessments.

J: Okay, February is the beginning of the course so I'll need to gather some baseline information about my students' knowledge of the subject. I think a simple knowledge quiz should cover that. [*pause*] February ... quiz.

Ms P: You should set the essay topics early in the year too, so they've got plenty of time to think about them. What assessment have you got planned for March?

J: Well, we've got a field trip organised for the second week in March. It's part of an on-going research project but it's too early for them to have gathered much information. They could do a poster I suppose, with photographs and other material from the field trip... and we could display them in the hall. [*pause*] March ... poster for display.

Ms P: And that could lead on very nicely to the next assessment—an oral presentation to be done in April, just before the first term break—they could use their posters as visual aids.

J: And after the break, in May, I'd like to see how they're getting on with the reading list—a series of quizzes, perhaps, just short-answer questions—to check that everyone is keeping up with the reading. It's the only way they'll get sufficient in-depth knowledge for the research assignment.

Ms P: Good idea. That brings us to June, mid-year exams—important for tracking students' progress.

J: And after the term break in July, the essays are due. [*pause*] 5,000 word essay—July.

Ms P: August is probably the month for handing in the research projects, right?

J: Yes, and we'll follow that up in September, before the third term break, with a seminar where they can report on their projects to the rest of the class. They'll be marked on their participation in that seminar.

Ms P: What about a test in October to assess student progress and identify any areas they need to study more before the final exam in November?

J: Yes, definitely.

Ms P: Well, I'll leave you now to work out the marking system and determine what proportion of the final mark each assessment is worth.

Listening 2

Narrator: *You will hear two students discussing their assessment schedule for the year. Listen carefully and answer questions 1-4.*

Eve: Hi, Jim. Have you looked at the geography assessment schedule yet?

Jim: Yes, and I'm worried I won't have time for a social life with all the homework!

Eve: Oh, come on! You just need good time-management skills, that's all.

Jim: It's quite different from last year's, isn't it? I really liked the on-line discussion group we had last year. I got good marks from participating in those discussions. There's nothing like that this year.

Eve: Well, there's the seminar in September—you get marks for participation in that. It's only worth 5% though.

Jim: Yeah, but it's not the same. And have you seen the required reading list? There must be half a dozen articles and 20 books at least!

Eve: Not quite, Jim. Only sixteen books and some of them we read last year. You're right, there are six articles though.

Jim: I wonder if we can find them on the internet or will we have to go to the library and look them up in journals?

Eve: Either way, you'll have to read them all or you won't score well in those quizzes scheduled for May. They're worth 10% of the overall mark for the year.

Jim: May's a long way off.

Eve: Time management, Jim! Start your reading now and then you won't have a last minute rush in May. Anyway, the more knowledge you gain, the more it'll help you to understand lectures and do your assignments.

Narrator: *Before you hear the rest of the conversation, you have some time to look at questions 5-10.* [*Pause*]. *Now listen to the dialogue and answer questions 5-10.*

Jim: What should we study for the quiz next week?

Eve: Just revise last year's notes. Anyway, the marks aren't

counted. I'm more worried about the poster next month—I'm not very good at artwork.

Jim: Just put it roughly on paper and I'll help you with graphic design on the computer. We're sure to get some good digital pictures on the field trip. A diagram, graph or flowchart and it's done in no time at all. That's an easy 5%.

Eve: Thanks. I'd feel silly using it as a visual aid in my presentation in April if it was really amateurish. But with your help it'll look more professional.

Jim: As for that oral presentation... I hate public speaking. I'd rather it was a power point presentation, and then the audience would be looking at the slides on the screen and not at me.

Eve: You'll be fine, Jim. Don't worry; it's only 5% of the final mark. Have you noticed the mid-year exam is worth almost as much as the final exam?

Jim: Really?

Eve: Yes, the end-of-year exam is just one fifth of the total; and the mid-year is 15%.

Jim: I'd better study hard for them both if I want a good pass mark when it's all over.

Eve: I see the 5,000 word essay is due after the July break. I suppose that means working on it over the holiday. And then the following month the big research project is due, worth 20%, twice as much as the essay. I really hate doing the references and bibliography for those projects.

Jim: Me too. Why do you think we're having a test in October just one month before the final examination?

Eve: I suppose it's to show up any weaknesses or gaps in our knowledge so we can target those areas for extra work before the last exam. It's worth the same as the essay, so we'd better study for it.

Jim: You know, Eve, this continuous assessment schedule means we're working hard all year.

Eve: Yes, but less stress at the end of the year. Now, let's see if it all adds up to 100%...

ANSWERS Unit 16 Commodities

1. no answers

2. no answers

3. no answers

4. Which word was not used?
   packet

5. Write the word or words to complete each sentence.
   a. factory; chewing   b. ingredients; tank
   c. contain; syrup   d. recipe; unique
   e. sample; packets

6. no answers

7. Match the process verbs, a-d, with the nouns from the same family i)-iv).

a. iii)　　　　　　b. i)
c. iv)　　　　　　d. ii)

8. Write the process verbs to complete each sentence.
    a. purify; add　　　　b. filter; sterilise
    c. collect; dry　　　　d. transfer; stir
    e. seal; wrap

9. no answers

10. Check your answers and your spelling.
    a. added; purified
    b. filtered; sterilised; tested
    c. collected; dried; processed
    d. transferred; stirred
    e. distributed; sealed; labelled

11. Write the missing words into these notes as you listen to a description.
    a. purified　　　b. stirred　　　c. distributed
    d. stirred　　　e. cut　　　　　f. secret

12. Write the words you hear to complete the flow-chart.
    a. cut　　　　　b. rolled　　　c. purified
    d. (sugar) syrup　e. dried

13. no answers

14. Check your answers.
    a. C　　　　　　b. B

Listening 1
    1. tested　　　　　2. different / unique
    3. syrup　　　　　4. bubbles　　　5. put / sealed
    6. distributed

Listening 2
    7. collected　　　　8. ground　　　9. purified
    10. flavours　　　　11. rolls　　　12. sealed
    13. labelled

SCRIPTS Unit 16 Commodities

1. no audio

2. Pay attention to how these words sound.

factory	tank	secret
chewing gum	soft drink	bubbles
syrup	contain	flavour
unique	pressure	packet
ingredients	recipe	sample

3. Tick the words as you hear them.

In a soft drink factory, the ingredients to make the drink are mixed in a big tank. Soft drinks contain flavour, sugar syrup and bubbles, which are created under pressure. The recipe for making soft drinks is often a secret because each flavour is unique. When you go on a factory tour, you can sample the different flavours.

4. no audio

5. Write the word or words to complete each sentence.
    a. In this **factory**, they make soft drinks and **chewing** gum.
    b. The **ingredients** used to make the gum are mixed in a big **tank**.
    c. Both products **contain** flavour and sugar **syrup**.
    d. The **recipe** for making soft drinks may be a secret because each flavour is **unique**.
    e. When you go on a factory tour, you can **sample** the different flavours and maybe take some **packets** home.

6. no audio

7. no audio

8. Write the process verbs to complete each sentence.
    a. We must **purify** the mixture before we **add** the other ingredients.
    b. The machines **filter** and then **sterilise** the mixture.
    c. The workers **collect** and **dry** out the ingredients.
    d. We must **transfer** the mixture to another machine before we **stir** the other ingredients in.
    e. It is important to **seal** and **wrap** the products.

9. no audio

10. Check your answers and your spelling.
    a. Before other ingredients are **added** A-D-D-E-D, the mixture must be **purified** P-U-R-I-F-I-E-D.
    b. It is **filtered** F-I-L-T-E-R-E-D and then **sterilised** S-T-E-R-I-L-I-S-E-D to remove impurities. Then it is **tested** T-E-S-T-E-D.
    c. The ingredients need to be **collected** C-O-L-L-E-C-T-E-D and **dried** D-R-I-E-D out before they can be **processed** P-R-O-C-E-S-S-E-D.
    d. The mixture is **transferred** T-R-A-N-S-F-E-R-R-E-D to another machine before the other ingredients are **stirred** S-T-I-R-R-E-D in.
    e. Before the products are **distributed** D-I-S-T-R-I-B-U-T-E-D, they must be **sealed** S-E-A-L-E-D. Bottles and packets need to be **labelled** L-A-B-E-L-L-E-D.

11. Write the missing words into these notes as you listen to a description.
    a. See the large tank over there? That's where the water is **purified**, so that it is clean and ready to drink.
    b. In this round machine here, the gum is **stirred** until it is smooth and silky.
    c. After they are labelled, the packets of gum are **distributed** around the country.
    d. The sugar syrup is gently **stirred** into the water, without adding too much air.
    e. The gum is dried and powdered with sugar, and then **cut** into small pieces.
    f. We can't show you the room where they make the flavours, because the recipe is a company **secret**.

12. Write the words you hear to complete the flow-chart.
Sugar can be made from either sugar beets or sugar cane. This

factory processes sugar cane. The cane is **cut** before it is brought to the factory in trucks. The cut pieces of cane are taken to a machine and **rolled** in order to get the juice. This juice is then **purified**, to make sure it is clean, and then it is boiled until it's thick. This thick juice is **sugar syrup**. The syrup is boiled for a long time, to grow sugar crystals. To make raw sugar, these crystals are **dried**.

13. no audio

14. Check your answers.

Narrator: *You will hear a factory tour guide explaining how soft drinks are made.*

Listening 1

Narrator: *You will hear a factory tour guide explaining how soft drinks are made.*

Good morning and welcome to our factory tour. As you all probably know, there'll be a free tasting session at the end of the tour. First, though, let's go and see how our soft drinks are made.

Before we go into the factory, could everyone please put on these special paper overalls? Thank you. Now, let's go through the control door and into the main factory building.

Right, here is the production line for making the soft drinks. The main ingredients in all our soft drinks are water, sugar, flavours and bubbles. We'll start at this large tank, where the water is purified. We have to make sure the water is very clean before adding it to our drinks and this process takes several hours. The water is filtered to remove any impurities and then sterilised. Finally, it is <u>tested</u> to make sure it meets our standards.

Next, you'll notice that the room on the opposite side of the building has a *Staff Only* sign. That's where we mix all the <u>different</u> flavours that give our drinks their <u>unique</u> taste. The exact recipes we use are a company secret, so I can't show you inside that room. I can assure you, though, that we use real fruit juice, not artificial flavours!

So, since I can't show you exactly how we make the flavours, let's come back to the factory line. In the second large tank, over there, we mix the flavours with sugar to make <u>syrup</u>. This mixture needs to be sterilised, to make sure that it will keep well. The syrup is then mixed gently into the purified water. It's important not to stir a lot of air into the drink mixture.

Next, we need to add the <u>bubbles</u>. That's when this machine, the carbonator, is used. The bubbles are actually carbon dioxide, which is kept under pressure. The carbonator adds the bubbles by force, so that the drink becomes fizzy.

Finally, the soft drink is ready to be <u>put</u> into bottles or cans. It needs to be transferred quickly and <u>sealed</u>, so that the bubbles don't escape. From there, the bottles are labelled, and bottles and cans are <u>distributed</u> around the country.

Right, now, let's go to the tasting room where you can try our newest flavours and, of course, your old favourites.

Listening 2

Narrator: *You will hear a factory tour guide explaining how chewing gum is made.*

Good afternoon and welcome to our factory tour. As you all probably know, we'll give out some free samples at the end of the tour. But first, let me show you how our chewing gum is made.

Before we go out onto the factory floor, could everyone please put on these special paper overalls? Thank you. Ok. Please follow me through the control door and into the main part of the factory.

At this point, I should tell you that the process for making chewing gum starts when the rubber gum is <u>collected</u> from the trees. It is <u>ground</u> and then dried in another factory. This product is then brought to our factory to be made into chewing gum.

How we make chewing gum from rubber gum is fairly simple. Let's start here, at this large tank, where the dried gum is heated and <u>purified</u>. Because the gum comes from a tree, it may contain dirt or small pieces of wood, so this step is very important. We have to make sure that the gum is very clean.

While the gum is still hot, we add sugar syrup, <u>flavours</u> and colours. As you can see, the room on the opposite side of the building has a *Staff Only* sign. That's where we test and mix our special flavours, so you can't go in there. Our recipes are, of course, a secret. I can assure you, though, that we use natural flavours for all our products!

Right, let's focus on the factory line again. This round machine in front of me mixes the gum until it's very smooth and silky. The gum must be kept at a constant temperature while this is done. Next, another machine <u>rolls</u> out the gum, with a special roller to control the thickness of each sheet. Both sides of the gum sheets are powdered, to prevent them from sticking to the machine during the rolling and cutting process. The sheets of gum need to be cooled and are then cut into small pieces.

Next, the pieces of gum are wrapped in foil and <u>sealed</u> in packets. It's important to seal the gum quickly, so that it does not dry out. From there, the packets are <u>labelled</u> and boxed, ready to be distributed around the country.

Right, now, let's go to the tasting room where you'll be given some samples of our latest and most popular flavours to take home.

ANSWERS   Unit 17   Dieting

1. no answers

2. no answers

3. no answers

4. Check your answers.
a. weight	b. lose	c. fitness
d. extreme	e. obsessed	f. realise

5. no answers

6. Check your answers.
a. weigh	b. dieting	c. loss
d. fit	e. invited	f. seriously

7. Write the number of the phrase 1-3 that matches the phrases a-e.
a. 2	b. 3	c. 1
d. 2	e. 1	f. 3

8. Write the phrase to complete each sentence.
   a. obsessed with her weight
   b. keep dieting
   c. gain; weight

9. Write prepositions to complete these sentences.
   a. for   b. in
   c. in   d. to

10. Write the words you hear to complete each sentence.
    a. big deal   b. right   c. true

11. Do the speakers have the same opinion?
    a. no   b. yes   c. yes

12. Write the possible consequence to complete each sentence.
    a. iv   b. ii   c. vi
    d. v   e. i   f. iii

13. no answers

14. Check your answers.

/s/	/z/	/iz/
		e.g. apologises
diets	gains	exercises
keeps	tells	loses
invites	tries	changes
	weighs	obsesses
	needs	realises

15. Write the word you hear to complete each sentence.
    a. obsesses   b. diets   c. gains
    d. invites   e. realises

16. Write the name of the speaker for each sentence.
    a. George   b. John   c. Sue
    d. George   e. John

17. Write the words to complete the last sentence.
    ... was going to ...

18. Complete each sentence to report what you heard.
    a. ... is / was going on a diet
    b. ... is / was going to get fit
    c. ... wants / wanted to meet for coffee
    d. ... had seen / saw John in the supermarket
    e. ... (had) gained weight last year
    f. ... (had) told John to say sorry

19. no answers

20. Check your answers.
    a. A   b. B   c. B

Listening 1
   1. feel like it   2. for coffee
   3. in restaurants / in public

4. was looking thin / looked thin
5. fruit or vegetables   6. in hospital
7. talk to her

Listening 2
   8. much happier   9. exercising as much
   10. try other sports   11. her eating habits
   12. keeps exercising   13. a bike ride

SCRIPTS   Unit 17   Dieting

1. no audio

2. Pay attention to how these words sound.

extreme	avoid	lose
continue	diet	concerned
obsessed	fitness	invite
weight	habits	realise
serious	public	gain

3. no audio

4. Check your answers.
   a. Your eating habits can affect your **weight**, and over time, your health.
   b. Many girls go on diets to **lose** weight and look slim.
   c. It is important to watch what you eat, but also to have a high level of **fitness**.
   d. An **extreme** diet is one where you make many changes to your eating habits.
   e. If you spend too much time thinking about something, you are **obsessed**.
   f. It's important to **realise** when you have unhealthy habits.

5. no audio

6. Check your answers.
   a. Many people don't know how much they **weigh**. W-E-I-G-H
   b. Some girls get really obsessed about **dieting**. D-I-E-T-I-N-G
   c. Extreme weight **loss** can be bad for your health. L-O-S-S
   d. To be healthy, it's important to keep **fit**. F-I-T
   e. We **invited** our friends around for a special dinner. I-N-V-I-T-E-D
   f. If you are training **seriously** for a sport, you may be on a special diet. S-E-R-I-O-U-S-L-Y

7. no audio

8. Write the phrase to complete each sentence.
   a. I'm worried about Jane. She is **obsessed with her weight**.
   b. I don't think she should **keep dieting**.
   c. I think she needs to **gain** some **weight**.

9. Write prepositions to complete these sentences.
   a. We always used to meet **for** coffee.
   b. I don't like to eat **in** public. I don't want people to see me.
   c. I often see people I know shopping **in** the supermarket.
   d. I think it's important to listen **to** your friends when they talk to you.

170

10. Write the words you hear to complete each sentence.
    a. I don't really think it's a **big deal**.
    b. You could be **right**.
    c. It's not a nice thing to say, but it's **true**.

11. Do the speakers have the same opinion?
    a. **B:** I think Jane needs to stop dieting.
       A: I don't really think it's a big deal. She'll be fine.
    b. **B:** I think Jane needs to stop dieting.
       A: You could be right. She is getting too thin.
    c. **B:** I think Julie is getting fat.
       A: It's not a nice thing to say, but it's true. She is much bigger than before.

12. Match the possible consequence to complete each sentence.
    a. If she keeps exercising, she may stop gaining weight.
    b. If she stopped her gymnastics training, she probably wouldn't exercise as much.
    c. If we don't do anything, she may diet until she ends up in hospital.
    d. If I tell her to change her eating habits, she may not listen to me.
    e. If you told her what to do, she might pay attention.
    f. If she gains a lot of weight, she may find it affects her health.

13. Look at the list of verbs and try to classify them.
    First, listen to the example: apologises

14. Check your answers.
    diets, exercises, gains, loses, tells, tries, keeps, changes, invites, obsesses, realises, weighs, needs

15. Write the word you hear to complete each sentence.
    a. I think she **obsesses** about her weight.
    b. If she **diets** too much, she may get sick.
    c. If she **gains** weight too quickly, that isn't healthy.
    d. He said he **invites** her to dinner every week, but she never goes.
    e. I hope she **realises** that she needs to change her habits.

16. Write the name of the speaker for each sentence.
    Sue: Hey George, did you hear what John said yesterday?
    George: Yes, and I thought it was very rude. He said that Jane is getting fat. She was very upset.
    Sue: I'm not surprised. I think that was a terrible thing to say.
    George: Yes it was. I think he should say sorry.
    Sue: Well, when I saw him, he said that he was going to apologise.

17. Write the words to complete the last sentence.
    Well, when I saw him, he said that he **was going to** apologise.

18. Complete each sentence to report what you heard.
    a. **Sue:** I'm going on a diet.

    b. **George:** I'm going to get fit.
    c. **John:** I want to meet for coffee.
    d. **Sue:** I saw John in the supermarket.
    e. **John:** I gained weight last year.
    f. **George:** I told John to say sorry.

19. no audio

20. Check your answers.
Narrator: *You will hear three friends, Annie, Blair and Carolyn, talking about their friend Sarah, who is on an extreme diet.*

Listening 1
Narrator: *You will hear three friends, Annie, Blair and Carolyn, talking about their friend Sarah, who is on an extreme diet.*
A: Hello! Fancy seeing you two here!
C: Hi Anna, long time no see. How have you been?
A: Good, keeping busy. Hey, have you seen Sarah lately?
B: No, not for ages.
C: She doesn't come out and meet us for dinner any more. The last three times I invited her, she said that she didn't <u>feel like it</u>.
A: It seems like she never wants to meet me <u>for coffee</u> either!
B: I was starting to think that she didn't like us anymore... Now I think that maybe she isn't avoiding us, she just doesn't want to eat with us <u>in restaurants</u>.
A: What do you mean?
B: Well, we think that she's too concerned about her weight— you know she's been dieting for a while now, and she seems to be getting more and more serious about it.
C: And, well, we're starting to wonder if maybe she's trying to avoid eating <u>in public</u> altogether.
A: You could be right. I saw her in the supermarket the other day, and she <u>was looking thin</u>. It looks like she's lost a lot of weight.
C: She seems to be obsessed with dieting. It's not healthy.
A: Well, you're not going to believe this—all she was buying was bottled water, tea and crackers! Not even any <u>fruit or vegetables</u>.
B: Oh, that's not good. I'm worried about her. What should we do?
C: I'm not sure if we can do anything. She said that she knows what she's doing. If we try and tell her to change her eating habits, she may not listen to us.
B: But, if we don't do anything, she may go on dieting, getting thinner and thinner, until she ends up <u>in hospital</u>!
A: We'd better do something. Why don't we have a party at my house and invite her? Then we can <u>talk to her</u> about it.
C: Good idea.

Listening 2
Narrator: *You will hear three friends, Donna, Peter and Helen, talking about their friend Tina, who has been gaining weight.*
D: Hello! Fancy seeing you two here!
P: Hi Donna, long time no see. How have you been?
H: Good, keeping busy. How about you?
D: Oh, same as always. Hey, have you seen Tina lately?
P: Yes, and hasn't she got fat?
H: Oh, Peter, you can't say that about a girl! It's rude!
D: It's not a nice thing to say, but it's true though, Helen. She looks much bigger than she used to.

P: Ever since she met her boyfriend who works at the pizza store!

H: When I talked to her the other day, she said she's <u>much happier</u> now, even though she's gained some weight. I really don't think it's a big deal.

D: If she keeps eating more and gains a lot of weight, then she may find it affects her health.

H: That's true, although it might not be because of what she's eating. Now she's stopped doing gymnastics, she isn't <u>exercising as much</u>.

D: She told me that she was sick of spending all her free time training. She wants to <u>try other sports</u> now.

P: But, if she continues getting bigger, then that will affect her fitness, and she won't be able to do gymnastics anymore.

D: It isn't nice to talk about people behind their backs. Don't you think we should say something to her?

P: I think we should. She needs to know it isn't healthy to gain weight so quickly.

H: Why don't we wait and see? I'm sure she'll realise and change <u>her eating habits</u>.

P: Do you really think so?

H: Well, she's not overweight, is she? She's just bigger than before.

D: That's true. I think if she <u>keeps exercising</u>, she'll stop gaining weight, and then she won't need to worry about being unhealthy.

P: Ok. I still think we should do something. Why don't we invite her to go for <u>a bike ride</u> with us tomorrow?

ANSWERS   Unit 18   International Events

1. no answers

2. Listen to the sentences and write down the dates you hear.

a. 776 B.C.	b. 772 B.C.	c. 393 A.D.
d. 1859	e. 1992	f. 1830
g. 1896	h. 2006	i. 1924
j. 708 B.C.	k. 1894	l. 2004
m. 2008		

3. Tick the number that you hear.

a. 1654	f. 859
b. 423	g. 1229
c. 992	h. 1010
d. 1377	i. 772
e. 1532	

4. Write the numbers that you hear.

a. 1783	f. 1905
b. 1873	g. 1939
c. 1890	h. 1950
d. 1900	i. 1907
e. 1903	

5. In pairs, quickly discuss the following questions.

   a. Letters   b. One   c. Time periods

6. Complete the classification questions.
   1. A   2. C   3. A

7. no answers

8. Check your answers.

/t/	/d/	/id/
worked	allowed	included
faced	planned	added
	offered	founded
	relied	permitted
	managed	lasted
		demonstrated

9. Write the words to complete each sentence.

a. included	b. added	c. allowed
d. founded	e. competed	f. permitted
g. planned	h. offered	

10. Tick the correct option.

a. in 776 B.C.	b. in 708 B.C.	c. in 1924
d. 1992	e. in June 1783	
f. between 1900 and 1909		g. in 1939

11. Classify the statements about computers according to these time periods.

History of Computers			
	Before 1938	**1939–1945 (World War II)**	**1946–now**
e.g.			✓ (1984)
a		✓ (1945)	
b	✓ (1801)		
c			✓ (1950s/60s)
d		✓ (WW II)	
e	✓ (before 1833)		
f	✓ (about 1933)		
g		✓ (1941)	
h	✓ (1600s)		
i			✓ (1971)
j		✓ (1943)	
k			✓ (1980s)

12. no answers

13. Check your answers.
   a. C   b. C

Listening 1

1. C	2. A	3. C
4. C	5. B	6. C
7. B		

Listening 2

8. B	9. C	10. A
11. C	12. A	13. B
14. A		

1. no audio

2. Listen to the sentences and write down the dates you hear.
   a. The first ancient Olympic Games were held in 776 B.C.
   b. King Shalmaneser IV of Assyria died in 772 B.C.
   c. Do you know why the Olympic Games were banned in 393 A.D.?
   d. The year 1859 started on a Saturday.
   e. The 1992 presidential election was a contest between Bush and Clinton.
   f. Joseph married Ann on New Year's Day in 1830.
   g. 1896 was a leap year.
   h. In 2006, the World Wide Web Conference was held in Edinburgh, Scotland.
   i. The 1924 Summer Olympics were officially known as the Games of the Eighth Olympiad.
   j. The first pentathlon was held in 708 B.C.
   k. 1894 is the year that Rewi Maniapoto died.
   l. Where were the 2004 Olympic Games held?
   m. The Olympic Games in 2008 were held in Beijing.

3. Tick the number that you hear.
   Narrator: *First, listen to the example: 1776   The answer is 1776.*
   Now, listen and complete the rest of the table.

a. 1654	b. 423	c. 992
d. 1377	e. 1532	f. 859
g. 1229	h. 1010	i. 772

4. Write the numbers that you hear.
   Narrator: *First, listen to the example: 1910*
   Now, complete the rest of the table.

a. 1783	b. 1873	c. 1890
d. 1900	e. 1903	f. 1905
g. 1939	h. 1950	i. 1907

5. no audio

6. Complete the classification questions.
   a. In 1801, punch card technology was introduced.
   b. The late 1950s and 60s saw the development of silicon chips, which led to the second generation of computers.
   c. Before 1833, Babbage designed a machine that could correctly calculate sums again and again.

7. Classify the list of regular verbs according to the way the '-ed' ending is said.
   First, listen to the example: devoted

8. Check your answers.

included	added	allowed
founded	permitted	planned
offered	worked	relied
faced	lasted	managed
demonstrated		

9. Write the words to complete each sentence.
   a. In 708 B.C., wrestling was **included** as an Olympic sport for the first time.
   b. Over t ime, other events such as boxing and horse racing were **added**.
   c. Women weren't **allowed** to watch or compete in the ancient Olympics.
   d. The International Olympic Committee was **founded** in 1894.
   e. In 1896, 241 athletes **competed** for medals.
   f. In 1924, women were finally **permitted** to compete.
   g. Organisers for the Beijing Olympics **planned** for 302 different events.
   h. The 2006 Winter Olympics **offered** seven sports, with 84 separate events.

10. Tick the correct option.
    a. The first record of the Olympic Games dates back to 776 B.C.
    b. In 708 B.C., the pentathlon (a 5-sport event) was held for the first time.
    c. In 1924, women were finally permitted to compete.
    d. Until 1992, the Winter Olympics were held in the same year as the Summer Olympics.
    e. Two brothers demonstrated their hot air balloon in June 1783 in France.
    f. By the end of the first decade of the twentieth century, many people were trying to be the first to fly a plane.
    g. The first flight of a jet plane didn't take place until 1939.

11. Classify the statements about computers according to these time periods.
    Narrator: *Listen to the example: In 1984, Apple launched the Macintosh. 1984 is in the period after World War II, so there is a tick in the third part of the table.*
    Now, listen and complete the table.
    a. The first completely electronic computer which could perform different tasks was built in the USA in 1945.
    b. In 1801, punch card technology was introduced.
    c. The late 1950s and 60s saw the development of silicon chips, which led to the second generation of computers.
    d. First generation computers were developed during World War II.
    e. Before 1833, Babbage designed a machine that could correctly calculate sums again and again.
    f. About a hundred years after Babbage, Alan Turing developed the idea of algorithms to solve problems.
    g. In Germany, Kruse completed the first general programmable calculator in 1941.
    h. The first mechanical calculators appeared in the 1600s.
    i. The 'third generation' of computers began with the development of the micro-chip in 1971.
    j. By December 1943, the British had a computer known as Colossus to decode language.
    k. Throughout the 1980s, personal computers became increasingly popular for many tasks.

12. no audio

13. Check your answers.
    Narrator: *You will hear a Community Sports Officer talking about the history of the Olympic Games.*

Listening 1

Narrator: *You will hear a Community Sports Officer talking about the history of the Olympic Games.*

Hello everyone. This evening I'm going to give you a brief history of the Olympic Games. Then we'll look at some photos and film clips of great sporting moments from the past 100 or so years of the Games.

The first record of the original Games in Greece dates back to 776 B.C., where there was one 200 metre race! By 722 B.C., there were 24 events. In 708 B.C., the pentathlon was held for the first time. This was a 5-sport event. Wrestling was also included. Over time, other events such as boxing, horse races and chariot racing were added. Women couldn't compete in any events; in fact, they were not even allowed to watch the games.

After a period of almost 1,170 years, the last of the ancient Games was held in 393 A.D. There was then a long time with no further Olympic Games.

During the 1830s, there was a campaign to revive the Games, with the first competition held in 1859, followed by some later Games also held in Greece.

Then the International Olympic Committee was founded in 1894, with the first modern international games being held in 1896. A total of 241 athletes from 14 nations competed for gold, silver and bronze. At the time, this was the biggest international sporting event ever held. From 1924, women were finally permitted to compete.

Since 1896 there has been a gradual increase in the number of countries taking part and the number of sports included. At the Athens Summer Olympics in 2004, there were almost 11,100 athletes from 202 countries. Events such as the marathon, cycling, sailing, soccer, judo, canoeing, basketball, water polo and rifle shooting have all been added to the modern Olympics. For the Beijing Olympics, planners planned for 302 events, over 28 sports.

The winter games were first held in 1924. Winter sports such as ice skating, ice hockey, bobsledding and skiing were held. These were not traditional Olympic sports, of course, as the climate in Athens was not cold enough.

Both the summer games and the winter games were held in the same year until 1992. Since that time, there has been a two-year gap between them. The 2006 Winter Olympics offered 7 sports with 84 separate events.

Right, now let's look at some early film clips of the great Olympic athletes.

Listening 2

Narrator: *You will hear a Museum Officer talking about the history of flight.*

Good evening everyone and welcome! Tonight I'm going to give you a brief history of flight. Then you can look more closely at the exhibition of pictures on the walls around you.

As you probably know, men dreamt of flying for hundreds of years. Finally two brothers demonstrated their hot air balloon in June 1783 in France, to the amazement of all who were watching. Later that year, in September 1783, the same men flew a hot air balloon with three 'passengers'—a sheep, a rooster and a duck! Their next flight a month later had two human passengers. In January 1784, they flew a giant balloon with seven passengers to a height of approximately a thousand metres.

Over the next one hundred or more years, various people devoted their lives to the mystery of flight. For example, an Englishman, Sir George Cayley, worked on it for more than 50 years, until his death in 1857. There were several key problems that faced anyone wishing to fly. These included things like how to get the 'lift' to get the plane in the air, and how to power the plane without adding too much weight.

By the first decade of the twentieth century, there was a fascination with flying and attempts to fly were being made in many parts of the world. Gliders had already been flown successfully in the 1890s, and the first successful airships flew in the early 1900s.

The Wright brothers in America were the first to truly fly a fixed-wing a plane, in 1903. Their first flight was only 35 metres, but by 1905 they could stay in the air for 30 minutes and fly in a circle.

Early planes relied solely on propellers. Although scientists had understood the principles of jet engines for ages, the first flight of a jet-driven plane didn't take place until 1939. By the 1950s, the use of jet engines in aeroplanes led to a revolution in aeroplane design.

The idea of helicopters dates back through the ages, with various designers working on vertical flight but lacking a lightweight engine with enough power to make it possible. The first successful manned flight by a helicopter took place in 1907, but only lasted very briefly. It was not until 1924 that a helicopter managed to fly for 14 minutes at a height of 15 metres.

Finally, let's consider rockets and space travel.

ANSWERS   Unit 19   Online Safety

1. no answers

2. no answers

3. no answers

4. Check your answers.
a. privacy	b. include	c. personal
d. publish	e. Strangers	f. false; trick

5. Write the number of each definition next to the matching word.
a. 4	b. 3	c. 6
d. 2	e. 1	f. 5

6. Write the pairs of words to complete each sentence.
a. personal details	b. identity theft
c. social networking	d. illegal downloads
e. Online bullying	

7. Write the phrase you hear to complete each sentence.
a. privacy settings	b. meet friends
c. home page	d. bank account
e. Digital dirt	

8. Write the prepositions that you hear to complete each sentence.
   a. out   b. on   c. up
   d. to   e. with

9. Choose whether the speaker is sure or unsure.
   a. sure   b. unsure   c. sure
   d. unsure   e. unsure

10. Complete the short-answer questions.
   a. (some) photos   b. People will see.
   c. name; contact details

11. Complete the sentences below.
   a. buy or sell   b. risky
   c. take your money   d. anybody can sell

12. Answer the questions below.
   a. no   b. no
   c. no   d. yes

13. no answers

14. Check your answers.
   a. B   b. A   c. C

Listening 1
1. online safety   2. identity theft
3. bank account   4. 5 (five) minutes
5. some reading   6. identity theft
7. risks and problems   8. trick people
9. privacy settings

Listening 2
10. new site   11. it's public
12. photo and details   13. face to face
14. make new friends   15. to give out
16. talk to strangers   17. meet (up with)

SCRIPTS   Unit 19   Online Safety

1. no audio

2. Pay attention to how these words sound.

obvious	include	identity
issue	personal	details
network	scary	illegal
download	copyright	false
trick	privacy	publish
strangers		

3. no audio

4. Check your answers.
   a. It's important to protect your **privacy** when using the internet.
   b. It may not be a good idea to **include** your address and phone number on your webpage.
   c. Check that your **personal** information cannot be viewed by the public.
   d. To **publish** to the internet means to put something on a website.

   e. **Strangers** are members of the public who you don't know.
   f. Some websites contain **false** information to try and **trick** you.

5. Write the number of each definition next to the matching word.
   1. —this is something that is easy to see or understand
   2. —this means something is not allowed by law
   3. —this is all your personal information, what makes you who you are
   4. —this means to meet people and make new friends
   5. —this is getting something from the internet, for example a music file
   6. —this is a topic, or a problem that people are trying to solve

6. Write the pairs of words to complete each sentence.
   a. It's a bad idea to give your **personal details** to strangers.
   b. When someone takes your personal information and pretends to be you, it is called **identity theft**.
   c. There are many **social networking** sites, where people can meet new friends.
   d. Music companies are trying to stop **illegal downloads** of their songs.
   e. **Online bullying** is when people use the internet to make someone feel bad.

7. Write the phrase you hear to complete each sentence.
   a. Check the **privacy settings** on your social networking site.
   b. It can be easy to **meet friends** online.
   c. A **home page** is your personal site or the first page of your website.
   d. Many people can access their **bank account** online.
   e. **Digital dirt** is a term for all your personal information on the internet.

8. Write the prepositions that you hear to complete each sentence.
   a. Never give **out** information to strangers.
   b. Information that is published **on** the internet is public information.
   c. Be careful when you meet **up** with new friends.
   d. Some people prefer talking face **to** face, rather than online.
   e. If you are going to meet someone, get some friends to go along **with** you.

9. Choose whether the speaker is sure or unsure.
   a. That's part of our topic, isn't it. (*falling intonation*)
   b. We have five minutes each, is that right? (*rising intonation*)
   c. He's always late, isn't he. (*falling intonation*)
   d. We're going to give advice, aren't we? (*rising intonation*)
   e. There isn't anything left, is there? (*rising intonation*)

10. Complete the short-answer questions.

Narrator: *You will hear two sisters, Deb and Jodi, talking about a social networking site.*

Jodi: Hey, Deb. Can you help me with my new site? I'm trying to upload some photos but there's something wrong.

Deb: I guess. But not for long. I'm really busy on my school project. What do you want me to do?

Jodi: Have a look here. The photos aren't showing ...

Deb: The photos are on your desktop, right? Let me look ... Oh Jodi, you shouldn't put photos like that on your site. People will see. And you girls are posing in your underwear!!

Jodi: But they're just for me and my friends to have a laugh about. No one can see them, can they?

Deb: They certainly can. You're posting them on the internet. Plus you've got your name and contact details on your site. That's just not safe.

11. Complete the sentences below.

Narrator: *You will hear two friends, James and Karl, talking about buying things online.*

James: Hey Karl, did you hear about this new website? You can buy all these great new products and they send them to you free.

Karl: That sounds cool. But I never buy or sell anything online. I don't like to give out my bank account details online.

James: It used to be risky, but most websites have safe payment options now, so you don't have to worry.

Karl: But, anyway, how do you know that they aren't going to take your money and not give you what you've paid for?

James: Do you think that really happens? Surely if you use a reputable website, they'll guarantee their products.

Karl: You could be right. I guess most of the bad stories I've heard have been those auction sites, where anybody can sell things.

12. Answer the questions.

a. Do you think that really happens? That sounds a bit extreme.

b. Wow. Is that right? That's awful. I'm going to learn a lot from this project.

c. Nope, that's not the way it works I'm afraid.

d. Most websites have safe payment options now, so you don't have to worry.

13. no audio

14. Check your answers.

Narrator: *You will hear 4 school friends planning a joint presentation on online safety.*

Listening 1

Narrator: *You will hear 4 school friends planning a joint presentation on online safety.*

Liz: Ok, you lot, let's get this project organised. We have to decide who is going to do what.

Ryan: Well, our topic's basically about online safety, isn't it? I guess that includes obvious things like giving out personal information and meeting strangers when you don't know who they really are.

Mary: But there's online bullying to worry about too. We should include that, shouldn't we?

Liz: Yeah. And identity theft...that's becoming a real issue overseas.

Ryan: What's identity theft? I'm not sure what you mean.

Liz: If someone gets all your personal details off your social site, they can pretend to be you. They may be able to fool the bank, for example, and access your bank account.

Mary: Do you think that really happens? That sounds a bit extreme.

Liz: Of course it does. You need to do some reading on this topic. It's scary once you look at what goes on.

Mary: Look, there's Jason coming now. He's always late, isn't he!

Jason: Hi all. Sorry, I had a flat tyre.

Liz: Right, now we're all here. Let's decide who will cover what section. Mary, are you OK to do online bullying? Maybe also include stuff on the risks involved in letting strangers access your social network site and going to meet people you don't already know.

Mary: Sure. That's OK with me. Just 5 minutes each, is that right?

Liz. Yep. And Ryan, maybe you could cover identity theft.

Ryan: Do I have to? I'd rather do illegal downloads and copyright. I've done some reading on that already. That's part of our topic, isn't it? I mean, it's about how to avoid breaking the law.

Jason: I could do the section on identity theft. I think it's fascinating. Most teenagers don't have any idea of the risks they're taking online. We're going to give advice on how to use the internet safely as well, aren't we?

Liz: Oh yes, I definitely think that should be part of our presentation ... give information on risks and problems, and then some advice.

Jason: I've read about identity thieves putting false job ads online, to trick people into giving out personal information after they answer the ad.

Ryan: Wow. Is that right? That's awful. I'm going to learn a lot from this project.

Mary: That's for sure. Hey, what are you going to do, Liz? There isn't anything left, is there?

Liz: Actually, there is. Something termed 'digital dirt'. It's really important. It's all about how employers and colleges can access personal sites and look at your personal messages and pictures.

Mary: Truly? You mean we'd better not put up silly photos and stories?

Liz: Nope. Not if you want to get a job or be admitted to grad school.

Ryan: It's pretty mean, isn't it? I mean, they're supposed to be social network sites, just for friends.

Liz: Well, there are some ways of controlling who can see your social profile. You just need to be sure to use the privacy settings on your website. And really limit who can see it. Don't allow 'friends of friends of friends' ...

Listening 2

Narrator: *You will hear 3 school friends talking about online safety.*

Mike: Hi you two, what're you up to? Not in the library studying?

Susie: Well, we were. We just came out here to have a break. I'm telling Pete about my new site on TeenSpace. It's really cool. I've got photos from a party last weekend up there already.

Mike: Do you realise that anything that is published on the internet, like in your social network site, can be used by anyone? 'Cos it's public?

Susie: What do you mean? It's private. It's just for me and my friends.

Mike: Nope, that's not the way it works I'm afraid. I just heard about someone in Australia who had her home page used by a TV program.

Pete: Wow! Is that right? That's a bit scary.

Mike: Well, yeah, especially as her name and photo and details were shown to millions of people and linked to a really unpleasant topic! I'd hate to have that happen to me.

Susie: But everyone has a social site these days. It's fun playing around with photos and graphics and messaging each other. I can't see how it's dangerous.

Pete: Well, actually I don't have one. I can't be bothered with it. I'd rather play music with my friends and talk to them face to face.

Susie: Oh yeah, you're so out of it! I'm going to make lots of new friends through my site.

Mike: You know, I don't think it's safe to give out your personal information to strangers. Nor to go and meet people that you've talked to online.

Susie: Why not? What's the problem? Lots of my friends do that.

Mike: Well ... you can't tell whether someone online really is another 16 year old girl, or is actually a middle-aged man.

Pete: That's so true. I've heard of cases like that. A girl was kidnapped just last week. Somewhere in Europe.

Mike: There was a report just the other day saying that lots of teenagers regularly talk to strangers online, and meet some of them face-to-face. That's really risky. You'd better be careful.

Susie: Ok, I'll try ... maybe you two can go along with me if I want to meet up with a new friend.

Mike: Yep. That's a good idea. I'll do that any time you need me. Right, I'm going to the computer labs to finish my project. See you at lunch!

ANSWERS Unit 20 Environment

1. no answers

2. Tick the word you hear.
   a. affects (v)   b. effects   c. effects

d. effect   e. affects (v)   f. effect
g. effect   h. affects (v)   i. effect

3. Write the word to complete each sentence.
   a. effects   b. affects   c. effect
   d. effect   e. affects   f. affects
   g. effect   h. affects

4. Tick the words that you hear.
   a. reduce   b. expansion   c. destruction
   d. improve   e. creation   f. provision

5. Write the word to complete each sentence.
   a. expansion   b. creation   c. provision
   d. improve   e. reduce   f. destruction
   g. provide   h. expand

6. Tick the correct column, to classify the words you hear.

Buildings and facilities / Methods of transport	
a. hotel	(B & F)
b. shop	(B & F)
c. diesel bus	(T)
d. road	(B & F)
e. airport	(B & F)
f. plane	(T)
g. restaurant	(B & F)
h. golf course	(B & F)
i. jeep	(T)
j. swimming pool	(B & F)
k. cruise ship	(T)
l. car park	(B & F)
m. camel	(T)

7. Match the events 1-3 to the time periods, A-E.
   1. E   2. D   3. A

8. Tick the correct option.
   a. it = tourism
   b. it = experience of other cultures
   c. These = problems
   d. this = increased population
   e. This = pollution
   f. These = many forms of pollution
   g. this = rubbish
   h. This = destruction of reefs and beaches

9. Complete the sentences with it, this, these or that.
   a. it   b. This   c. this
   d. These   e. This   f. These
   g. it   h. this

10. Match the sentences you hear, 1-4, to the sentences a-d below.
   a. 4   b. 1
   c. 2   d. 3

11. Read the summary below and choose the correct options.
   1. adjective   2. noun   3. noun
   4. noun   5. noun

12. no answers

13. Check your answers.
   a. C   b. A   c. A

Listening 1
   1. C   2. B   3. local
   4. Tourism / The tourist industry
   5. understanding   6. (local) education   7. (local) roads

Listening 2
   8. A   9. C   10. B
   11. D   12. C   13. A
   14. B

SCRIPTS   Unit 20   Environment

1. no audio

2. Tick the word you hear.
   a. First, consider how tourism **affects** the global economy.
   b. Then, think about the local **effects** of tourism.
   c. The local **effects** of tourism relate to the general area of a tourist attraction.
   d. The noise of helicopters has a significant **effect** on people visiting the Grand Canyon.
   e. Tourism **affects** the world in a variety of ways.
   f. One positive **effect** is the increased awareness that tourists have of people in poorer countries.
   g. An important local **effect** of increased tourism is the creation of jobs.
   h. Tourism also **affects** local supplies of food, water and energy.
   i. The loss of wildlife habitat is another **effect** of the tourist industry.

3. Write the word to complete each sentence.
   a. First, think about the global **effects** of tourism.
   b. Tourism certainly **affects** the world as a whole.
   c. One positive **effect** is the increased awareness that tourists have of people in poorer countries.
   d. The loss of wildlife habitat is a negative **effect** of the tourist industry.
   e. Next, consider how tourism **affects** the local economy.
   f. The noise of helicopters **affects** people walking the Inca Trail.
   g. Tourism has a positive **effect** on the number of jobs available for local people.
   h. Tourism **affects** local supplies of food, water and energy in a negative way.

4. Tick the words that you hear.
   a. People are trying to **reduce** the impact of tourists in popular areas.
   b. The **expansion** of tourism in poor areas can cause problems such as water shortages.
   c. The **destruction** of habitat affects animals and birds.
   d. The income generated by tourism should be used to **improve** local roads and rubbish disposal systems.
   e. One positive effect of tourism is the **creation** of new jobs.
   f. Another is the **provision** of money to look after wildlife in those areas.

5. Write the word to complete each sentence.
   a. The **expansion** of tourism in poor areas can cause problems such as water shortages.
   b. One positive effect of tourism is the **creation** of new jobs.
   c. Another is the **provision** of money to look after wildlife in those areas.
   d. The income generated by tourism should be used to **improve** local roads and rubbish disposal systems.
   e. People are trying to **reduce** the impact of tourists in popular areas.
   f. The **destruction** of habitat affects animals and birds.
   g. Tourism income can be used to **provide** for conservation of animals and plants.
   h. Tourist facilities often **expand** over good farm land, which puts pressure on food supplies.

6. Tick the correct column, to classify the words you hear.
   a. hotel   b. shop   c. diesel bus
   d. road   e. airport   f. plane
   g. restaurant   h. golf course   i. jeep
   j. swimming pool   k. cruise ship   l. car park
   m. camel

7. Match the events 1-3 to the time periods, A-E.
   a. The first computers built with silicon chips went on sale in 1964.
   b. The British had a computer known as Colossus to decode language by December 1943.
   c. The first mechanical calculators appeared in the 1600s.

8. Tick the correct option.
   a. What are some advantages that tourism brings to an area and its economy? Well, **it**'s certainly a way a region can make money ...
   b. I think both tourists and local people can benefit from the experience of other cultures; **it** increases understanding of how and why people have different customs.
   c. Now, sadly, there is also a variety of problems that go with tourism. **These** can be broadly grouped in three categories ...
   d. As population numbers may increase by as much as 10 times at peak season, **this** can lead to shortages of food for local people.
   e. Next, another significant issue for any major tourist area is pollution. **This** takes many forms ...
   f. Pollution takes many forms, such as air pollution, noise pollution, littering problems, rubbish disposal, the amount of chemicals used for golf courses and swimming pools and the disposal of human waste. **These** all have to be managed ...

g. Each cruise ship passenger generates about 3.5 kgs of rubbish daily. Quite a lot of **this** ends up in the sea and along the shorelines ...

h. Finally, there are other physical effects of tourism such as the destruction of coral reefs and beaches to use the coral and sand as building materials. **This** has happened in the Philippines.

9. Complete the sentences with it, this, these or that.

a. I think both tourists and local people can benefit from the experience of other cultures; **it** increases understanding of how and why people have different customs.

b. Finally, there are other physical effects of tourism such as the destruction of coral reefs and beaches to use the coral and sand as building materials. **This** has happened in the Philippines.

c. As population numbers may increase by as much as 10 times at peak season, **this** can lead to shortages of food for local people.

d. Now, sadly, there is also a variety of problems that go with tourism. **These** can be broadly grouped in three categories ...

e. Next, another significant issue for any major tourist area is pollution. **This** takes many forms.

f. Pollution takes many forms, such as air pollution, noise pollution, littering problems, rubbish disposal, the amount of chemicals used for golf courses and swimming pools and the disposal of human waste. **These** all have to be managed.

g. What are some advantages that tourism brings to an area and its economy? Well, **it** is certainly a way a region can make money.

h. Each cruise ship passenger generates about 3.5 kgs of rubbish daily. Quite a lot of **this** ends up in the sea and along the shorelines.

10. Match the sentences you hear, 1-4, to the sentences a-d below.

[Audio—not seen by students; numbers to be stated clearly by narrator]
Listen to the audio and match the sentences you hear [1-4] to the sentences below [a-d].
1. There are a number of benefits of tourism for a local region and its people.
2. Sadly, there is also a variety of problems that go with tourism.
3. A problem for a lot of tourist regions is the large amount of water used by tourists.
4. We need to consider how tourism affects the world as a whole.

11. no audio

12. no audio

13. Check your answers.

Narrator: *You will hear an Education Officer at a museum discussing the impact of tourism.*

Listening 1

Narrator: *You will hear an Education Officer at a museum discussing the impact of tourism.*

Hello. Today I'm going to talk to you about the advantages and disadvantages of tourism.

To start off, I want to make clear that we can consider the impact of tourism at two levels. First of all, there are the global effects of tourism, which means the way any tourism affects the world as a whole. Then there are the local effects, which relate to the area of any particular tourist attraction, such as Mt Everest or the Grand Canyon.

On the global level, there can be positive effects, such as increased awareness by tourists of environmental and social issues in other places. On the other hand, there are many negative effects, such as factors leading to climate change. Note, for example, that about 60% of air travel is generated by tourism. In addition, there is the loss of various animals and plants as their habitat is reduced or destroyed by the expansion of tourism.

Right, now let's look at the local picture in more detail. What are some advantages that tourism brings to an area and its economy?

Well, it's certainly a way a region can make money and perhaps avoid 'dirty' industries such as steel mills or paper factories. In addition, the tourist industry creates jobs—many types of jobs, for people of various ages and skills. For example, the hotels, restaurants and shops all need staff; the people who make local arts and crafts are able to sell their goods; there are jobs for guides, for people supplying all sorts of food and local transport—including things like camel rides at the Pyramids.

Another important benefit is the opportunity local people have to improve their skills—for example, a hotel maid may move on to working in the restaurant, or a waiter may start training as a chef. Other people are able to start up small businesses supplying the hotels or restaurants.

I think both tourists and local people can benefit from the experience of other cultures; it increases understanding of how and why people have different customs.

Finally, of course, the income generated by tourism will ideally be used to set up better local education and health systems, improve local roads and waste disposal systems and provide for the conservation of animals, birds and plants in that region. In this way, the local area benefits from the tourists it provides for.

Listening 2

Narrator: *You will now hear the rest of the Education Officer's talk.*

Now, sadly, there is also a variety of problems that go with tourism. These can be broadly grouped in three categories: pressure on natural resources, various kinds of pollution and other physical effects.

A huge problem is the amount of water that is required in a tourist area. Water is needed for the hotels and restaurants, the swimming pools, gardens and, of course, the golf courses. It is claimed that a golf course in a tropical country uses as much water in a year as 60,000 village people. Often these are areas that already have a water shortage. Also, tourists use a lot more water when on holiday, especially in hot climates.

As population numbers may increase by as much as <u>10 times</u> at peak season, this can lead to shortages of food for local people. All fresh vegetables, meat and fruit tend to be bought for the tourists. Similarly, tourism puts pressure on supplies of energy as large amounts are needed for heating or cooling of rooms, hot water for showers and so on. Good farm land is taken up by buildings, airports, golf courses and car parks.

Next, another significant issue for any major tourist area is pollution. This takes many forms, such as air pollution, noise pollution, littering problems, rubbish disposal, the amount of chemicals used for golf courses and swimming pools and the disposal of human waste. These all have to be managed—but often this isn't done well, as poor countries don't have modern technology and facilities. That means, of course, that in the end the area becomes <u>less attractive to tourists</u>, because of the rubbish and the damage to the environment.

Air pollution results from the use of planes and diesel buses. For example, tourist buses often keep their engines running for hours at a site, so the tourists can return to a heated bus in winter, or a cool one if it's summer. <u>Air pollution and acid rain cause significant damage to ancient buildings, such as the Taj Mahal.</u>

As an example of <u>noise pollution, so many tourists now travel around Yellowstone Park</u> on snow mobiles that the engines can be heard all over the park. As for <u>rubbish—a cruise ship in the Caribbean</u> on average has 600 crew members and 1400 passengers. Each passenger generates about 3.5 kgs of rubbish daily. Quite a lot of this ends up in the sea and along the shorelines, killing sea birds and other marine life.

Finally, there are other physical effects of tourism such as the destruction of <u>coral reefs and beaches to use the coral and sand as building materials. This has happened in the Philippines.</u> In addition, cruise ships dropping anchor can destroy large areas of reefs and the development of marinas can affect currents and change coastlines. The loss of wildlife habitat because of construction of tourist facilities is another effect. In addition, the pursuit of wildlife by tourists in jeeps and small planes can cause injuries and stress animals so much that their behaviour changes; they may neglect their young or fail to mate.

As you can imagine, all these problems have to be managed or else such tourist attractions will seem less attractive and the tourists will go somewhere else.

新东方独家引进

《剑桥雅思考试全真试题集9》
（含光盘2张）
剑桥大学考试委员会　编著

定价：110元　开本：16开　页码：176页

《剑桥雅思考试全真试题集8》
（含光盘2张）
剑桥大学考试委员会　编著

定价：110元　开本：16开　页码：176页

《剑桥雅思考试全真试题集7》
（含光盘2张）
剑桥大学考试委员会　编著

定价：110元　开本：16开　页码：176页

《剑桥雅思考试全真试题集6》
（含光盘2张）
剑桥大学考试委员会　编著

定价：110元　开本：16开　页码：176页

《剑桥雅思考试全真试题集5》
（含光盘2张）
剑桥大学考试委员会　编著

定价：110元　开本：16开　页码：176页

◎ 4套完整的学术类雅思全真试题
◎ 2套培训类雅思阅读与写作全真试题

《剑桥雅思真题精讲9》
周成刚　主编

定价：28元　开本：16开　页码：232页

《剑桥雅思真题精讲8》
周成刚　主编

定价：28元　开本：16开　页码：208页

《剑桥雅思考试全真试题集7精讲》
周成刚　主编

定价：28元　开本：16开　页码：234页

《剑桥雅思真题精讲4、5、6》
周成刚　主编

定价：55元　开本：16开　页码：500页

◎ 洞悉雅思出题规律，精确剖析雅思真题
◎ 针对中国雅思考生的特点和需求，分题型全面破解

《剑桥雅思常见错误透析》
Pauline Cullen，Julie Moore 编著

定价：18元　开本：32开　页码：136页

《剑桥雅思语法》（附MP3）
Diana Hopkins，Pauline Cullen 编著

定价：45元　开本：16开　页码：272页

◎ 雅思备考资料官方出版机构推出的权威雅思语法教程
◎ 剑桥资深语法专家为全球雅思考生量身定做

《剑桥雅思核心词汇精讲精练》
（附MP3）**Pauline Cullen** 编著

◎ 错误警示：帮助考生避免常见错误
◎ 单元测试：协助考生检验自己的进步
◎ 试题练习：涵盖学术类、培训类阅读以及写作、听力测试内容

定价：40元　开本：16开　页码：180页

《剑桥雅思写作高分范文》（附MP3）
刘巍巍　方林　编著

◎ 收集十年雅思写作题目，全部写作话题一网打尽
◎ 从雅思写作题目出发，全面提高考生写作能力

定价：38元　开本：16开　页码：248页

《剑桥雅思12周完全攻略——阅读》
耿耿　乐静　孙吉芯　梅晗　编著

定价：35元　开本：16开　页码：320页

《剑桥雅思12周完全攻略——听力》
（附MP3）　　　　　王超伟　编著

定价：29.8元　开本：16开　页码：184页

《剑桥雅思12周完全攻略——口语》
（附MP3）　　孙涛　王冬　编著

定价：29元　开本：16开　页码：204页

◎ 针对中国雅思考生的学习特点，制定12周科学备考方案
◎ 覆盖雅思阅读、听力、口语考试核心话题，提供权威答案，帮助考生有的放矢地备考

《雅思词汇词根+联想记忆法（加强版）》

（附MP3）　　　　俞敏洪　编著

◎ 完整收录雅思常考词汇，大量真题例句

◎ "词根+联想"实用有趣，配有插图，加深记忆

◎ 按字母顺序编排，增加返记菜单，便于考生进行自测

定价：58元　开本：16开　页码：528页

《雅思词汇词根+联想记忆法（乱序版）》

（附MP3）　　　　俞敏洪　编著

◎ 完整收录雅思常考词汇，大量真题例句

◎ "词根+联想"实用有趣，配有插图，加深记忆

◎ 增加返记菜单和索引，便于查找定位

定价：58元　开本：16开　页码：528页

《雅思词汇词根+联想记忆法》

（附MP3）　　　　俞敏洪　编著

◎ 原汁原味的真题例句，收词全面，涵盖雅思四大题型词汇

◎ 标出听力、口语单词，有针对性进行记忆

定价：32元　开本：32开　页码：368页

《雅思词汇词根+联想记忆法——写作》

（附MP3）　　　　俞敏洪　编著

定价：12元　开本：64开　页码：200页

《雅思词汇词根+联想记忆法——听力》

（附MP3）　　　　俞敏洪　编著

定价：12元　开本：64开　页码：160页

《雅思词汇词根+联想记忆法——口语》

（附MP3）　　　　俞敏洪　编著

定价：12元　开本：64开　页码：192页

《雅思词汇词根+联想记忆法——阅读》

（附MP3）　　　　俞敏洪　编著

定价：12元　开本：64开　页码：232页

◎ "词根+联想"实用有趣，配有插图，加深记忆

◎ 涵盖雅思阅读词汇，收词全面，分类科学

《雅思考官口语实战指导》

（附MP3）　　　　Mat Clark　编著

◎ 分析中国考生的成绩现状，阐释评分系统的逐项要求

◎ 详尽介绍考试三部分程式，收录最新问题与话题卡片

定价：35元　开本：16开　页码：212页

《101雅思制胜法则：学术类》

（附MP3）Garry Adams, Terry Peck　编著

定价：45元　开本：16开　页码：312页

《101雅思制胜法则：培训类》

（附MP3）Garry Adams, Terry Peck　编著

定价：45元　开本：16开　页码：312页

《202雅思技能强化训练》

（附MP3）Garry Adams, Terry Peck　编著

定价：30元　开本：16开　页码：184页

《互动式三步搞定雅思1001词》

（附CD-ROM）　Keith Burgess　编著

定价：28元　开本：16开　页码：160页

《404雅思精编模考试题：学术类》

（附CD-ROM）

Donna Scovell, Vickie Pastellas,
Max Knobel　编著

定价：34元　开本：16开　页码：224页

《404雅思精编模考试题：培训类》

（附CD-ROM）

Donna Scovell, Vickie Pastellas, Max
Knobel　编著

定价：35元　开本：16开　页码：224页

　　这套教材由澳大利亚雅思培训专家编写，自出版以来受到全球考生的广泛赞誉，是备战雅思考试的必选材料。这套教材主要包含：《101雅思制胜法则》，分为学术类和培训类两册，内含101条实用雅思备考技巧及大量的模拟练习；《202雅思技能强化训练》，包含针对雅思题型而设置的202道英语技能练习题及拓展练习；《404雅思精编模考试题》，分为学术类和培训类两册，内含4套完整的雅思模考题及针对雅思考试各题型的备考建议；《互动式三步搞定雅思1001词》，帮助考生通过识记、转述、应用"三步走"轻松记忆雅思常考词。

《词以类记：IELTS 词汇》

（附 MP3） 张红岩 编著

◎ IELTS最新词汇：覆盖听说读写
◎ 按学科和意群分类：细分至最小同义词区间，符合大脑分类记忆规律

定价：38元 开本：32开 页码：400页

《雅思词组必备》

俞敏洪 编著

◎ 紧扣真题，选词科学
◎ 例句经典，原汁原味
◎ 收录同义词组，扩充词汇量
◎ 幽默插图，巧妙助记

定价：22元 开本：32开 页码：224页

《雅思口试话题高分妙语——旁征博引助你赢》

（附 MP3） 陆文佳 编著

◎ 新颖性：以全新的视角剖析雅思口语考试，灵活运用名言引证
◎ 全面性：覆盖雅思口语常考话题，提供大量名言素材与使用范例
◎ 专业性：融多年课堂教学经验，深入讲解引证法在雅思口语考试中的运用

定价：28元 开本：32开 页码：264页

《剑桥雅思官方模考题精讲精练》

（附 MP3）

Louise Hashemi, Barbara Thomas 编著

◎ 6套官方雅思模拟测试题，设题科学，难度仿真
◎ 具体、实用的答题指导和建议
◎ 特设的语法、词汇和写作练习

定价：49元 开本：16开 页码：236页

《雅思写作论证论据素材大全》

韦晓亮 刘剑 编著

◎ 全面性：覆盖雅思写作话题涉及的英文论证和论据素材
◎ 权威性：精选《经济学家》、《时代周刊》、《科学》、《大英百科全书》等权威刊物文章
◎ 文化性：囊括西方教育、法律、文化、科技、历史等领域

定价：28元 开本：32开 页码：280页

《IELTS 9分必考短语·学术类》

（附 MP3） 李伯庆 著

定价：25元 开本：32开 页码：272页

《IELTS 9分必考短语·培训类》

（附 MP3） 林昱伶 著

定价：25元 开本：32开 页码：272页

从记忆、理解到应用，一次搞定IELTS应考短语！① 记忆公式：不用死记，让你迅速掌握短语意义；② 英语理解：英语释义，让你直接领略短语的精确含义；③ 例句应用：通过例句让你学会如何应用短语。

《雅思核心词汇》（第2版）

（附 MP3） 陆文玲 编著

◎ 根据雅思考试出现频率分为"高频单词"、"精选单词"及"挑战单词"三大类，由浅入深，循序渐进
◎ 15项主题式单词分类，涵盖政治、经济、科技、教育与休闲等领域。核心单词配合实用例句，活学单词，即学即用

定价：38元 开本：16开 页码：272页

《雅思9分口语》（第2版）

（附 MP3） Patrick Hafenstein 编著

◎ 给出4大口试评分标准及QPS口试应考策略
◎ 提供实用笔记速记法及口语测试现场模拟
◎ 全面囊括12大常考主题，依照口语测试标准题型编排

定价：40元 开本：16开 页码：280页

《雅思9分写作》（第2版）

Julian Charles 编著

◎ 60篇高分写作范文
◎ 阶段式写作学习法
◎ 高分词汇精准运用
◎ 综合练习精进写作

定价：45元 开本：16开 页码：380页

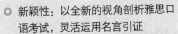

《雅思9分听力》（第2版）
（附MP3）　　　　Justine Ball　编著

◎ 5大题型深入分析
◎ 8种要领彻底掌握
◎ 4套完整模拟试题
◎ 全真听力测试原文

定价：40元　开本：16开　页码：288页

《雅思9分阅读》（第2版）
Patrick Hafenstein　编著

◎ 3阶段进阶，逐步提高
◎ 说明式解答，题题详尽
◎ 5大题型精辟剖析
◎ 4套考题全真模拟

定价：40元　开本：16开　页码：308页

《雅思9分模考》（第2版）（附MP3）
Daniel Sansoni, Patrick Hafenstein
编著

◎ 4套完整模拟考题
◎ 8篇高分写作范文
◎ 常用词汇完整收录
◎ 全真听力测试原文

定价：40元　开本：16开　页码：292页

《雅思口语特训》（附MP3）
孙涛　编著

◎ 收录最新口语真题和话题卡片，将常考话题进行分类、分级，实现逐级突破
◎ 随书配有420分钟录音光盘，内含所有话题题目及经典答案

定价：45元　开本：16开　页码：292页

《雅思听力特训》（附MP3）
彭新松，Stuart Perkins　编著

◎ 洞悉雅思听力出题规律，提供最新模拟试题
◎ 针对中国雅思考生的特点和需求

定价：35元　开本：16开　页码：176页

《雅思口语必备核心话题》
（附MP3）　孙涛　王冬　关新　编著

◎ 话题全面，分类合理，提供一个小型"口语语料库"
◎ 答案精准，表达地道，奉上最佳口语练习模板
◎ 选材丰富，语言生动，展示英语语言无限魅力

定价：40元　开本：16开　页码：260页

《雅思考前突破与冲刺试题》
（附MP3）　　　　Lin Lougheed　编著

◎ 四套全真模拟练习题，提供真实的考场氛围
◎ 包含详细题解、答案及听力原文，供考生自我检测

定价：48元　开本：16开　页码：356页

《雅思听力》（附MP3）
新东方教育科技集团雅思研究院　著

定价：48元　开本：16开　页码：192页

《雅思口语》（附MP3）
新东方教育科技集团雅思研究院　著

定价：48元　开本：16开　页码：204页

《雅思阅读》
新东方教育科技集团雅思研究院　著

定价：45元　开本：16开　页码：176页

《雅思写作》
新东方教育科技集团雅思研究院　著

定价：45元　开本：16开　页码：212页

◎ 新东方团队倾力打造，雅思基础培训指定辅导教材
◎ 符合中国雅思考生学习特点，听说读写全部搞定

《强化培训：雅思口语》（附MP3）
新东方教育科技集团雅思研究院　著

定价：35元　开本：16开　页码：160页

《强化培训：雅思写作》
新东方教育科技集团雅思研究院　著

定价：32元　开本：16开　页码：160页

《雅思全真模拟试题集》（附MP3）
新东方教育科技集团雅思研究院　著

定价：45元　开本：16开　页码：304页

◎ 新东方团队倾力打造，雅思强化培训指定辅导教材
◎ 重点攻破中国学生口语和写作薄弱环节，提供雅思试题全攻略